Raising Reading Achievement

Second Edition

in Middle and High Schools

In memory of David Kent Holmquist

April 1, 1951 to June 12, 2006

Dave Holmquist was an inspirational instructional leader. One of his many legacies is the role he played in his high school's literacy achievements. I knew him as that rare high school administrator who was as supportive of literacy as he was of his football team's record. I am most appreciative to Dave for the contributions that he and his faculty made to this book.

SECOND EDITION

Raising Reading Achievement

IN MIDDLE AND HIGH SCHOOLS

FIVE

SIMPLE-

TO-

FOLLOW

STRATEGIES

Elaine K. McEwan

CORWIN PRESS
A SAGE Publications Company
Thousand Oaks, CA 91320

For information:

Corwin Press
A Sage Publications Company
2455 Teller Road
Thousand Oaks, California 91320
www.corwinpress.com

Sage Publications Ltd.
1 Oliver's Yard
55 City Road
London EC1Y 1SP
United Kingdom

Sage Publications India Pvt. Ltd.
B-42, Panchsheel Enclave
Post Box 4109
New Delhi 110 017 India

Printed in the United States of America

Library of Congress Cataloging-in-Publication Data

McEwan, Elaine K., 1941-
Raising reading achievement in middle and high schools:
Five simple-to-follow strategies / Elaine K. McEwan. — 2nd ed.
      p. cm.
Includes bibliographical references and index.
ISBN 1-4129-2434-0; 978-1-4129-2434-4 (cloth : alk. paper) — ISBN 1-4129-2435-9;
978-1-4129-2435-1 (pbk. : alk. paper)
   1. Reading (Secondary) 2. Reading (Middle school) 3. Middle school principals.
4. High school principals. I. Title.
LB1632.M35 2007
428.4071'2—dc22   2006014232

This book is printed on acid-free paper.

06   07   08   09   10   9   8   7   6   5   4   3   2   1

Acquisitions Editor:	Robert D. Clouse
Editorial Assistant:	Jessica Wochna
Production Editor:	Melanie Birdsall
Typesetter:	C&M Digitals (P) Ltd.
Copy Editor:	Marilyn Power Scott
Cover Designer:	Anthony Paular
Graphic Designer:	Audrey Snodgrass

Contents

List of Teaching
for Learning Tips

Preface

Raising reading achievement in middle and high schools is a challenging undertaking, even for the most effective educators. There are many reasons: (a) most adolescents read less, not more, as they mature, preferring to spend time on jobs, sports, and extracurricular activities; (b) technology is consuming more and more of their interest and free time that was devoted to reading in the past; (c) most middle and high school teachers have not been trained to diagnose specific reading difficulties or expected to teach students how to read strategically; (d) achievement in middle and high school is highly dependent on the preparation students have received in their elementary schools which may or may not use research-based programs in early reading instruction; (e) peer pressure often creates an antiachievement mindset among adolescents; (f) rigid scheduling and graduation requirements limit options for struggling students to receive the instructional time they need to catch up; and (g) high turnover among building and central-level administrators makes meaningful change difficult to bring about and sustain.

Educators, corporate CEOs, and politicians periodically elevate secondary school achievement to the top of their agendas. Hope springs eternal that a promising new program or a fresh infusion of money will provide easy solutions for low literacy levels and high dropout rates. But results are seldom instantaneous, leading educators to abandon reforms and lapse into yet another cycle of doing what they've always done. However, with the passage of the No Child Left Behind Act (NCLB, 2002), raising literacy levels in secondary schools has taken on a new urgency. Absent the ability to read proficiently, a significant percentage of young people have always fallen through the cracks or been left behind, but *now*, their failure to make annual yearly progress (AYP) carries consequences and sanctions for educators.

In 1998, I wrote *The Principal's Guide to Raising Reading Achievement* and developed a workshop based on my personal experiences with raising achievement in a suburban Chicago elementary school. Thus began the exhilarating experience of working with thousands of educators across the United States and Canada. Many middle and high school principals attended the programs, frustrated by how little they knew about reading instruction and how few success stories were available to inspire and inform them. They were overwhelmed with the enormity of the task and desperate for solutions. In response to their need for help, I wrote *Raising Reading Achievement in Middle and High Schools: Five Simple-to-Follow Strategies for Middle and High School Principals* (McEwan, 2001). The book introduced five "big ideas" for winning the battle against illiteracy. In this second edition, these practices have taken on a new urgency.

There are no *easy* answers to the problems of helping adolescents become more proficient readers, but there are increasing numbers of (a) teachers who are embracing their new roles as content literacy specialists, (b) research-based programs that are successfully teaching nonreading adolescents to read, and (c) courageous principals who are refusing to accept failure as the norm. This second edition contains updated descriptions of current research, suggestions from successful practitioners, and descriptions of new programs especially designed for adolescent learners.

A CHANGE IN FOCUS

While the role of principals as instructional leaders is as important as ever, the focus of this revised edition has been broadened to include teacher leaders as well. The five simple-to-follow strategies of the first edition have been enhanced with over twenty research-based "teaching for learning" tips and seven cognitive strategies of highly effective readers that teachers can infuse into their content instruction on a daily basis.

THE GOALS OF THIS BOOK

I have written with these goals in mind:

- To remind you of the power and possibilities that you and your colleagues have at your disposal to make a difference in the lives of your students.
- To focus your attention on ten instructional and environmental variables that can be altered to raise reading achievement.
- To give you a short course in how children learn to read, regardless of age or grade, so that you can make informed decisions about curriculum and instruction.
- To demonstrate the importance of systematically teaching every student, even the best and brightest, how to employ the cognitive strategies that skilled readers routinely use.

- To inspire you to take on the assignment of motivating your students to do three things: (a) read more than they are currently reading, (b) read more challenging and well-written books, and (c) be accountable for understanding and remembering what they read.
- To show you how to build a reading culture in your school.

WHO THIS BOOK IS FOR

This book has been written for several audiences. It is primarily intended for secondary educators to help them develop and implement literacy plans for raising reading achievement in their schools. It can also serve as a resource for site-based literacy and improvement teams as they grapple with what needs to change in their schools. The addition of the following professional development tools will aid central office administrators, principals or department chairs seeking to lead faculty book study groups or other professional development activities: (a) a prereading assessment, (b) reflection and discussion questions at the end of each chapter, and (c) a postreading assessment.

New administrators and teachers or those without backgrounds in reading instruction or curriculum will find the book especially helpful. Reading specialists, special education teachers, literacy coaches, intervention specialists, and central office administrators can use it to evaluate middle and high school reading programs and formulate school and district improvement goals. Last, the book provides a source of information for reading educators at colleges and universities as they seek to make their classroom experiences more relevant to practitioners.

WHAT THIS BOOK IS NOT

Although there are certainly many practical suggestions contained herein (dozens more than in the first edition), this book is not intended as a comprehensive instructional guide nor does it contain explicit lesson plans for classroom teachers. It is designed to help you explore a variety of options so that you might be better prepared to exercise leadership in your learning community. The guaranteed-to-work prescription for which you may have been searching does not exist. School improvement initiatives must be rooted in a school's culture and are better framed by a team of educators, parents, and students in response to the unique challenges posed by the community and its students. This book cannot take the place of developing teacher leaders and building internal professional development capacity. There are many ways to address the challenges posed by low or declining achievement, but determining what is best for your school will require research, data gathering, study, discussion, and consensus building by a site-based team.

OVERVIEW OF THE CONTENTS

Chapter 1 provides a brief history of secondary reading achievement in the United States that includes: (a) an examination of the results of the National Assessment of Educational Progress (NAEP) reading tests; (b) a consideration of the recommendations made by recent task forces; and (c) the costs to students, their families, and the economy of illiteracy. Chapter 2 introduces the first of the five strategies: *Focus on changing what you can change.* You will be challenged to examine your beliefs regarding why students don't learn to read and then asked to consider ten variables that can be altered to raise achievement.

Chapter 3 describes the second strategy: *Teach the students who can't read how to read.* Regardless of how desperately some may cling to the idea that the job should have been done by someone else or that the ability to read text will develop magically, we must provide nonreaders and struggling readers with the explicit, systematic instruction they need now. If they cannot decode words, we must begin there. You will be given a short course in how students learn to read and then be introduced to multiple programs that get results with the lowest-achieving readers.

Chapter 4 explains the third strategy: *Teach every student how to read to learn.* This strategy is a major key to improving overall reading achievement in your school; it is also the strategy that will require the most dramatic and systemic change. If students are unable to "use reading for their personal and professional needs in such a way that their prior knowledge gets synthesized and analyzed by what they read" (Curtis & Longo, 1999, p. 10), we can and must teach them how to do this. Teachers will be introduced to the power of personally modeling their cognitive processing for students and then incorporating strategy instruction into content lesson plans. The chapter defines and describes the seven strategies of highly effective readers that all students need in order to be successful.

Chapter 5 introduces a strategy that is underappreciated and misunderstood: *Motivate all students to read more, to read increasingly more challenging books, and to be accountable for what they read.* The vicious cycle that paralyzes students when they fail to read enough must be reversed. Reading a lot increases fluency, vocabulary, and knowledge. E. D. Hirsch, Jr., (2000) puts it this way: "The more you know, the more readily you can learn something new." But merely reading a lot is not enough. Students must read increasingly challenging text and also be held accountable for understanding and in many cases retaining what is read. There are no manuals that show teachers how to motivate students to read more. There are no programs that can share the joy of books with students. All teachers must undertake this assignment with their own brand of enthusiasm and creativity.

Last, Chapter 6 sets forth the final strategy of the five simple-to-follow strategies: *Create a reading culture in your school.* Twelve benchmarks of a reading culture will be examined as they relate to building a community that not only provides instruction and motivation for reading but demands that students and teachers be committed to daily reading as a skill and a practice. A case study illustrating one school's successful efforts to raise reading achievement will be presented.

A NEW FEATURE

One of the biggest challenges faced by secondary teachers is how to organize their classrooms and design lessons to maximize success for all students—struggling readers, gifted scholars, and all of the students in between. To that end you will find more than twenty "teaching for learning" tips. These tips can be found in one-page sidebars throughout each chapter and include research-based best practices for raising achievement, not only in reading but also in every content area. Each tip contains a "how to get started" section, one or two recommended resources for individual or group study, and brief research citations that support the power of the practice for raising student achievement. Reading and using the Teaching for Learning Tips can easily be done independently of reading the text in each chapter. While all of the tips are related to raising student achievement, they are not all directly connected to the topics of the chapter where they are found. So be sure to browse through the complete list of the Teaching for Learning Tips located at the end of the Contents, page x.

THE CHALLENGE

I hope that after reading this book, you will be motivated to set about raising reading achievement in your school. Changing the attitudes, accountability, and achievement of your students with regard to reading may require some changes on your part as well. Begin today by reading a book—a professional book, a classic that you missed when you were growing up, or a novel or biography for pure enjoyment. Think aloud with others about your processing of the text. Ask colleagues and students about what they are reading and why they chose a particular book. If you are really ambitious, sign up for a reading methods course at your local university. Exercise your leadership and creativity to lead your colleagues and students to higher levels of literacy.

I invite you to visit me at www.elainemcewan.com where you can learn more about my writing and workshops and enroll in online seminars based on my books, or contact me directly at:

emcewan@elainemcewan.com

Acknowledgments

This book would not have been possible without the encouragement and support of dozens of middle and high school principals and teachers throughout the country who have invited me into their schools and classrooms, shared materials and lesson plans, and offered their insights regarding raising adolescent literacy levels. My special thanks to Val Bresnahan, Allyson Burnett, TerraBeth Jochems, Beth Balkus, Linda Nielsen, and Michelle Jones-Gayle for sharing their expertise relative to raising reading achievement in secondary schools.

Last, I am profoundly grateful for the overflowing love, support, and encouragement I receive from my husband, business partner, and copy editor extraordinaire, E. Raymond Adkins. When deadlines loom and pressures mount, he is always there with a gentle word and a calming touch.

Corwin Press gratefully acknowledges the contributions of the following people:

Patti J. Larche
Director of Curriculum
    and Instruction
Phelps-Clifton Springs
    School District
Clifton Springs, NY

Marsha Sobel
Assistant Superintendent,
    Curriculum and Instruction
Newburgh Enlarged School District
Newburgh, NY

Rosemarie Young
President, NAESP
Principal
Watson Lane Elementary
    School
Louisville, KY

Claudia Thompson
Director of Curriculum and
    Staff Development
Peninsula School District
Kent, WA

Bess Scott
Principal
Goodrich Middle School
Lincoln, ME

Rena Richtig
Professor, EACL
Central Michigan University
Mt. Pleasant, MI

Donald Poplau
Principal
Mankato East High School
Mankato, MN

Ray Van Dyke
Principal
Kipps Elementary School
Blacksburg, VA

Erin Rivers
Principal
DeLa Salle Middle School
Mission, KS

About the Author

 **Elaine K. McEwan** is a partner and educational consultant with The McEwan-Adkins Group, offering workshops in instructional leadership, team building, and raising reading achievement, K–12. A former teacher, librarian, principal, and assistant superintendent for instruction in a suburban Chicago school district, she is the author of more than thirty-five books for parents and educators. Her Corwin Press titles include *Leading Your Team to Excellence: Making Quality Decisions* (1997), *The Principal's Guide to Attention Deficit Hyperactivity Disorder* (1998), *How to Deal With Parents Who Are Angry, Troubled, Afraid, or Just Plain Crazy* (1998), *The Principal's Guide to Raising Reading Achievement* (1998), *Counseling Tips for Elementary School Principals* (1999) with Jeffrey A. Kottler, *Managing Unmanageable Students: Practical Solutions for Educators* (2000) with Mary Damer, *The Principal's Guide to Raising Math Achievement* (2000), *Raising Reading Achievement in Middle and High Schools: Five Simple-to-Follow Strategies for Principals* (2001), *Ten Traits of Highly Effective Teachers: How to Hire, Mentor, and Coach Successful Teachers* (2001), *Teach Them ALL to Read: Catching the Kids Who Fall through the Cracks* (2002), *7 Steps to Effective Instructional Leadership, Second Edition* (2003), *Making Sense of Research: What's Good, What's Not, and How to Tell the Difference* (2003) with Patrick J. McEwan, *Ten Traits of Highly Effective Principals: From Good to Great Performance* (2003), *7 Strategies of Highly Effective Readers: Using Cognitive Research to Boost K–8 Achievement* (2004), *How to Deal With Teachers Who Are Angry, Troubled, Exhausted, or Just Plain Confused* (2005), and *How to Survive and Thrive in the First Three Weeks of School,* (2006).

Elaine was honored by the Illinois Principals Association as an outstanding instructional leader by the Illinois State Board of Education, with an Award of Excellence in the Those Who Excel Program, and by the National Association of Elementary School Principals as the National

Distinguished Principal from Illinois for 1991. She received her under-graduate degree in education from Wheaton College and advanced degrees in library science (MA) and educational administration (EdD) from Northern Illinois University. She lives with her husband and business partner E. Raymond Adkins in Oro Valley, Arizona.

The Five Simple-to-Follow Strategies for Raising Reading Achievement

1. Focus on changing what you can change.

2. Teach the students who can't read how to read.

3. Teach every student how to read to learn.

4. Motivate all students to read *more* books, to read increasingly *more challenging* books, and to be *accountable* for what they read.

5. Create a reading culture in your school.

Reading Achievement

Where Do We Stand?

Ten years ago it was visionary to assure that each student read at or above grade level by third or fourth grade. Today it is the law. Ten years from now it may be a civil right.

—Lynn Fielding in Fielding,
Kerr, and Rosier (2004, p. 150)

Many adolescents who struggle with reading have much in common with the Mexican revolutionary leader portrayed in the film *Viva Zapata!* His charismatic personality mesmerizes his followers, but he is powerless to conquer the printed page. In the film, we see him staring at a book, putting his hand across his eyes, pounding the desk, and shouting with frustration, "I can't read." (NOTE: Although I have viewed the film, I cannot take credit for noting the scene I describe here. Robert Karlin [1984] cited it in *Teaching Reading in High School: Improving Reading in the Content Areas*.)

Robert Uber, a young adult whose academic career I have followed closely for several years, can relate to the anger of the illiterate in this cinematic classic. By the time he entered high school in 1997, Robert had been in and out of a variety of self-contained classes for students with behavior difficulties. He was on course to become a dropout statistic when his academic trajectory took a sharp turn upward. What was behind this dramatic turnaround?

A gifted special education teacher in a small, northern Michigan high school learned the source of Robert's frustration when his older brother shared this remarkable insight: "All Robert wants is to learn to read." It seemed that when former teachers ignored Robert's inability to read, focusing instead on controlling his behavior, he became aggressive and unmanageable. On the auspicious day that Robert met his new teacher, she offered him a way out: If he would stick with her, she would teach him to read. During his high school career, Robert not only reached his reading goal, he also received a citizenship award, worked in the media center, and attended vocational school. (NOTE: Robert was taught to read by the Spalding Method, a multisensory, direct instruction approach [Spalding & Spalding, 1957/1990]. See Resource B for a detailed description of the program.)

Since his graduation in 2001, Robert has married his prom date, fathered a son, and realized his dream of owning his own business, All Vehicle Repair. A high school diploma, combined with the ability to read and write, changed Robert's life forever. His life story is still being written, but the first chapter has a very happy ending—thanks to a gifted teacher using a research-based methodology (R. Uber, personal communication, October 16, 2005).

The toll that illiteracy takes on dropouts can be seen in a variety of traumatic events—emotional, criminal, psychological, physical, and financial catastrophes that pervade their lives. Irrespective of what a high school diploma may represent for any given individual, for the majority of students, "*high school graduation has been a necessary (but not sufficient) prerequisite for making it in America*" (Rouse, 2005, p. 1).

Economists project the cost of school failure to be in the billions:

- A high school dropout earns about $260,000 less over a lifetime than a high school graduate and pays about $60,000 less in taxes. Annual losses exceed $50 billion in federal and state income taxes for all 23 million of the nation's high school dropouts aged 18 to 67.
- The United States loses $192 billion—1.6 percent of its current gross domestic product—in combined income and tax revenue losses with each cohort of 18-year-olds who never complete high school. Increasing the educational attainment of that cohort by one year would recoup nearly half those losses.
- Increasing the high school completion rate by 1 percent for all men aged 20 to 60 could save the United States up to $1.4 billion a year

in reduced costs from crime. A one-year increase in average years of schooling for dropouts would correlate with reductions of murder and assault by almost 30 percent, motor vehicle theft by 20 percent, arson by 13 percent, and burglary and larceny by about 6 percent (Teachers College Columbia University, 2005).

There are potential dropouts in every school in America. We label them remedial, at risk, learning disabled, emotionally disturbed, or behaviorally disordered. You know who they are in your school. They achieve at levels far below their peers, often drop out of school, seldom attend college, and are frequently unable to obtain or hold meaningful jobs. However, these students are not the only reading underachievers.

There is a second category of readers who have mastered the science of reading (decoding) but still do not have the "art" (meaning and understanding). They believe that if they have read it once, they've read it, even if they have no clue about the meaning of the text. They have never received explicit instruction in how to access the cognitive strategies employed by skilled readers and often lack the vocabulary and background knowledge to tackle challenging textbooks with success. The solutions to the problems of these readers are more subtle and systemic. To teach all students to be more strategic readers, all teachers must be involved, not just a remedial teacher or two.

There is a third category of readers that is often ignored altogether. This group contains the students who are capable of reading far more than they do as well as reading books that are more challenging. Instead, these active adolescents are watching television, playing computer games, or hanging out at the mall. Granted, there are many teens who volunteer, participate in extracurricular activities, and hold down part-time jobs and are hard pressed to find time in their schedules to read. But unless we raise our expectations, our students will never make reading a priority in their lives. Take a moment to read the Teaching for Learning Tip 1.1. Thinking aloud for students regarding your personal processing of text is a practice that has the power to revolutionize your teaching of content.

RAISING ACHIEVEMENT EXPECTATIONS

The challenge before us is, as it has always been, to secure equal educational opportunity. Every American child should have the same opportunities for an excellent education. . . . The real issue . . . is whether the schools are good enough to prepare students for the challenges that confront them.

—Ravitch (2003, p. 36)

TEACHING FOR LEARNING TIP 1.1

Think Aloud Daily for Students

How to Get Started

Select a piece of content-related text. Alternate reading aloud short sections of the text with thinking aloud about how you are mentally processing what you have read. Use the seven strategies of highly effective readers as described in Chapter 4. Make statements about your thinking similar to the following:

Activating: *What I just read reminds me of something I learned when I was in high school.*

Monitoring-Clarifying: *I got confused here because of the way the word was used, so I used the context to figure it out. It helped that I knew a related word in a foreign language.*

Questioning: *I wonder why the author chose this word to describe the Civil War. It seems to me that another word would have made more sense.*

Visualizing: *I pictured what was happening here, and it helped me understand how the crime was committed.*

Searching-Selecting: *I had a question when I read this section, and I'm either going to ask my friend John who knows a lot about this topic or I'll Google it later.*

Organizing: *To help me remember the order in which these events happened, I'm going to construct a time line in my notes.*

Inferring: *I'm sure I know what's going to happen next because the same thing happened to me several years ago.*

Your students will be mesmerized by hearing you speak your thoughts. Some teachers pair up with a colleague, combine their classes, and each read and think aloud from the same text to show students that readers process text in different ways based on their backgrounds, experience, and strategy usage.

Resist the temptation to teach, explain, and lecture about the text. The purpose of thinking aloud is to show students how *you* personally process and respond to what you read. In so doing, you become the "master reader-thinker-problem solver," and your students serve as *cognitive* apprentices.

Resources to Help You Implement

McEwan, 2004. *The 7 Strategies of Highly Effective Readers.*
Schoenbach, Greenleaf, Cziko, & Hurwitz, 1999. *Reading for Understanding*

Research on Teacher Modeling During Strategy Instruction

Afflerbach, 2002; Collins, Brown, & Holum, 1991; Duffy, 2002; Pressley, 2000; Pressley, Gaskins, Solic, & Collins 2005; Trabasso & Bouchard, 2000, 2002.

Concerns about the quality of secondary schools rise to the top of the national agenda periodically. In fact, the country often looks to the public schools for solutions when anything goes wrong. The first such occurrence in my lifetime was precipitated by a cataclysmic current event. On October 4, 1957, the Russians launched the first satellite, Sputnik, into outer space. The happening stunned the nation. Politicians and pundits immediately launched an attack on the public schools for having fallen behind Soviet schools in training students for careers in the sciences and other fields. Congress quickly passed the National Defense Education Act (1958) that provided aid to education at all levels, both public and private. Its primary purpose was to stimulate the advancement of science, mathematics, and foreign language; materials flooded into classrooms and libraries to support instruction in these content areas. And as all too often happens, before long, most educators had shelved the books and materials, abandoned the special institutes and training programs for promising math and science students, and moved on to other more pressing priorities and enticing innovations.

In the early 1980s, a thought-provoking study triggered a flurry of activity focused on higher standards, revised curricula, and stricter high school graduation requirements. Titled *A Nation at Risk*, it not only sounded an alarm regarding quality, but it also called for equity. "All, regardless of race or class or economic status, are entitled to a fair chance and to the tools for developing their individual powers of mind and spirit to the utmost" (National Committee on Excellence in Education, 1983, p. 5).

In the twenty-first century, professional organizations, political coalitions, think tanks, and a variety of foundations have caught what appears to be a "new" wave of middle school and high school reform. The reports they have generated are impressive at first glance but offer more questions than answers. They all seem to agree on one thing, however: "Whether one looks at standardized test scores, at graduation rates, or at college admission test results, American high school performance [and middle school as well] has hardly budged over the past three decades. To say that improving high-school student achievement is like turning a supertanker around would be an insult to the speed and maneuverability of supertankers" (Greene, 2006, p. 1). Teaching for Learning Tip 1.2 suggests that helping students to comprehend the various types of text found in content classrooms is an assignment that *only* the teacher of that content can accomplish.

> "Without professional development, ongoing formative assessment of students and programs, and ongoing summative assessment of students and programs as the foundation of any middle or high school literacy program, we cannot hope to effect major change in adolescent literacy achievement; no matter what instructional innovations are introduced."
>
> —*Biancarosa and Snow (2004, p. 29)*

TEACHING FOR LEARNING TIP 1.2

Teach the Structure of Your Discipline

How to Get Started

There is no one better suited to teach students how to read and write about the disciplines of science, social studies, and mathematics than the teachers who teach those subjects. Here are some questions to consider in your planning:

1. How does your discipline typically present information? *For example, in social studies, history texts are organized in a chronological fashion. Economics and civics texts use a problem-solution or goal-action-outcome format. Geography texts emphasize description with an emphasis on comparing and contrasting various places and cultures. Science texts contain explanations of difficult concepts and complicated processes, descriptions of scientific experiments, and the juxtaposition of conflicting sources and theories* (International Reading Association, 2006, p. 31).

2. How might you explicitly teach students how to read the text of your discipline?

3. What are the essential literacy skills for your discipline? For example, in social studies, they include the abilities to
   • Locate and use primary and secondary source documents
   • Recognize and evaluate author perspective and bias
   • Synthesize information from multiple sources
   • Make connections across chronological eras, across geographical regions, or between civic and economic issues
   • Present findings in a variety of forms, including oral presentations or debates and written documents that may take the form of research papers, position papers, or writing from a specific role or perspective (International Reading Association, 2006, p. 32).

Resources to Help You Implement

Kobrin, 1996. *Beyond the Textbook: Teaching History Using Documents and Primary Sources.*
Their & Daviss, 2002. *The New Science Literacy.*

Research on Teaching the Structure of Your Discipline

Alexander, 1997; Alexander & Jetton, 2003; Beck & Dole, 1992; Craig & Yore, 1995; Hand, Prain, & Wallace, 2002; Shanahan, 2004; Stahl & Shanahan, 2004; Wade & Moje, 2000.

Despite the discouraging realities of secondary achievement, there are still commentators who delight in discounting stagnant test scores and cavernous achievement gaps. They pronounce our educational system competitive and blame achievement problems on inalterable variables or flawed tests (Berliner, 2005; Bracey, 2002, 2005, 2006; Kohn,

2000). Some even suggest that schools focus on developing an *aptitude* for learning (i.e., "the ability to process new information quickly and solve problems creatively") rather than improving instruction so that *all* students can acquire the skills and knowledge they need to be successful in life (Klein, McNeil, & Stout, 2005).

The aforementioned individuals hypothesize that beleaguered students "are caught in an 'achievement trap,' an academic arms race that requires kids to demonstrate their ability to learn by actually learning more and more facts, at more and more advanced levels, all the hours of their young days that are not filled by such demonstrable time-eaters as soccer practice and violin recitals" (Klein et al., 2005, p. 32). Perhaps these commentators can afford to take this perspective because the students with whom they work have already mastered the basics of reading, writing, and mathematics. But for millions of students in this country, illiteracy and innumeracy are facts of life (Hanushek, 2003; Rouse, 2005).

THE STATE OF READING ACHIEVEMENT IN THE NATION

The National Assessment of Educational Progress (NAEP) is the only wide-scale and somewhat rigorous test of reading achievement in the United States. It is a federally sponsored assessment that is periodically given in reading (and other subjects) to a nationwide sample of students in fourth, eighth, and twelfth grades. Although all states have their own mandated reading assessments at various grade levels, these tests vary widely in content and difficulty as well as in their definitions of what constitutes a proficient reader. Therefore, NAEP is a critical tool for comparing reading achievement uniformly across the states and determining literacy levels in the United States as a whole at any given point in time.

The test is not without its problems, however (Cavanagh, May, 2005/June, 2005; Cavanagh & Robelen, 2004; Innes, 2005; Viadero, 2005a, 2005b). There are several troubling issues regarding the NAEP that make it challenging to draw subtle conclusions about current achievement levels and long-term trends, but there is one undeniable fact: Reading achievement hasn't budged at the secondary level since the test's inception in 1992. The first problem concerns the voluntary nature of the test. Prior to 2003, individual states could opt in or out of the NAEP testing, thereby resulting in a sample that although demographically representative was not drawn from the country as a whole. While that problem has been solved at the fourth-grade and eighth-grade levels by the federal No Child Left Behind Act of 2001 (2002) that mandates testing a representative sample from every state, one still cannot draw firm conclusions about state trends since 1992 except in individual states that have participated continuously.

A second and related issue concerns the testing of twelfth-grade students. Although NCLB mandated testing at fourth and eighth grades, no such provision was included for the twelfth grade. The motivation and participation rate of high school seniors has been dropping over time, jeopardizing the credibility of the twelfth-grade results. Various solutions to the problem have been advanced, including publishing individual scores and offering incentive gifts to students who participate (Cavanagh, 2005, May 23).

A third and more perplexing problem is the wide variation in the percentage of students excluded from the NAEP testing in individual states, thereby skewing the results. For example, in 2004, an average of 35 percent of students with disabilities was excused from taking the 2004 reading test (Viadero, 2005a).

> "The NAEP is a 'no-stakes' test. [T]here are no consequences attached to student performance on the NAEP exams, nor are instructional hours spent specifically preparing for the NAEP. Furthermore, while a national goal of academic excellence for all students has been implicit in previous surveys and analysis of the American education system, no explicit goals for student performance or progress on the NAEP have ever been articulated."
> —*SchoolMatters (2005, p. 1)*

Despite its current flaws, the NAEP is the only nationwide test we have. It has the potential to level the playing field from state to state, giving educators and policy makers the ability to compare like schools in various demographic areas or compare individual states with each other. Figures 1.1 and 1.2 illustrate the overall proficiency levels of the students who have taken the eighth and twelfth grades Reading NAEP since its inception. Figure 1.3 describes the three categories into which students are placed based on their scores: Basic, Proficient, and Advanced. Students whose scores fall below the cutoff point for Basic are placed in the fourth category, aptly titled Below Basic. The picture is dismal.

- There are far too many students whose reading levels consign them to failure in middle and high school—between one-fourth and one-third of the students tested fall in the Below Basic category.
- There are even more students—close to 40 percent at both grade levels—who have only a partial mastery of the knowledge and skills they need to be considered grade-level readers. With skilled teaching, strong motivation, and very hard work, these students might be able to make it. But motivation and hard work are not typical characteristics of struggling adolescent readers, and most secondary teachers do not have the expertise needed to work miracles.

Figure 1.1 Percentage of Students in NAEP Reading Achievement Levels: Grade 8, 1992–2004

		Below Basic	Basic	Proficient	Advanced
*Accommodations Not Permitted	1992	33	41	25	2
	1994	33	40	25	2
	1998	29	41	28	2
**Accommodations Permitted	1998	29	42	27	2
	2002	26	43	28	2
	2003	28	42	27	3
	2005	29	42	26	3

SOURCE: U.S. Department of Education, Institute of Education Sciences, National Center for Education Statistics, NAEP (1992, 1994, 1998, and 2002 Reading Assessments).

*Students with disabilities who took the test were not granted accommodations such as extended time, large print tests booklets, and so forth.

**Students with disabilities who took the test were provided with accommodations as recommended by their individual education plans (IEPs).

- If we add up the percentages of students at either grade level in the Below Basic and Basic categories, at least two out of every three students did poorly on the test.
- On the opposite end of the achievement continuum, only 5 percent or fewer of secondary students are Advanced: able to synthesize and learn from specialized reading material. That percentage is far smaller than the percentage of students who enter college every year, suggesting a possible reason why 53 percent of college students are forced to enroll in remedial courses (Greene & Forster, 2003; Swanson, 2004).

> "In many states, standards are set far too low to ensure a [high] level of skills. . . . Standards that don't set challenging goals for student learning ultimately stunt the academic growth of our young people."
>
> —*Education Trust (2005, p. 2)*

Figure 1.2   Percentage of Students in NAEP Reading Achievement Levels:
Grade 12, 1992–2002

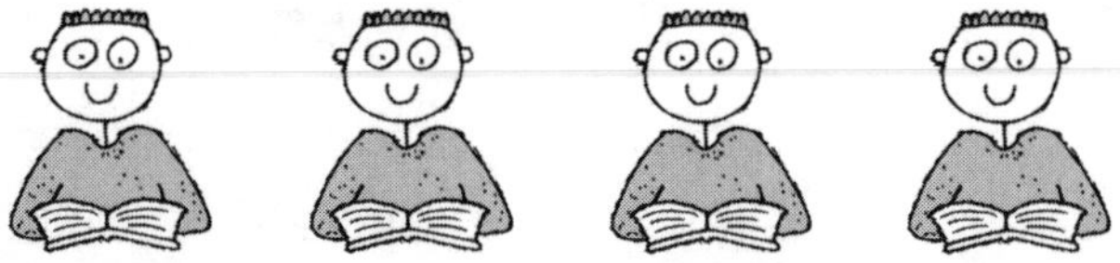

		Below Basic	Basic	Proficient	Advanced
*Accommodations Not Permitted	1992	22	41	34	3
	1994	27	39	31	4
	1998	24	37	33	5
**Accommodations Permitted	1998	25	37	33	5
	2002***	28	38	30	4

SOURCE: U.S. Department of Education, Institute of Education Sciences, National Center for Education Statistics, NAEP (1992, 1994, 1998, and 2002 Reading Assessments).

*Students with disabilities who took the test were not granted accommodations such as extended time to take the test, large print tests booklets, and so forth.

**Students with disabilities who took the test were provided with accommodations as recommended by their IEPs.

***Testing results for 2004 are scheduled to be released in Spring 2006.

- Since the NAEP was first administered in 1992, there has been little significant change in achievement levels at either the eighth or twelfth grades.

THE RESPONSE OF EDUCATORS

What is the response of educators to this discouraging news? After the release of the 2004 NAEP Reading Test results, the Association for Supervision and Curriculum Development (ASCD) posted the following question on its Web site: *What is the most effective strategy for improving reading and math scores on assessments such as NAEP?* ASCD officials offered the following choices for respondents (in the same order as they are printed here) and provided a running total of the percentage of individuals who chose each answer (ASCD, 2005):

Figure 1.3 Levels of Student Performance on NAEP Reading Tests

Basic	**Partial mastery** of prerequisite knowledge and skills. Includes the abilities to demonstrate a literal understanding of what students read, make some interpretations, identify specific aspects of the text that reflect overall meaning, extend the ideas in the text by making simple inferences, and recognize and relate interpretations and connections.
Proficient	**Solid academic performance** at the tested grade level. Students reaching this level have demonstrated competency over challenging subject matter, including subject-matter knowledge, application of such knowledge to real-world situations, and analytical skills appropriate to the subject matter.
Advanced	**Superior performance** includes the abilities to describe the more abstract themes and ideas of the overall text; analyze both meaning and form and support their analyses explicitly with examples from the text, and extend text information by relating it to their experiences and to world events.

SOURCE: U.S. Department of Education, Institute of Education Sciences, National Center for Education Statistics, NAEP (1992, 1994, 1998, and 2002 Reading Assessments).

1. Embrace a whole-child philosophy (24.46 percent).

2. Improve teacher quality (32.45 percent).

3. Increase funding for education (15.74 percent).

4. Focus more closely on math and reading (22.11 percent).

5. I don't think assessment scores are important (5.25 percent).

This poll is not scientific (respondents self-selected into the sample), but the responses do suggest how some educators respond to unfavorable assessment results. The good news is that only 5.25 percent of the respondents felt that assessment scores aren't important. The bad news is that fewer than 25 percent of the respondents identified a more intense focus on math and reading as the answer to helping students master the challenges of reading and mathematics. Instead, respondents indicated that a solution to the lack of knowledge and skills in reading and math might be an ephemeral concept called the "whole-child philosophy." Recall that Robert's teacher did not promise to treat Robert as a "whole child" if he would stick with her for four years. She promised to teach him to read.

When considering the results of a large-scale, summative evaluation like the NAEP, one can easily attack the test, overlooking the fact that the data represent not only the actual students who took the test but also those that the sample represents—millions of adolescents whose low achievement levels are predictive of their academic and vocational failures. It's not about test scores per se. It's about the ability of our students to "understand and use those written language forms required by society and/or valued by the individual" (Elley, 1992, p. 3), the ability to gain meaning from the printed page. Your students will approach the reading of textbooks and literature in a new way once you teach them how to question the author as described in Teaching for Learning Tip 1.3.

TEACHING FOR LEARNING TIP 1.3

Teach Students How to Question the Author

How to Get Started

Introduce students to the idea of a fallible author or, in the case of textbooks, a committee of fallible authors. Explicitly teach and model for students how to

- Identify difficulties with the way the author has presented information or ideas
- Question the author's intent or particular choice of vocabulary
- Zero in on the precise meaning an author is trying to convey
- Recognize when an inference about the author's intentions is needed because the author's conclusions are not clearly articulated

The purpose of questioning the author is to make public the *processes of comprehension.* This questioning ideally takes place immediately following a guided reading session in which the teacher encourages students to grapple with ideas in order to construct meaning.

Students can question authors of both narrative and expository texts. Questioning the author is a particularly useful approach when reading primary sources in history.

A Resource to Help You Implement

Beck, McKeown, Hamilton, & Kucan, 1997. *Questioning the Author: An Approach for Enhancing Student Engagement With Text.*

Although this book is written for elementary teachers, don't let that fact discourage you from reading it. Its thesis is a powerful one that all readers need to grasp: Every text has a human, fallible author with whom the reader can (and should) interact in a questioning mode.

Research on Questioning the Author

Underwood & Pearson, 2004.

The NAEP results do not engender passionate discussion during faculty meetings or even raise most teachers' levels of concern. The test is often viewed as an annoyance by administrators, teachers, *and* students. What is getting attention in the faculty lounge and the principal's office, however, is NCLB. The idea that low achievement among particular groups of students (e.g., minorities, students with disabilities, or English Language Learners [ELLs]) can put seemingly successful middle schools or comprehensive high schools in upscale suburbs on a "watch list" fills educators with both anger and anxiety.

Whether NCLB is unfair, underfunded, and unfocused (Sunderman, Kim, & Orfield, 2005) or the only logical way to bring about change in schools where expectations are low and teaching is ineffective is a question that is hotly debated in op ed pages, graduate classes and letters to the editor. The arguments are familiar ones.

Those who abhor the march toward accountability as measured by a group-administered, standardized test assert that the results of teaching and learning cannot be measured by a single test. "How can a paper-and-pencil assessment measure creativity, ingenuity, motivation, and perseverance?" they ask. Critics of the standards and assessment movement in the United States paint a bleak picture of where we are headed if we continue down the testing trail: cookie cutter educations, drill and kill, "ram, remember, and regurgitate" (Renzulli, 2000, p. 48), trivial pursuit, and back to the boring basics. If these naysayers are to be believed, there will be no joy left in learning when the "standardistos" (Thompson, 1999) take over. We will all be too busy "prepping for the test."

John Bishop (1993, 1995, 1998a, & 1998b) of Cornell University disagrees with this mindset. His research has shown that educational systems that have established content standards and then used curriculum-based tests to determine whether students have learned have improved achievement for all students, including those from less advantaged backgrounds.

> "The . . . focus on literacy cannot end in third grade. To meet the requirements of colleges and employers in the 21st century, students must receive explicit literacy instruction throughout their adolescent years, defined in this guide as beginning in the fourth grade and continuing through the end of twelfth grade."
>
> —*National Governors Association (2005, p. 4)*

THE STATE OF READING ACHIEVEMENT IN THE STATES

Since the first edition of this book was published in 2001, almost all of the states have come online with reading assessments based on their own unique standards and curricula. Almost half of the states reported a jump in achievement in the number of eighth graders rating proficient on those tests from 2003 to 2005. However, the difference between the number of students rated proficient in reading on individual state assessments and those who received the proficient rating on the 2005 eighth-grade NAEP is startling. Seven states (Alabama, California, Idaho, Arizona, Maryland, Virginia, and Kentucky) reported an additional 5 to 11 percent of eighth-grade students receiving a proficient rating in 2005 than did in the 2003 testing. None of these states, however, showed any progress on the eighth-grade NAEP test from 2003 to 2005. In fact, five of the seven states actually showed a decline on the NAEP test (Dillon, 2005). We can only speculate about the reasons for the discrepancies between state results and the NAEP, but one issue that must be considered is the pressure states feel to lower their standards in order to appear successful in raising achievement. Although summative assessments seem to be dictating the agendas in many districts and schools, take a moment to discover the power of assessing your learning as described in the Teaching for Learning Tip 1.4.

ROADBLOCKS TO RAISING READING ACHIEVEMENT IN MIDDLE AND HIGH SCHOOLS

Raising reading achievement in secondary schools is undeniably difficult. To succeed, educators need to think outside the box and grapple with long-standing beliefs and practices that interfere with raising literacy levels.

Here are some restraining forces that are likely to impede or even prevent progress:

- Dysfunctional bureaucracies made up of transient, upwardly mobile superintendents; politicized school boards; and multiple layers of entrenched central office administrators (Haberman, 2003)
- Educators who doubt their abilities to make a difference with adolescents who are unable to read at grade level
- Educators who believe that someone else should have done it in the past
- Educators who believe that someone else should do it now (e.g., special education, alternative schools, special reading teachers)
- Educators who believe that they are already doing as much as they possibly can
- Educators who believe they deserve credit for trying, even if they don't get results
- Tentative principals who lack the courage, will, or knowledge base to lead for reading improvement

---

TEACHING FOR LEARNING TIP 1.4

Assess for Learning

How to Get Started

Teachers generally assess their students to gather grades for reporting their progress to parents. These assessments do nothing to advance learning. Instead, assess students with these two purposes in mind: (a) to determine the status of their learning and (b) to gain information regarding how to adjust your instruction. The power of formative assessment to increase learning and achievement lies in the immediacy of its impact on your teaching as well as on your students' learning. A test given at the end of a unit for purposes of assigning a report card grade is useless both to you as a teacher and to your students who need to know specifically what to do in order to improve. When students are compared to one another at regular intervals during the semester with no opportunity for a "do-over," you are creating a competitive classroom environment in which some students win and some lose.

Assessment for learning grows out of a mastery mindset in which teachers provide feedback to students so they can improve their work products and thereby achieve mastery of the content or process. Similarly, a test given at the end of the unit (when you have *finished* teaching the content) does not permit you to adjust your instruction to ensure higher levels of learning by your students or give students the extended opportunities they may need in order to be successful.

A Resource to Help You Implement

Black, Harrison, Lee, Marshall, & Wiliam, 2003. *Assessment for Learning: Putting It Into Practice.*

Research on Assessment for Learning

Assessment Reform Group, 2002; Reeves, 2004; Wiliam, 2003.

- Aggressive principals who mandate, order, intimidate, or harass their subordinates
- Marginal or ineffective teachers who do just enough to get by

Here are some common initiatives that are unlikely to result in meaningful or sustained change:

- Hiring one or two reading teachers to provide one class period of reading instruction for a year to struggling students
- Massive infusions of money into a school or system without instructional leadership and accountability

- Reduced class sizes across the school
- Literacy and school improvement plans that do not include a data-based assessment component, meaningful and measurable goals, and realistic time lines
- Professional development for teachers that is not attended by and supported by *all* building administrators
- Mandated districtwide middle and high school literacy initiatives that do not involve staff, students, and parents in the planning
- Mandated strategy instruction programs for teachers that do not provide at least two to three years of intensive training and coaching
- Installation of a motivational reading program in the library
- Institution of a schoolwide sustained silent reading program
- Installation of a program to teach students how to read strategically in text that is unrelated to the content they encounter daily in their classes
- Installation of a program to teach students how to read strategically that is not also taught and supported by content teachers on a daily basis
- One-time workshops that are unrelated or even in conflict with ongoing professional development goals
- Hiring of untrained and unsupported literacy coaches who know little about secondary content instruction
- Professional development that is only available to teachers on a volunteer, unpaid basis

THE RESPONSIBILITY OF SCHOOL LEADERS

How do school leaders meet top-down regulations from outside their districts while still fostering an enhanced collegial on-line sense of initiative and control within their schools? The principal must be in charge to meet this challenge.

—Goldring and Rallis (1993, p. 18)

Educators have a difficult mission—to remain focused on the ability of their students to read and succeed in content-laden classrooms. If you permit yourself to be diverted by the often contentious debate surrounding standards, testing, and NCLB, you can easily forget that raising achievement is about helping individual students make quantum leaps in learning every single year of their academic careers. To keep yourself, your colleagues, and your students focused on learning while policy makers argue issues is like driving in a downpour. The experts may be predicting rain, but it's time for you to start building the boat (Harvey & Housman, 2005, p. 5).

To raise reading achievement in the midst of a cacophony of excuses and distractions requires that educators zero in with laserlike precision on the following strategies:

1. Identify the instructional and environmental variables that need to be changed in your classroom or school, and develop a plan to change them.

2. Teach the students who can't read how to read (whether special education, ELL, at-risk, unmotivated, or behavior disordered students).

3. Teach all students how to read strategically.

4. Motivate students to read larger amounts of text as well as more challenging text while also being accountable for understanding and remembering what they have read.

5. Create a reading culture in your school or district.

> "While the literature identifies instructional leadership (that is, efforts to improve teaching) as being key, principals spend time on necessary administrative tasks, such as maintaining physical security of their school, and on managing facilities, resources, and procedures. There is a disconnect between the more lofty goals articulated in the literatures and the realities of the everyday tasks required of an effective operations manager."
>
> *—Juvonen, Le, Kaganoff, Augustine, and Constant (2004, p. xviii)*

Ron Edmonds (1981) was ahead of his time when he said,

> We can, whenever and wherever we choose, successfully teach all children whose schooling is of interest to us. We already know more than we need to do that. Whether or not we do it must finally depend on how we feel about the fact that we haven't so far. (p. 53)

A similar visionary statement in *Reading Next: A Vision for Action and Research in Middle and High School Literacy* echoes Edmonds's long-ago challenge:

> Enough is already known about adolescent literacy—both the nature of the problems of struggling readers and the types of interventions and approaches to address these needs—in order to act immediately on a broad scale. (Biancarosa & Snow, 2004, p. 10)

How do you feel about the fact that you and your colleagues haven't done it so far? If not you, then who? If not now, then when?

REFLECTION AND DISCUSSION QUESTIONS

1. What are the roadblocks standing in the way of reaching literacy goals in your school or district? What initiatives have been tried? What are the results?

2. What should be your response to the ever-increasing number of secondary students who are unable to read at grade level?

3. How do the expectations of your school, district, and state regarding reading proficiency compare to those in other states?

4. How might you better deal with the increasing numbers of special education referrals that are being made at the secondary level?

5. What does the trend data in your school or district show with regard to changing demographics, and how do you plan to respond to these changes?

6. What kind of professional development opportunities do teachers need in order to acquire the attitudes and skills to teach all students how to read to learn?

Focus on Changing What You Can Change

Making catch-up growth in middle school is perhaps twice as hard as doing it in elementary school and even harder in high school. The curriculum, master schedules, limited expertise in reading instruction by language arts instructors, materials, and student motivation all work against catch-up growth, especially when it must be double or triple the annual growth.

—Fielding, Kerr, and Rosier (2004, p. 165)

When I assumed the principalship of a suburban Chicago elementary school in the early 1980s, reading achievement was at an all-time low—the 20th percentile for Grades 2 through 6 on the Iowa Test of Basic Skills. The news was depressing, and the superintendent made it clear that he was looking for improvement. I was brand new to administration and knew nothing about raising test scores. My teaching experience was in communities similar to the imaginary Lake Woebegon, Minnesota, where all the students are above average.

At the first faculty meeting, I asked the teachers why they thought achievement was so low. They offered plenty of reasons for the dismal state of affairs: the students, the parents, the community, and central office, to name just a few. The teachers didn't mention any role they might have personally played in the test results, but their reactions were not unlike those of most educators faced with failing students: "We say we believe that all children can learn, but few of us really believe it" (Delpit, 1995, p. 172).

The responses of my faculty mirrored the conclusions of James Coleman's (1966) work, a massive education research project funded by the federal government. Coleman shocked educators when he reported that differences in the resources of schools were not a consideration in how well students achieved. Rather, he concluded, it was the background of students that made the difference. His report, which set in motion the large-scale busing plans of the late 1960s, completely overlooked school-wide and classroom variables that affect student achievement.

In response to Coleman's (1966) indictment of schools, a group of researchers began to examine school effectiveness, demonstrating in both quantitative and qualitative studies that the following variables clearly made an impact on students' academic success, even in schools where demographics seemed to dictate failure:

- Administrative leadership
- Climate conducive to learning
- Schoolwide emphasis on learning
- Teacher expectations of achievement
- Monitoring system of pupil progress tied to instructional objectives
- Parent involvement
- Time on task (Edmonds, 1979; Purkey & Smith, 1983; Rutter, Maughan, Mortimer, & Ouston, 1979).

To help my staff shift their thinking in a new direction, I gave them a short course in what Benjamin Bloom (1980) called "alterable variables." He scolded educators for whining about things over which they had no control (e.g., the demographics of their students and parents). As we brainstormed what those variables might be at Lincoln School, the list began to grow. So did our excitement and motivation to change the way we conducted the business of schooling. During the eight years we worked together, reading achievement climbed to the 70th and 80th percentiles. And if we had known then what is known now about reading instruction and the importance of early intervention (see Chapter 3), we could have boosted achievement to at least the 95th percentile (Hall, 2006).

In spite of the depth and durability of evidence demonstrating that demographics don't have to determine the destiny of our students, there are some who continue to expend their energies on dissecting inalterable variables rather than applying their scholarship to changing what needs to be changed in today's schools (Berliner, 2005).

While I cannot claim that the specific changes we made "caused" our achievement to go up, we did indeed experience a steady upward trend in our students' literacy levels as we began to tinker with variables that we could definitely point to as being out of alignment with research and best practices (e.g., amount of allocated and academic learning time devoted to explicit reading instruction, low expectations for students, and absence of cooperative learning).

Your challenge lies in determining just which variables need to be altered and in what ways they need to be changed in your classroom, school, or district. No one can give you a recipe that's guaranteed to work. Replication of what another school has done is difficult, if not impossible, without the vision of a strong leader and the collective efforts of all of the stakeholders. Your school community is unique, and any changes you make must address the needs of those that work and live there. The vision to guide your school's direction must come from a strong instructional leadership team, but everyone must have a stake in the planning and implementation—parents, students, staff, and administration.

Here are ten variables that you do have the power to change. You will undoubtedly think of several more that apply to your unique setting as you read:

1. Your educational paradigm

2. How goals are set

3. How teachers teach

4. The curriculum and how it is chosen

5. The alignment of the curriculum

6. The amount of time allocated to the teaching of reading

7. Where strategic reading is taught

8. How learning is assessed

9. Expectations for students

10. How professional development is provided

Teaching for Learning Tip 2.1 explains the importance of giving students the background knowledge they need *prior* to assigning textbook readings.

TEACHING FOR LEARNING TIP 2.1

Figure Out What's Hard for Students and Teach It

How to Get Started

Step into the shoes (or the brains) of your students, whether struggling or gifted, and figure out what is most difficult about the text or topic you are planning to teach. Even the brightest students may lack background knowledge or be confused by poorly written text. Is there too much information? Do students lack sufficient background knowledge to understand? Is the text poorly written or disorganized? Is there a great deal of unimportant information in the text?

After you have determined the most difficult aspects of your content, directly teach students what they need to know to be successful. For example, using the text, model for students how you distinguish between important and trivial information when you are reading. Show a video clip, draw a diagram on the board, or read aloud from a primary source document to provide background information that students may not have. If the main idea is especially difficult to understand, make a summarizing statement in advance of giving the reading assignment. Make difficult content as accessible and comprehensible as possible for all students.

Resources to Help You Implement

Deshler & Schumaker, 2006. *Teaching Adolescents with Disabilities: Accessing the General Education Curriculum.*

Don't assume that this recommended resource would be useful *only* to special educators. There are many struggling students in your classroom who don't qualify for special education but *could* be far more successful with these approaches. See especially Chapter 3 by Bulgren and Schumaker on teaching practices that optimize curriculum access.

Research on Curricular Access

Afflerbach, 1990a, 1990b; Bransford, 1983; Dole, Valencia, Greer, & Wardrop, 1991; Pearson, Roehler, Dole, & Duffy, 1992.

CHANGE THE EDUCATIONAL PARADIGM

> *Twenty years ago all I needed to do was keep the teachers and the parents happy. Now I have to get results.*
>
> —Anonymous Principal

As I travel the country working with principals and teachers to raise achievement in low-performing schools, I ask them to identify the differences between the old (only some students are capable of learning) and new (all students are expected to learn and educators will be held accountable) paradigms in education. A paradigm is a way of looking at or thinking about an idea or practice—a set of shared assumptions. The paradigm defines the needs that are addressed, the students who are served, and how those services are provided. Your current educational paradigm has no doubt been around for decades. It is probably solid, providing both continuity and stability to your school or district, if not results. It may seem impossible to shift. Many administrators, teachers, and even parents will defend the current paradigm and some will actively resist changing it. Only new discoveries, new knowledge, or revolutionary concepts advanced and supported by strong instructional leadership can change a paradigm.

Here are some of the old paradigm's assumptions to which many educators are still clinging: (a) activity counts for more than achievement; (b) teachers and students deserve to have fun (activity); (c) teachers should be able to teach what and how they choose (autonomy); (d) principals should focus on keeping the buses running, the budgets balanced, and the boilers humming and stay out of classrooms unless specifically invited; (e) all students aren't capable of learning; (f) some teachers are better suited to teaching gifted students and should not have to teach struggling students; (g) teachers and principals are not accountable to the public; (h) students and teachers are overworked.

Recall the Ron Edmonds quote at the end of Chapter 1. Embracing the new paradigm with commitment and enthusiasm requires some soul searching regarding how teachers and administrators feel about the fact that to this point in time they haven't done an adequate job of teaching at-risk students. The new paradigm requires raising expectations, changing instructional methodologies, and adopting research-based programs so that all students have increased opportunities to learn. The new paradigm requires principals with courage and character who are willing to be instructional leaders rather than merely managers of administrivia. The new paradigm requires that everyone—including students and parents—work collaboratively toward a common goal. As one courageous principal told his staff, "Well, folks, if all of our students were successful and achieving at the 99th percentile, you could be just as creative and autonomous as you pleased. But since we are in decline with no signs of stopping, you need to get with a program that works and start teaching them all to read [and read to learn]."

CHANGE HOW GOALS ARE SET

Tangible and unyielding goals are the focus of high-performing schools.

—Carter (1999, p. 5)

Every school and district in the United States engages in an annual frenzy of setting goals and writing improvement plans. It is, without question, a rite of spring in education. The plans are sent to the board of education for approval, printed on card stock, and then posted in offices and classrooms where they are promptly ignored. Here are some typical district goals from one such exercise:

- Implement the new computerized reading program.
- Assess the learning styles of low-achieving readers.
- Train teachers in the use of reading strategies.

If your goals are similar to these, you are unlikely to raise achievement. Your efforts will be like those of a basketball team I watched during a recent NBA playoff game. The commentator was lamenting the losing team's lackluster performance as its players raced up and down the court with no evidence of teamwork. "What we need here," he wryly observed, paraphrasing revered former UCLA basketball coach John Wooden (1997, p. 20), "is less activity and more achievement." The commentator could have been describing the average school in America. Many well-meaning professionals are so busy innovating and implementing that they have no idea if what they are doing actually works.

We had only one goal in the first year of our reading-improvement initiative at Lincoln School: reduce the number of students scoring in the bottom quartile by 10 percent. We called them *target students* because we targeted our efforts toward improving their reading abilities. We used a standardized test to determine our ultimate success, but teacher-made tests, performance assessments, and curriculum-based measurements were used frequently during the year to monitor our students' progress at key points. We focused on the numbers—not a natural mindset for many educators. Schmoker (1999) points out that "schools have an almost cultural and ingrained aversion to reckoning with, much less living by, results" (p. 3). We want to get credit for our good intentions, but unfortunately, good intentions do not necessarily result in improvement.

The staff and students at Lincoln exceeded the initial goal, reducing the number of students scoring in the bottom quartile by nearly 15 percent. If we had set a global achievement goal at the outset (e.g., to have all of our students reading on grade level at some distant point in the future), its sheer magnitude would have rendered it meaningless for many staff members. Instead, we set a reasonable and measurable goal, thus rallying staff members to what Glickman (1990) calls "a cause beyond oneself" (p. 18).

One powerful way for teams or departments to focus their efforts is by setting measurable mini-goals to be achieved during a one-month period. The 30-Minute-30-Day Rapid Results Meeting Agenda shown in Form 2.1 provides a template to help teachers conduct thirty-minute goal-setting meetings. During the first meeting, the group may take a little

Form 2.1   30-Minute-30-Day Rapid Results Meeting Agenda

Timekeeper _____ Recorder _____ Facilitator _____

Purpose of this meeting _____

Rank the students on a teacher-made, standardized, or state-mandated assessment.

_____

_____

Identify the students who are most in need of extra help or the outcome or standard that is the lowest overall for the class.

_____

_____

_____

Write a clear, measurable, attainable, and compelling goal for what your students should be able to do for the one area you have chosen as most important. (5 minutes)

_____

_____

Brainstorm possible solutions to reach this goal. (8–10 minutes)

List the best ideas from the brainstorming session. **Describe** how they will be measured. **Set priorities** based on which are perceived to be most effective. (8 minutes)

Best Ideas	Measure	Priority

Team Members Present _____

_____

Next team meeting is on _____ to share results and set a new goal. The recorder is to give a copy of this completed form to principal and team members today.

Thank you.

_____

SOURCE: McEwan (2002). Form by C. Quinn, San Diego County Office of Education. Reprinted by permission.

longer than thirty minutes, but stick with the process, always begin on time, and expect results. Gather pretreatment data to bring specific focus to the goal. After thirty days of implementation, collect posttreatment data and present the results to the principal or share findings with the entire faculty. Highly focused, time-intensive goals serve as a powerful incentive for teachers to notch up their own performance and in turn raise expectations for their students while at the same time motivating all faculty to pay attention to results.

For example, a high school science department might decide to include a regular writing-to-learn activity according to an agreed-upon schedule for thirty days (i.e., "the treatment"). Student work products from every student enrolled in a science class would be collected prior to beginning the treatment to assist teachers in identifying specific areas needed for improvement (e.g., use of complete sentences, relevance of the answer to the question, ability to provide supporting statements, etc.). The responses would be evaluated with a collaboratively developed rubric similar to the one shown in Exhibit 2.1 developed by the Science Department of Alief Hastings High School (Houston, Texas). Summative work products would then be collected after the thirty-day treatment period and be evaluated by an outside evaluator from another department using the supplied rubric. Teachers who want to translate the scoring rubric into grades can do so using the point totals and corresponding percentages in Exhibit 2.2.

CHANGE HOW TEACHERS TEACH

> *We believe teachers and teaching are the heart of the educational enterprise. . . . We further believe that a teacher's skill makes a difference in the performance of students, not only in their achievement scores on tests (as important as that might be), but in their sense of fulfillment in school and their feelings of well-being.*
>
> —Saphier and Gower (1987, p. v).

If too many students are being left behind in your school or classroom, consider an alternative instructional mindset—one that can simultaneously meet the needs of both struggling and gifted students. I recommend *mastery learning,* an approach we used in our district with astounding success in the early 1980s, after reading the work of Benjamin Bloom (1971) and James Block (1971).

Regrettably, at some point during the past two decades, mastery learning was reconceptualized as a rigid, teacher-directed approach suitable

Exhibit 2.1 Scoring Rubric for Writing in Response to Science Prompt

Performance Element	3 Points Exemplary Work Product	2 Points Adequate Work Product	1 Point Insufficient Work Product	No Points Absent Work Product
Topic Sentence	Topic sentence specifically addresses the prompt, completely prepares the reader for what will be discussed in the remaining sentences of the paragraph in a defensible way, and does not overreach by including evidence and explanations that are inappropriate for a topic sentence.	Topic sentence partially addresses the prompt and prepares the reader for what will be discussed in a general way.	Attempts to address the prompt. Attempts to prepare the reader for what will be discussed in the remaining sentences of the paragraph.	No topic sentence.
Supporting Statements	Supporting statements provide sufficient evidence in support of the topic sentence. Includes at least two of the following elements: definitions of scientific terms, quotations, scientific principles, data, or a scientifically sound argument.	Provides adequate evidence or proof in support of the topic sentence. Includes only one of the following elements: definitions of scientific terms, quotations, scientific principles, data, or a scientifically sound argument.	Provides insufficient evidence or proof in support of the topic sentence. Attempts to include additional elements are incomplete.	No supporting statements.
Further Insight	Work contains a well-developed explanation that relates to the real world or larger context.	Contains an explanation that only partially relates to the real world or larger context.	An insufficient attempt to develop an explanation that relates to the real world or larger context.	No explanation.

SOURCE: Adapted by permission of the Alief Hastings High School Science Department and Chairperson Craig Smith, Alief Hastings High School, Alief ISD, Houston, Texas.

Exhibit 2.2   Point Totals and Corresponding Percentages

9 = 100%	4 = 55%
8 = 95%	3 = 45%
7 = 85%	2 = 35%
6 = 75%	1 = 25%
5 = 65%	0 = 0%

only for dishing up rote skills and trivial information. This may have resulted in some measure from the descriptions given to it in popular educational psychology textbooks: an anticonstructivist, behavioral management technique in which instruction proceeded in a lockstep manner at the pace of the slowest students in the class (R. Gentile, personal conversation, November 17, 2005).

In reality, mastery learning combines the critical attributes of standards-based learning, differentiated instruction, and strategic reading instruction in one of the few instructional packages that works at any level or for any content *and* can truly promise that no student will be left behind (Gentile & Lalley, 2003, p. 129). Here are the four basic principles around which the "reconstituted" mastery learning is organized:

1. Explicit instructional objectives, hierarchically sequenced, which all students are expected to attain

2. Criterion-referenced assessments to evaluate and provide feedback on the achievement of those objectives

3. Remedial instruction for students who do not achieve the desired standard of performance

4. Enrichment activities and a corresponding grading scheme to encourage students to go beyond initial mastery of essentials to higher-order thinking that includes a variety of applications of their newly acquired knowledge and skills (p.156).

Mastery learning is grounded in a criterion-referenced mindset (i.e., all students can learn) as compared to a norm-referenced or competitive approach to learning (i.e., only some students can learn). Note the parallels to the old and new paradigms. James Lalley explains, "Although a norm-referenced mindset may not at first glance appear to be competitive in nature, consider that many teachers typically teach to their best students and move on when those students are able to do well on the test. With this approach, some students achieve less (the losers) than others (the winners) in terms of grading, credit, *and* learning. Unfortunately, if learning new content is contingent upon the mastery of earlier content (more losing), a substantial number of students will fall even farther behind" (J. Lalley, personal communication, November 18, 2005). See the Teaching for Learning Tip 3.4, Teach for Mastery, in Chapter 3 for further suggestions regarding how to implement this approach.

CHANGE THE CURRICULUM AND HOW IT IS CHOSEN

When even a small percentage of students in your school are failing to pass high-stakes assessments, remediating their deficiencies requires a careful consideration of research-based programs and methodologies— different programs and methodologies than those offered in regular reading and language arts classrooms. At Millard Central Middle School (MCMS) in Omaha, Nebraska, 85 percent of sixth graders, 93 percent of seventh graders, and 90 percent of eighth graders met the specified benchmarks in reading at the end of 2005, but principal Jim Sutfin wasn't ready to rest on his laurels just yet. Students in the Millard District are required to pass a "high-stakes" graduation exam, and they must be prepared before they leave MCMS.

Twenty percent of the students at MCMS receive special education services and, in addition, the demographics of the school are rapidly changing. (NOTE: The 20 percent figure includes not only students from MCMS's attendance area, but also students enrolled in districtwide programs housed at MCMS: ELL, Structured Behavior Skills, Multi-Categorical, and Montessori.) Jim is cognizant of the challenges that lie ahead for his staff and is leading the school improvement team to plan ahead, developing a coordinated instructional delivery system that meets the needs of at-risk students.

The goals at MCMS are two: (a) All students will achieve one year or more of academic growth for each year they attend MCMS and (b) each grade level, irrespective of the students enrolled, will raise its achievement during each successive year. To achieve these goals, the administrative and school improvement teams determined a need for additional reading classes at all grade levels to address serious reading deficiencies using solid research-based instruction. Jim relied on his assistant principal, Beth Balkus, to select the curriculum. After investigating a number of possibilities, she chose *Corrective Reading* (Engelmann, Hanner, & Johnson, 1999), a research-validated direct-instruction program that produces remarkable results when teachers are well trained and the program is taught with fidelity to the model.

All sixth-grade and seventh-grade students at MCMS receive reading (a class focused on teaching students how to read to learn, i.e., use cognitive strategies in their content reading) *and* language arts (a class where grammar, writing, and the study of literature are the focus), while all eighth-grade students are enrolled in a combination reading and English class. These classes, while offering more reading instruction than found at many middle schools, did not provide specific instruction for the very lowest students.

The new classes are remedial in nature (i.e., they provide interventions to bring below-grade-level students to grade level) and were introduced at sixth and eighth grades for the first time during the 2005–2006 school year. A seventh-grade class is planned for the 2006–2007 school year when the entire schedule is being redesigned to accommodate a districtwide change to six-week electives. Enrollment in the remedial classes is based on test scores, and the class sizes range from five to ten students at the sixth- and seventh-grade levels and five students to one teacher at the eighth-grade level. Beth and her colleagues are proactively meeting the challenges of the school's changing demographics and refuse to let demographics determine their students' academic destinies.

CHANGE THE ALIGNMENT OF THE CURRICULUM

Adrienne Hamparian Johnson is an eighth-grade literature teacher at West Chicago Middle School, Illinois, where raising reading achievement is a priority. A finalist for Illinois teacher of the year in 1999 and a National Board Certified Teacher in Adolescent Language Arts, Adrienne works tirelessly with her principal and colleagues to make sure that everyone takes the school's mission seriously. Her choice for the most influential variable in raising achievement: consistency. "A school or a district must be tightly woven," she explains, "with everyone on the same page." The middle school teachers have collaborated with the elementary staff on a districtwide language arts committee to ensure that everyone is pulling in the same direction. Together, they are working to overcome the "this too shall pass" mentality that derails many well-intentioned improvement plans (A. Johnson, personal communication, November 20, 2005). Adrienne feels so strongly about the importance of standards and alignment she also serves as a member of the state of Illinois' Language Arts Advisory Committee.

Fenwick English (1992) described the challenges of creating a district that is seamless:

Curriculum design and delivery face one fundamental problem in schools. When the door is shut and nobody else is around, the classroom teacher can select and teach just about any curriculum he or she decides is appropriate. This fact of organizational autonomy represents the shoals of many so-called "reforms" in education: innumerable board policy pronouncements, state testing mandates, national goals, superintendent's decisions, or principal/supervisory dicta. (p. 1)

Working to create a tightly woven or aligned curriculum is not an easy undertaking, but, without alignment, achieving success may be an elusive goal. To raise achievement, aim for curricular quality control: "a process that concerns the internal capability of a school system to improve its performance over time . . . by developing goals and objectives, employing people to reach the goals, periodically assessing the differences between desired and actual performance, and then using the discrepancy data to adjust and improve day-to-day operations" (English, 1992, p. 19).

The Attributes of an Aligned District or School

- The mastery of certain key skills and concepts is required at some point (i.e., there are expectations that students will achieve certain benchmarks at each grade level).

- Teachers use a common language, employ research-based methodologies, and teach the same cognitive strategies schoolwide so that students are able to build on their learning from grade to grade rather than starting over each year.

- Teachers use a standardized assignment notebook and subscribe to similar homework and grading policies.

- Teachers exercise reasonable amounts of autonomy and creativity in their classrooms but never to the detriment of their students' achievement.

- Teachers teach the routines, rubrics, and rules they expect all students to master during the first three weeks of school and use during the remaining thirty-three weeks of the school year (McEwan, 2006).

- Teachers have a clear understanding of what students are expected to learn in their grade levels as well as in prior and subsequent grades and can explain to parents how the curriculum and instruction in their classrooms relate and contribute to that learning continuum.

- Teachers at the same grade levels coordinate their efforts to ensure instructional equity (e.g., all of the sophomore English students are exposed to the same titles and genres, receive the same amount of instructional time, and are evaluated using the same rubrics).

- All students are told what they are expected to learn, shown how they will be evaluated, and presented with examples and role models that demonstrate excellence.

CHANGE THE AMOUNT OF TIME ALLOCATED TO READING INSTRUCTION

> *Students who are behind do not learn more in the same amount of time as students who are ahead. Catch-up growth is driven primarily by proportional increases in direct instructional time. Catch-up growth is so difficult to achieve that it can be the product only of quality instruction in great quantity.*
>
> —Fielding et al. (2004, p. 52)

If you want to raise achievement, you must allocate more instructional time to reading instruction than you have in the past, particularly for those students who are well below grade level, and then use every minute of that time wisely. Middle and high school educators, under pressure to raise achievement, are examining every option to find extra time for reaching low-achieving students: before and after school, Saturday school, summer academies, and multiple periods of reading instruction during the school day.

Dave Bond, principal of Kamiakin High School (KHS) in Kennewick, Washington, is a man in a hurry. There's no time to waste when it comes to catching up the ninth graders who are academically deficient. Dave explains, "We have a philosophy that when kids come to us and they can't read, we're going to get them reading on grade level as fast as we can. By the spring of their eighth-grade year, we know which kids are in trouble and which kids are in good shape, and we select the students that we're going to put into intensive reading help" (D. Bond, personal communication, February 2, 2006).

Dave has mobilized a literacy coach who provides intensive, ongoing training for teachers (often one to one), four ninth-grade English-reading support teachers, and an entire faculty of content teachers who are all committed to teaching reading in their content areas. The team has two years to reach their goal with each incoming freshmen class: meeting the standards on the Washington Assessment of Student Learning (WASL) reading test given in the spring of tenth grade.

Four years ago, when Dave and his staff began to build the program, only 69 percent of students met the standards. Now, 89 percent of students are hitting the target. "Last spring (2005), 336 sophomores took the reading test. Only 36 didn't meet the standard, and half of those students were special education (SPED) students. We sat down with the teachers and went through the list, student by student. In spite of our best efforts, there are students who fall through the cracks. They're in the juvenile justice system, they've been absent for thirty-five days, or there are other variables that have made it almost impossible for teachers to meet their needs. We don't control every facet of students' lives. But there were kids about whom we said, 'We could have had this kid if we'd done this or that differently'" (D. Bond, personal communication, February 2, 2006).

Here's how the Kamiakin personalized learning system works: Four English teachers are assigned a ninth-grade reading class as part of their schedule. Each of these English teachers also has at least two and sometimes three sections of ninth-grade English. The reading classes are limited to fifteen students. A student who comes to Kamiakin High School with below-ninth-grade reading skills is assigned a reading teacher and has English with the same teacher later in the day. Each English teacher is teamed with a ninth-grade social studies teacher and a ninth-grade science teacher. All students assigned to that English teacher also have the same teacher for science (although not all in the same class period) and for social studies (although not all in the same period). The reading teacher coordinates with these two other content area teachers. The reading teacher then assists the students with their reading challenges in English, social studies, and science.

The reading teacher also has a wide array of data to use in determining how to best help the students to improve their reading skills. The data comes from the Measures of Academic Progress (MAP) test (Northwest Evaluation Association, 2006) and in-building tests that the school administers, as well as data from software programs, such as the Academy of Reading program. The reading teacher uses all of the data to determine appropriate individualized or small group instruction for each student.

English teachers assigned to reading classes are supported by as many as five colleagues who also teach one section of reading, a literacy coach, a paraeducator, and instructional software support from Auto-Skill, publishers of the Academy of Reading software.

In math, a slightly different approach is used. Four different math teachers teach two or three sections of ninth-grade math. Each teacher is assigned thirteen to fifteen students who have been identified as having below-ninth-grade math skills and who are scheduled across that teacher's sections of ninth-grade math. In addition, the students are scheduled for a second period of math later in the day with the same teacher. During the second period of math, the teacher validates students' understanding of the earlier lesson, reteaches the material individually or in small groups as necessary, and introduces the concepts to be covered in upcoming lessons. In addition, the students work on a software program (Academy of Math) that is designed to help them review and learn the basic skills in which they are weak.

Ninth-grade students are retested on the MAP test just before the end of the first semester. Students who have caught up to grade level are exited from the second reading or math class. Additional testing is done for the students who were identified by teachers as struggling during the first semester in their regular ninth-grade English or math classes. Some of those students are added to the second math class if the testing indicates that they need it. Both of these models are repeated at the tenth-grade level.

Scores are moving up in Kennewick School District and at KHS, but not without massive infusions of quality instructional contact time for students who are behind. In 1995, well in advance of NCLB, visionary administrators and school board members set a district goal to have 90 percent of third-grade students (including all ELL and special education students) reading at or above grade level. When they launched their improvement initiative, 57 percent of Kennewick third graders were reading at or above grade level. They reached 77 percent in 2000, 82 percent in 2001, 86 percent in 2003, and 88 percent in 2004. Dave and his faculty have reaped the benefits from the increased emphasis on raising reading achievement in the lower grades, but they also know that there are still kids falling through the cracks before they reach high school. They have chosen to use the precious time their students have left in school to focus on literacy (L. Fielding, personal communication, January 23, 2006; P. Rosier, personal communication, January 30, 2006; D. Bond, personal communication, February 2, 2006).

See Teaching Tip 2.2 and Exhibits 2.3–2.5 for information about using rubrics to communicate standards and expectations to students.

CHANGE WHERE STRATEGIC
READING INSTRUCTION IS PROVIDED

> *For too long, reading and writing have been taught as "subjects." They are not subjects like history, geography, or physical science, they are processes, strategies, or tools. . . . We read and write about something. It is impossible to learn or use these language strategies separately from content.*
>
> —Irvin (1998, p. 42)

The nation's governors are concerned about adolescent literacy. Their report, *Reading to Achieve: A Governor's Guide to Adolescent Literacy* (National Governors Association, 2005), estimates that about half the incoming ninth graders in urban and high-poverty schools read three years or more below grade level. The report recommends that educators address literacy skills by teaching them within the context of core academic subjects rather than apart from challenging content instruction (Johnston, 2005).

TEACHING FOR LEARNING TIP 2.2

Develop and Use Scoring Rubrics

How to Get Started

Rubrics are scoring guides in which students' work products or performances are evaluated using specific, preestablished performance criteria along a continuum of excellence. When rubrics are well constructed and explicitly taught to and modeled for students in advance of giving assignments, they have the potential to accomplish the following goals:

1. Define in precise and age-appropriate language what you want your students to know, do, or be while they are in your classroom as well as when you send them on to the next level.

2. Communicate those expectations to students in positive and empowering ways through the collaborative development of rubrics.

3. Objectively assess students' progress toward meeting the academic and behavioral goals you have set forth and provide helpful information for modifying your instruction.

4. Provide students with ongoing opportunities to self-assess their own academic, social, and behavioral progress.

5. Assist you in teaching your students not only the what, but also the how and why, in more explicit, systematic, and supportive ways (McEwan, 2006).

Rubrics are even more powerful when developed in collaboration with colleagues to align student expectations across departments or with students to empower them and increase motivation. See Exhibit 2.3, a rubric developed by the staff at Aki Kurose Middle School Academy to help their students understand what it takes to do well on state assessments in terms of attitude and effort. Exhibits 2.4 and 2.5 are samples of materials used by the Alief Hastings High School in developing the rubric for scoring writing to learn assignments in science. Remember to provide excellent models that show students specifically what a "good one" looks like.

Resources to Help You Implement

McEwan, 2006. *How to Survive and Thrive in the First Three Weeks of School.*
Mertler, 2003. *Classroom Assessment: A Practical Guide for Educators.*

Research on the Power of Using Rubrics

Goodrich Andrade, 2001; Reeves, 2004.

Exhibit 2.3 My Best Performance Rubric

My Best Performance Rubric	Exceeds Standards	Meets Standards	Approaching the Standard; Needs Improvement	Standards Not Met
Preparedness	I am quiet and in my seat on time with my pens, pencils, notebook, planner, and any other supplies I need.			
Respectful attitude	I am polite to my classmates and adults and respectful of their right to work without disruption.			
Confidence and a positive attitude	I *always* show that I believe in myself by being serious and focused and by taking pride in doing my very best. I know that confidence will positively impact my work.	I *consistently* show that I believe in myself by being serious and focused and by taking pride in my work. I know that confidence will positively impact my work.	I *sometimes* show that I believe in myself by being serious and focused. Sometimes I get discouraged, and it becomes hard for me to be proud of my work.	I *do not* take my work or achievement seriously. I often get discouraged and *do not* show that I am confident.
Time management	I use *all* of the time I am given to work on my task and check my work. I keep my attention focused on doing my very best.	I use the *majority of the time* I am given to work on my task and check my work. I consistently keep my focus on doing my very best.	I *sometimes* use only a portion of the time I am given to work on my task and check my work. I am frequently unfocused and inattentive.	I *do not* stayed focused on doing my best. I use only the minimum amount of time I am given to work attentively on my task. I rarely check my work.
Reading the questions carefully (being sure about what I'm being asked to do)	I use *all* of these strategies to follow the instruction correctly: I underline key words of the instructions. I number the steps of the instructions. I restate the question in my answer.	I use *at least two* of these strategies to follow the instructions correctly: I underline key words of the instructions. I number the steps of the instructions. I restate the question in my answer.	I *sometimes* rush through reading the instructions and am in a hurry to answer the questions. I *sometimes* do not use many of the strategies that are needed to help make me successful.	I *do not* read the instructions or I carelessly rush through reading the instructions. I *do not* use any set strategies effectively.

My Best Performance Rubric	Exceeds Standards	Meets Standards	Approaching the Standard; Needs Improvement	Standards Not Met
Perseverance and determination	I *always* push myself to continue working on the task even when difficulties arise or a solution is not immediately clear.	I *consistently* try to continue working even when the task is difficult or a solution is not immediately clear.	*Sometimes* I get discouraged and give up. The task seems to take too long and *sometimes* I decide not to continue to try.	I often become frustrated and tired. I *do not* feel like I can do well on my task and *do not* continue to try my best.
Making an attempt on every task	I *always* pay attention to places where the instructions say things like, "show all your work," "describe or show," "give two examples."	I *consistently* pay attention to places where the instructions say things like, "show all your work," "describe or show," "give two examples."	I *sometimes* pay attention to places where the instructions say things like, "show all your work," "describe or show," "give two examples."	When I turn in my assignments, I *do not* check to see that I've answered everything completely.
Resourcefulness	When I am confused or unsure of how to do something, I brainstorm all of the different ways I might solve the problem. Then I try several approaches until I feel comfortable with my answer.	When I am confused or unsure of how to do something, I think about how to solve the problem using strategies I know. I *consistently* use a strategy I felt comfortable with.	When I am confused or unsure about how to do something I *sometimes* get frustrated and give up. Every now and then, I try to answer the question or solve the problem using a strategy that I think will help. As a result, I often leave answers blank or give incomplete responses.	I *do not* think of any strategies that will help me solve the problem or answer the question. I frequently get frustrated and give up. As a result, I often leave answers blank or give partial responses.
Using resources and tools to check my work	I use *all* of the resources and tools that I am allowed to use to make my work stronger (*calculator, thesaurus, dictionary, graphic organizers*). I use my finger or a pencil to scan my work to be sure I'm not leaving blanks where there should be an answer.	I *consistently* use all of the resources and tools that I am allowed to use to make my work stronger (*calculator, thesaurus, dictionary, graphic organizers*). I use my finger or a pencil to scan my work to be sure I'm not leaving blanks where there should be an answer.	I *sometimes* use the resources and tools that I am allowed to use to make my work stronger. My original draft or response rarely shows that it's been improved. I *sometimes* use my finger or a pencil to scan my work to be sure I'm not leaving blanks where there should be an answer.	I *do not* use the resources and tools that I am allowed to use to make my work stronger. My work does not show that I've improved upon the original draft or response. I *do not* scan to be sure that I'm not leaving any blanks where there should be an answer.

SOURCE: Copyright © 2004 by Aki Kurose Middle School Academy. Reprinted by permission.

Exhibit 2.4 Definitions for Developing a Rubric

Science Department

Definitions for Rubric

Paragraph

A *paragraph* is a collection of related sentences dealing with a single topic. An effective paragraph contains a topic sentence (the essential idea of the paragraph), unity (all ideas are related to and focused on the topic sentence), coherence (all sentences are related and connected to one another), and adequate development.

Topic Sentence

A *topic sentence* is a sentence that indicates in a general way the ideas the paragraph will develop. It is often the first sentence of the paragraph—but does not have to be. It is the most general sentence in the paragraph, and it is considered a "contract" between the writer and reader. The writer is promising to limit the discussion in the paragraph to the idea(s) stated in the topic sentence.

Support

Support includes all ideas that are acceptable and reasonable methods a writer can use to prove his/her answer is accurate or correct. One nearly indisputable form of support is to quote direct words from a source.

Insight

Insight is a particularly thoughtful conclusion or interpretation. Insight shows a depth of understanding that goes beyond the literal or superficial—an understanding of the nuances.

SOURCE: Reprinted by permission of Allyson Burnett, Interventionist Specialist, Alief Hastings High School, Alief ISD, Houston, Texas.

Exhibit 2.5 Model Response for Science Teacher Scoring

Title of Article: Human-Animal Chimeras

Prompt Given by Science Teacher: What is this article mainly about?

Topic Sentence: This article is mainly about the chimeras.

Support: On the one hand, researchers need to study how stem cells behave inside the body and due to the risk, preferably not a human body! This will require "freedom to test in animals and thereby make chimeras." For example, scientists might make a mouse with human brain tissue. On the other hand, those who oppose these experiments are seeking support with laws that would "outlaw several kinds of chimeras" as well as the "introduction of animal cells into human blastocysts."

Insight: There is concern over the blurring of the boundaries that separate people from animals. Could the line be crossed enough to ever have a human female give birth to a litter of puppies?

SOURCE: Reprinted by permission of Allyson Burnett and Andi Malin, Alief Hastings High School, Alief ISD, Houston, Texas.

In many secondary schools, reading instruction is limited to a few remedial classes, often held in portable units in the parking lot. Oh, there may be a handful of English teachers who include some strategy instruction in their literature classes, but rarely do teachers in other content areas concern themselves with reading instruction. Carol Santa (1986) says, "Secondary teachers feel their job is to impart particular content information. All too often they forget that their fundamental role is to teach the process of learning" (p. 303). Increasing numbers of educators are recognizing, however, that meaningful strategy instruction is best done in the context of content classes where all students can reap the benefits of instruction, not just a few.

Larry Snyder is a strategic teacher at Robert A. Taft Middle School in Canton, Ohio. At the beginning of each school year, he introduces his students to the concept of strategic reading by asking them, "What do good readers do while they are reading? What mental tools do they have that enable them to comprehend, analyze, and interpret a text? How do they make sense of challenging material?" After a brief discussion, he models strategic reading and thinking for his students. To do this, he alternates reading aloud and thinking aloud from a primary source document like the Bill of Rights.

Let's observe Larry. He is reading aloud when we slip into the classroom. During his reading, he frequently stops to think aloud, pausing to activate prior knowledge and experiences that relate to the text, question the author's intent, infer the meaning of unfamiliar words, summarize what he has read so far, and visualize what he thinks the setting may have looked like at the time the document was written.

During his year-long American History course, Mr. Snyder will not only teach the required content, he will also teach his students how to learn the content in more efficient and effective ways. He will teach one or two strategies at a time, introducing new ones only when his students are well on their way to mastering the previous ones. He will continue to model the use of all of the strategies for his students but will gradually expect them to think aloud about their processing during class discussions and choose appropriate strategies for use in assigned readings. His goal is to help students understand and remember the content of his course in more effective ways than they would have if taught through typical lectures and class discussions. Larry encourages others to begin integrating cognitive strategy instruction into their content classrooms:

> My advice to fellow educators is to take things one step at a time. You don't eat a whole pizza in one bite and you can't do it with cognitive strategy instruction either. For example, I've found read-alouds and think-alouds are an excellent way to introduce

primary source documents that are difficult to read. I begin from the first day breaking these down and showing students the process. We're still doing it [as of November, 2005], and some of them are beginning to catch on. They aren't ready to fly on their own just yet, but we have time. (L. Snyder, personal communication, November 12, 2005)

CHANGE HOW LEARNING IS ASSESSED

Diagnostic testing, proportional increases in instructional time, focused teaching to the deficient sub-skill, and retesting to assure that learning has actually occurred are common-sense strategies and central to how we catch up students who are behind.

—Fielding et al. (2004, p. 23)

Standardized assessments are here to stay. They provide an objective and cost-effective way to gauge generalized growth in reading. But for the real work of raising reading achievement, summative tests have limitations. Douglas Reeves (as quoted in Olson, 2005) calls them autopsy reports. "They tell you why the patient died at the end of the year" (p.13). Summative assessments can't help you choose programs, teach individual students, or plan tomorrow's lessons. For those tasks, schools need a comprehensive system that includes three additional types of assessments: (a) *diagnostic* to determine precisely why students are having certain kinds of reading difficulties, (b) *placement* to determine at precisely what instructional levels students should be placed, and (c) *formative* to determine the effectiveness of classroom instruction.

At the Boys Town Reading Center, every student is tested within a week of arrival using the Diagnostic Assessments of Reading (DAR) test (Roswell & Chall, 1992). The DAR is a criterion-referenced test that can be used to establish mastery levels (ranging from first-grade through twelfth-grade levels) in six areas of reading and related language skills: (a) word recognition, (b) oral reading or connected text, (c) knowledge of word meanings, (d) silent reading comprehension, (e) spelling, and (f) word analysis (Curtis & Longo, 1999, p. 12). Once the DAR results are compiled, decisions are made about course assignments and the need for special help. Content area teachers are informed immediately of a student's reading skills so that accommodations can be made if needed. The students who come to Boys Town are typically two to three years behind in reading, and some are reading as many as five to six years below grade level. Based on the DAR results, these students receive intensive services in the Boys Town Reading Center, a laboratory for older adolescents with reading problems. Students with word recognition difficulties receive direct instruction in word analysis along with computer and spelling-related instruction. Students with depressed vocabulary knowledge receive direct instruction in word meanings. Those with difficulties in comprehension are taught strategies and study skills. Some students receive simultaneous instruction in multiple areas; others begin at the beginning with word analysis and progress to reading a lot to gain fluency. Curriculum-based measures (i.e., procedures for assessing a student's ongoing performance with course content) are used weekly to determine progress toward goals. Results are discussed frankly with students who are usually grateful to have finally found people who recognize they have a problem, know exactly what the problem is, and have a plan to solve the problem. For more information about the Boys Town Reading Center, see the discussion in Resource B.

Assessments, whether summative or formative, are essential to the improvement process. They provide a way to monitor learning closely, they can demonstrate what students still need to learn, and they can show us how we need to adjust instruction to ensure success. See also Teaching for Learning Tip 1.4, Assess for Learning.

CHANGE EXPECTATIONS FOR STUDENTS

> *To assume that a problem is inherent in the learner leaves the teacher without any influence, because the problem is framed as being outside of the teacher's province of control (i.e., in the learner's head).*
>
> —Kameenui and Simmons (1990, p. 13).

Some educators believe students are incapable of meeting academic standards because of their demographics (e.g., poverty, limited English proficiency), low ability, or lack of motivation (laziness). Others have gradually lowered their expectations in response to pressure from parents who think their children need "less homework, more downtime, and a life outside of school" (Bempechat, 2000, p. 64). Still others have been seduced by the current wave of "self-esteem" proponents who preach that standards, pressure, hard work, frustration, challenges, and setbacks are somehow dangerous for adolescents.

Carol Jago (2000), high school English teacher in Santa Monica, California, stands in sharp contrast to these educators. She gives reading assignments to her students that make the average high school English teacher cringe—*Crime and Punishment, Beowulf,* and *The Odyssey.* She expects, requires, and even demands hard work from her students.

"What irks students," she reports, "is the work: paying attention, doing the reading, taking notes, studying for tests, writing papers. I don't blame them. But students who fail to discipline themselves to these onerous tasks learn very little." Jago (2000) is honest with her students. "Yes, *Crime and Punishment* is a very long book. It is also a heavy book. Get over it. Trust me. I would never assign this novel if it weren't a glorious story and if I didn't love it myself" (p. 27).

Hard work and high expectations don't necessarily warm parents' hearts either. The *Wall Street Journal* reported that some parents are pulling their students out of elite public high schools well-known for their histories of sending students on to highly competitive colleges because they were too focused on academics, especially math and science (Hwang, 2005).

There is another trend that is resulting in lowered expectations for students—the notion that the students themselves should be in charge. An unfortunate effect of this strong emphasis on student choice has been that teachers, swept up in the enthusiasm of creating a learner-centered curriculum, often feel guilty when their instincts tell them to take some control over the structure of their classrooms or the content of student learning. While on the one hand teachers can never place too much emphasis on the worth and dignity of the individual learner and the empowering effects of personal choice, there are times when teachers must be empowered to lead students in directions they might not take on their own (Hynds, 1997, p. 8).

Gregory Hodge, the principal of the Frederick Douglass Academy (Grades 7–12) in the central Harlem area of New York City, gives students few choices. He and his staff are focused on one goal: to get every graduate a full scholarship to college. Parents support Mr. Hodge; he gets positive results. Increasing numbers of students graduate from Frederick Douglass every year with scholarships to attend highly competitive and very prestigious universities. "You have to demand more of your students while providing them with the structure to meet those demands," says Hodge (as quoted in Carter, 1999, p. 15). He believes that the degree of student effort determines whether or not they will be successful. The Frederick Douglass Academy is a real-world example of what Lauren Resnick (1999) calls an "effort-based" school" (p. 40).

Merely telling students to work harder is not enough, however. Most students who are failing have adopted the attitudes of some of their teachers: "I can't learn because I'm not smart." "Many low-achieving students deny the importance of learning and withhold the effort it requires in order to avoid the stigma of having tried and failed" (Tomlinson, 1992, p. 1). These reluctant students need to be shown specifically and directly that their learning difficulties are simply due to their lack of knowledge regarding the right strategies (or shortcuts to learning) to use and their own lack of effort. Borokowski, Carr, Rellinger, and Pressley (1990) believe that changing low-achieving students' beliefs about themselves as learners at the same time as providing direct instruction in the cognitive strategies used routinely by high-achieving students (see Chapter 4 for the seven strategies of highly effective readers.) can have a profound effect on their achievement.

Students who have continually failed at learning to read need to be

- Taught to understand that their deficiencies are treatable.
- Shown that self-discipline and hard work are better predictors of academic performance (grades) than intelligence (Duckworth & Seligman, 2005).
- Given general problem-solving skills and accompanying attributional and motivational components.
- Explicitly taught (as opposed to merely having explained) specific strategies for a wide variety of tasks (Duffy et al., 1987).
- Given the opportunity to teach what they have learned to someone else in a reciprocal teaching situation (Borokowski et al., 1990, p. 77).

CHANGE HOW PROFESSIONAL DEVELOPMENT IS PROVIDED

The most effective staff development programs are embedded in the culture of the school. They take time, resources, money, commitment, and expertise.

—Learning First Alliance (2000, p. 27)

Providing professional development that translates to more effective classroom instruction requires long-range planning, a commitment of resources, and patience. At Millard Central Middle School, principal Jim Sutfin and his assistants, Beth Balkus and Heather Phipps, were concerned that the rapidly shifting demographics of their school would soon make it far more difficult for teachers to achieve the results to which they had become accustomed. The school improvement team identified several problems: (a) instruction in regular reading classes was focused on isolated skills without a coherent program to remediate below-grade-level students; (b) although the district had adopted a published reading comprehension program for use in reading classes, the program was not being implemented by content teachers; and (c) the majority of teachers failed to see how reading instruction fit into their responsibilities.

Beth, a former English teacher, was delegated to lead the literacy initiative and went searching for possible solutions to the identified problems as well as professional development to help Central's teachers become more skilled at teaching their students how to use cognitive strategies in their content areas. Beth knew that teachers would need a great deal of background knowledge, coaching, and practice to become skilled at integrating strategy instruction into their content areas and that implementation would take a minimum of two to three years for most teachers to feel comfortable. She especially wanted to raise expectations for teachers to integrate more modeling and thinking aloud of their own processing of text into their daily content instruction (something she had done regularly in her own classroom). She drafted a two-year plan in which all scheduled professional development would focus on a single goal: helping teachers to become skilled at strategic reading instruction. She read several books and chose one to use for a facultywide book study. Once the study groups were underway, she identified faculty members (one from each department) who were currently experimenting with strategic reading instruction and asked for permission to videotape lessons in their classrooms. With the help of the technology assistant, she produced a DVD of model lessons and used it in a professional-development session to facilitate discussion around what strategic reading teachers look and act like in their classrooms.

It was only after several months of reading, discussion, and peer observations that Beth invited a consultant in to work with teachers. After a large group session that was introductory in nature, the expert met with each department to talk about the unique aspects of literacy in their disciplines. Department teams were given two large blocks of time during the day-long session to develop think-alouds to be used in their classrooms. Although the task seemed a simple enough one at the outset, the teachers found it to be challenging to stick to their own thoughts during thinking aloud and not revert to the lecturing and explaining modes.

The next step for teachers was the development of lessons to teach specific cognitive strategies directly to students using instructional activities of their own choosing specifically related to their content. As the first year progressed, teachers were encouraged to invite colleagues in to observe their strategy instruction lessons and to visit other classes as their schedules permitted. There were once-a-week meetings in professional learning communities to discuss their progress and gain assistance from colleagues. At monthly professional development sessions, teachers began to share lesson plans and PowerPoint presentations with one another. Gradually, even some of the most vocal resistors discovered how engaged their students became in the content when they modeled the act of skilled reading for them. The implementation was not without its challenges, however.

There were a few experienced and outspoken teachers who felt certain they were already strategic teachers and needed no further professional development. Providing professional development for these experienced veterans was focused on showing them very precise models and raising their awareness regarding just what direct instruction in cognitive strategies looked like (J. Sutfin, B. Balkus, & H. Phipps, personal communication, January and February, 2006).

MCMS's plan differs in several respects from those found in many schools where a one-day "make and take" or "sit and get" is the typical model. The administrators at MCMS are planning for long-term success by building internal capacity, providing opportunities for collaboration, and giving teachers the time they need to feel at ease with a radically different approach to teaching their content.

REFLECTION AND DISCUSSION QUESTIONS

1. Describe the educational paradigm that governs how business is done in your school or district.

2. Do you and your colleagues believe that it is possible to meet the needs of gifted students, at-risk students, and all of the students in the middle?

3. What variables do you think need to be changed in your district or school?

4. Is your district or school out of alignment? What specific actions might be taken to get it into alignment?

5. What is your current approach to professional development? What else do you think Beth could do to ensure that all of the teachers at MCMS are successful?

Teach the Students Who Can't Read How to Read

Useful knowledge of the spelling-to-speech correspondences of English does not come naturally. For all children, it requires a great deal of practice, and for many children, it is not easy. The acquisition of this knowledge depends on developing a reflective appreciation of the phonemic structure of the spoken language; on learning about letter-sound correspondences and spelling conventions of the orthography; and on consolidating and extending this knowledge by using it in the course of one's own reading and writing.

—Adams (1998, p. 74)

How many students would you estimate enroll in the average kindergarten class each year already knowing how to read? I'm not talking about reading a few simple words but fluently reading the daily newspaper or an unfamiliar piece of children's literature. The hundreds of kindergarten teachers and principals to whom I've posed this question over eight years of workshops on raising reading achievement report that it is a rare class that contains more than two or three students who can read; most classes around the country have none. Steven Pinker (as quoted in McGuinness, 1997) summarizes the critical issue: "Children are wired for sound, but print is an optional accessory that must be painstakingly bolted on" (p. ix).

We aren't alarmed by this state of affairs. After all, most kindergartners have had no formal reading instruction. We don't expect them to know how to read yet.

At the other end of the educational continuum, however, the question of how many students in your middle or high school's entering class have actually read and understood the most recent Harry Potter book or even the daily newspaper is more than just academic. Some have been learning to read for years and still have miles to go. Although standardized tests are much maligned for their inability to assess the total student, they can reveal serious generalized problems. Consider these results from just one question on a standardized test of reading comprehension (Meichenbaum & Biemiller, 1998, p. 2):

"A plain, as all agree, is a great stretch of level or nearly level land."

Question: "What is true of all plains?"

Correct multiple-choice alternative: "They have no high mountains."

Two-thirds of entering high school students who took the test failed to answer the question correctly. To understand why so many students cannot answer even this simple question requires an understanding of what the current research says about how students learn to read. The problem could be a phonemic awareness (PA) deficiency, an inability to decode, dysfluency, a lack of vocabulary or background knowledge, a lack of motivation or concentration on the task at hand, or some combination of these difficulties. Fluency, the topic of Teaching for Learning Tip 3.1, is the missing piece of the reading puzzle for many secondary students. They can decode, but they cannot do it automatically and accurately enough to comprehend the text.

HOW CHILDREN LEARN TO READ: A SHORT LESSON

Reading is one of the most uniquely human and complex of all cognitive activities.

—van den Broek and Kremer (2000, p. 1)

There has never been a more exciting time to be involved in improving reading achievement. The publication of the National Reading Panel's report (National Institute of Child Health and Human Development [NICHD], 2000) summarized the available research to that date regarding what methodologies are most effective for teaching nearly every child to read. In addition, there are increasing numbers of schools where outstanding

TEACHING FOR LEARNING TIP 3.1

Develop Fluency Using Content-Based Texts

How to Get Started

Choose either commercially available fluency passages that relate to your content or write your own passages based on the critical content objectives you expect your students to master. Follow these steps in writing your own passages:

1. Identify the "big ideas" of the chapter or unit.

2. Select five to eight key words that are essential for students to automatically and accurately identify and understand when they encounter them.

3. Then either choose a section of text to rewrite at a lower reading level or write an original 125-150 word sample that explains the big ideas you have chosen and contains the key words.

4. If you are using textbook material, compact the text (reduce the amount) by deleting unimportant or repeated information and collapsing long lists of items into a single word or phrase.

5. Write a passage of 150 words that includes the big ideas and uses all of the key concept words. Pretend you are "talking the text" to your students. Write as simply as possible using short sentences and a minimum of unfamiliar words (except for new vocabulary).

6. Ask a colleague to read your passage for clarity and accuracy.

7. Determine the reading grade level of your sample using an online resource like www.interventioncentral.org/htmdocs/tools/okapi/okapi.shtml. Your goal is to lower the reading level by at least two to three grades.

8. Prepare copies for students to practice reading aloud to family members several times each evening, Monday through Thursday.

9. After you hand out the fluency passage on Monday, give a pretest of oral reading fluency (words correct per minute). Give a posttest on Friday after students have practiced reading the passage aloud for four evenings.

10. Graph the results.

See also Teaching for Learning Tips 3.2 and 5.3 for suggestions to help you teach the pronunciations and meanings of the new words in each unit.

A Resource to Help You

Adams & Brown, 2003. *The Six-Minute Solution: A Reading Fluency Program.*

Research to Support the Worth of Building Fluency

LaBerge & Samuels, 1974; Samuels, 1979.

instructional leaders and their teams of teachers are demonstrating that even the most at-risk students are capable of high achievement if exposed to the right combination of the variables (Carter, 1999; Pressley et al., 2005; Pressley, Raphael, Gallagher, & DiBlla, 2004; Reeves, 2004; Sadowski & Willson, 2006; Worthington, 2005). Figure 3.1 illustrates the pieces of the reading puzzle that must be assembled for and eventually by every student, regardless of age and Figure 3.2 describes them in more detail. Keep in mind, however, that learning to read is a far more synergistic, interactive, and simultaneous process than can be depicted in a simple puzzle such as this. As noted by early reading expert Louisa Moats (2004), "teaching reading is rocket science" (p. 1).

Figure 3.1   The Reading Puzzle

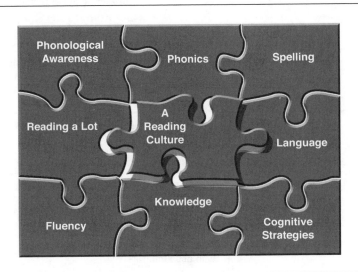

One of the most exciting developments in reading instruction has occurred in the past two decades as researchers have shown that phonological awareness—the ability to hear and manipulate the sounds (phonemic awareness), syllables, and words of the language—is an essential prerequisite to mastering the sound-spelling correspondences (i.e., phonics). Students who fail to learn to read with phonics instruction, even excellent phonics instruction, are often shown to be deficient in phonemic awareness (PA). They lack the abilities to distinguish rhyming words, blend phonemes into words, and hear the individual sounds in a word. They are sometimes diagnosed as dyslexic, reading disabled, slow learners, or learning disabled.

Figure 3.2   Reading Puzzle Definitions

Puzzle Piece		Definition
	Phonological awareness	The ability to hear and manipulate sounds (e.g., words, syllables, and phonemes)
	Phonics	A teaching method aimed at matching individual letters of the alphabet with specific sounds of English pronunciation (Fries, 1963, pp. 143-144); a method to teach students how to decode
	Spelling	The ability to recognize, recall, reproduce, or obtain orally or in written form the correct sequence of letters in words (Graham & Miller, 1979, p. 76); encoding
	Fluency	Automaticity and flow in the act of reading
	Language	Speech and sound system; the meanings of words; how words are put together to construct a message; and how discourse of various kinds is carried out
	Knowledge	What an individual knows about a specific discipline or domain
	Cognitive strategies	Mental processes used by readers during the act of reading to extract and construct meaning
	Reading a lot	Reading a lot of text, at increasing levels of difficulty, with accountability
	Reading culture	The collective attitudes, beliefs, and behaviors of all of the stakeholders in a school regarding any and all activities associated with enabling students to read at the highest level of attainment possible for both their academic and personal gain.

SOURCE: Adapted from *Teach Them ALL to Read: Catching the Kids Who Fall Through the Cracks* by Elaine K. McEwan. Copyright © 2002. Corwin Press, Inc. All rights reserved.

There are three ways for students to acquire PA: (a) inheriting genes that predispose them to distinguish and manipulate phonemes (sounds) without difficulty; (b) living in a print-rich environment where read-alouds, conversations about books, and word games are routine; or (c) good instruction. Students who begin school without PA are totally dependent on the quality *and* quantity of instruction they receive in kindergarten. The fact that we *can* teach PA to students who don't have it is the best news educators have had in a long time. After an extensive investigation of the experimental and high-quality quasi-experimental research, The National Reading Panel (NICHD, 2000) reported the following: Teaching phonemic awareness to children is clearly effective. It improves their ability to manipulate phonemes in speech. This skill transfers and helps them learn to read and spell. PA training benefits not only word reading but also reading comprehension. PA training contributes to children's ability to read and spell for months, if not years, after the training has ended. Effects of the PA training are enhanced when children are taught how to apply PA skills to reading and writing tasks (sec. 2, p. 40).

PA training is not just for kindergartners. The research shows that older disabled readers who have already developed reading problems can benefit from PA instruction as well (NICHD, 2000, sec. 2, p. 41). Intensive instruction using explicit, systematic approaches can overcome deficits of both nature and nurture (Burke, Howard, & Evangelou, 2003). Once students are able to hear and manipulate discrete sounds (phonemes), they can then benefit from instruction in the sound-spelling correspondences (i.e., the alphabetic code or phonics). The National Reading Panel (NICHD, 2000) makes it clear that "systematic phonics instruction is significantly more effective than non-phonics instruction in helping to prevent reading difficulties among at-risk students and in helping to remediate reading difficulties in disabled readers" (sec. 2, p. 86).

All the while that students are learning to decode words, they should regularly be exposed to a wide variety of children's literature, both fiction and nonfiction, and have ample opportunities to hear text read aloud and discussed. Activities of this type enhance students' vocabulary, general knowledge, and comprehension abilities. However, once students can independently decode words, they must read large amounts of decodable text in phonics readers at their independent reading levels to develop fluency and automaticity. Some basal reading programs provide few phonics readers, thus depriving students of the practice that is needed to develop fluency (i.e., accuracy and automaticity in decoding text). Absent sufficient opportunities to practice newly learned phonetic skills in phonics readers containing only words made up of sounds students have mastered, students' abilities to develop accuracy and automaticity during reading will be severely hampered. These same principles hold true for teaching beginning reading to students in middle and high school.

Fluency, "rate and accuracy in oral reading" (Hasbrouk, Ihnot, & Rogers, 1999; Shinn, Good, Knutson, Tilly, & Collins, 1992), is frequently the forgotten aspect of reading instruction, particularly in middle and high schools. Although Anderson suggested in 1981 that fluency training was the missing ingredient in classroom reading instruction and Allington reminded us in 1983 that oral reading fluency was a neglected reading goal for both good *and* poor readers, fluency has never generated the popular books, workshops, and cultlike followings that have arisen around other components of a balanced reading curriculum.

The National Reading Panel (NICHD, 2000) chose to investigate fluency as part of its comprehensive review of reading research and concluded that "repeated reading and other procedures that have students reading passages orally multiple times while receiving guidance or feedback from peers, parents, or teachers are effective in improving a variety of reading skills." The Panel went on to explain, "these procedures are not particularly difficult to use; nor do they require lots of special equipment or materials" (sec. 3, p. 20).

Fluency difficulties are directly attributable to the inability of readers to identify words quickly and accurately (Lyon, 1995; Torgesen, et al., 2001; Wise, Ring, & Olson, 1999). During the past two decades, research has provided educators with overwhelming evidence of the critical role that phonological awareness skills play in learning how to accurately identify words (Wagner, Torgesen, & Rashotte, 1994). Dysfluent or reading disabled students are almost always phonologically deficient.

Developing fluency (for a little smoother flow) for the majority of students first means making certain they have acquired the appropriate phonemic decoding skills and then giving them continuous opportunities to practice those skills through reading a lot in text at their independent reading levels: (a) orally and repeatedly with peers and parents, (b) along with their teachers in guided reading sessions, and (c) on their own in smaller amounts of silent reading that gradually increase in length as reading competence increases. The process sounds quite simple, but making it happen in middle and high school classrooms takes a master teacher. See Teaching for Learning Tip 3.1 and Linda Nielsen's story at the end of the chapter.

Dysfluent readers decode in a laborious fashion that interferes with gaining meaning from the text. In fact, fluency rates (the number of words correct per minute students can read) are an excellent proxy for comprehension. The working memories of dysfluent readers are so consumed with word identification, they have few if any cognitive resources remaining for extracting or constructing meaning from the text. Lacking fluency, students are unable to achieve the ultimate goal of reading: "to understand the messages conveyed in the text" (Pressley, 1998, p. 142).

Jeanne Chall's (1983/1986) theory of reading development organizes the pieces of the reading puzzle (except for reading culture) into a five-stage continuum. As you read about these stages, think of the students in your school and where they might fall along this continuum. Furthermore, reflect on what is being done instructionally to move them from the stage in which they are currently reading to the next one. We should never stop working toward the ultimate goal of having all students reach Stage 5, the most proficient stage, but our short-term goals *must* focus on moving all students from whatever stage they are currently in to the next higher stage. That goal is readily attainable. We know how to do it. The question is this: How do we feel about the fact that we haven't done it so far?

If you have preschoolers at your house (or in your extended family), they are likely to be in the first stage, *prereading*. Readers in this stage of development are able to repeat materials that have been read to them over and over, particularly if those books are predictable and contain lots of rhyming words. Although they are not actually reading yet, in the sense of identifying words on the page, prereaders are able to engage in "pretend reading" because they understand that books have meaning. They also know that groups of letters written on a page stand for words. Most adolescents, but certainly not all, have made it beyond this stage. Teaching for Learning Tip 3.2 offers content teachers one way to help their dysfluent readers develop fluency.

Readers in the *decoding stage* are beginning to associate letters with sounds and spoken words with printed ones. Because they are still in the process of learning how to sound out words, Stage 1 readers are able to read only a fraction of the words whose meanings they know. Many adolescents, particularly those in very-low-achieving schools, are still in the decoding stage. They are easily frustrated and do a lot of guessing if they even attempt to read. Because they are unable to read the literature or textbooks on their grade level, they often either act out or tune out in class. These young people would rather be seen as students who won't read than as students who can't read.

Readers in the *confirmation stage* are becoming fluent in dealing with print. Chall (1983/1986) refers to this process as "ungluing" (i.e., becoming less and less dependent on having to painstakingly sound out each word and able to focus more of their attention on the meaning of what has been read). Rates of reading increase steadily for students who move through this stage without difficulty. By the end of Stage 2, students are able to read and understand about 3,000 words, and about 9,000 words can be understood when heard. Adolescents in Stage 2 read slowly and are often teased by their peers when caught reading easy books.

The *reading-to-learn stage* marks a transition from learning to read to an emphasis on using reading as a tool for learning new information. Readers in this stage are able to decode in a fairly automatic way. As such,

TEACHING FOR LEARNING TIP 3.2

Teach Students How to Fluently Read
Multisyllabic Content Vocabulary

How to Get Started

Many middle and high school students have never had instruction in how to divide multisyllabic words into parts (syllables) to make them pronounceable. Unfortunately, most of the "meaning" or content words in middle and high school texts contain more than one syllable. Therefore, even if your students have the appropriate vocabulary and background knowledge to understand a word, their inability to decode and pronounce it prevents them from accessing the text. Although you probably won't have the time to embark on a full-scale program to teach this skill, there are several simple things you can do on a daily basis to increase the likelihood that your students will learn how to fluently identify the vocabulary of your discipline. To that end, choose five to eight key words each week and follow these steps:

1. After you have identified the key words, look them up in a dictionary to see how they are divided into syllables.

2. Write out the divided words on chart paper or poster board.

3. At the beginning of a week or unit, point out the list of words to students and tell them that to become a historian, scientist, mathematician, musician, and so forth, they will need to know how to identify the important words of the subject quickly and accurately. Assure them that you will help them to do so.

4. As you run your hand or a pointer under each new word, say it slowly once, so students can hear the various parts of the word, and then blend the parts together and say the word quickly.

5. Practice the list together one or two more times, and then move your hand or pointer around to prompt students to say the words with you.

6. Provide a sheet of flashcards for each student with the syllabicated words on one side and a student-friendly definition of the word on the reverse side.

7. Review the words once or twice every day for both pronunciation and meaning. When you say the word in the context of an explanation or discussion, run your hand or the pointer under the word to affix the sounds and corresponding spelling firmly in students' minds. Even bright students who may know the meanings of words can have problems pronouncing them correctly if they have not had the benefit of instruction in earlier grades. Here's the strategy recommended in the following resource: (a) Look for word parts at the beginning and end of the word and vowel sounds in the rest of the word, (b) say the parts of the word, (c) say the parts fast and (d) make it a real word.

A Resource to Get You Started

Archer, Gleason, & Vachon, 2005. *Rewards: Multisyllabic Word Reading Strategies.*

Research on Decoding

Adams, 1990; Nagy & Anderson, 1984; Perfetti, 1985; Share & Stanovich, 1995.

they may be able to read words for which they do not know the meanings. Adolescents in this stage of reading development may also begin to encounter words that, although somewhat familiar, have not been mastered. Without a great deal of teacher assistance, adolescents in this phase may tune out during difficult content area instruction and appear to be lazy and unmotivated.

Students in the *multiple-viewpoints stage* are able to read and understand a broad range of materials. Still developing, however, is their ability to integrate the different viewpoints and perspectives they experience through their reading. They are also in the process of acquiring the ability to use a number of different sources of reading materials as a way to answer questions and to solve problems. Stage 4 reading usually develops during high school if the appropriate instruction is provided and students read a sufficient quantity and quality of text.

In the final stage, *construction and reconstruction,* readers are able to use reading for their personal and professional needs in such a way that their prior knowledge gets synthesized and analyzed by what they read. Regrettably, few high school students reach Stage 5 reading. According to Chall (1983/1986), getting to this stage may be the most difficult transition of all, because it depends on broad knowledge of the content being read, a high degree of efficiency in reading it, and the courage and confidence to form an opinion.

FAILING TO LEARN

> *My students . . . taught me as much as I taught them, and their strongest lesson was a frightening one: adolescents who have not been successful—have failed—in traditional classrooms are at risk. Unless we find ways to engage them, they will shut down. If we continue to focus only on identifying deficits and devising sterile remedies, these students will surely use their energy and talent for unproductive purposes—or not at all.*
>
> —Krogness (1995, p. 1)

Why do so many students fail to learn to read well or even to learn at all?

There are dozens of possible reasons: lack of PA skills, a learning or reading disability, attendance in multiple schools, ineffective teachers in kindergarten or first grade, exposure to one or more ineffective methodologies or programs, truancy, and emotional or behavioral problems. Students with these profiles will have one or more of the following three "big" problems that need immediate attention: (a) inability to decode, spell, and pronounce words; (b) inability to use already learned decoding skills to rapidly process words (i.e., lack of reading fluency); and (c) inability to comprehend either written or oral content. Students who have one or more of these problems may already be labeled as dyslexic, learning disabled, or behavior disordered when they reach middle or high school, as was Robert, the young man you met in Chapter 1.

These students have been "taught" by so many different teachers (e.g., classroom, remedial, special education, outside tutors, or their parents) using so many different methods, they are convinced that *they* are the problem, not the methods or the teachers. They are confused, frustrated, and often very angry. The reading deficits of these students will *not* be remediated by any of the following band-aid approaches: (a) placement with proficient readers in heterogeneous classes, (b) placement in cooperative groups, (c) placement in tutoring programs with volunteers, (d) placement in remedial reading taught by a paraprofessional, or (e) placement in overcrowded special education classes containing students with vastly diverse reading levels using a variety of ineffective curricula. Students with severe reading disabilities need direct, intense, research-based instruction that meets their specific needs. They need small groups or even one-to-one settings in which to learn, and they need to be taught by highly skilled and nurturing teachers. Students with the most severe reading disabilities will require at least eighty hours of intensive one-to-one instruction from highly trained professional staff to learn to read and much more time after that to develop fluency and acquire cognitive strategies for comprehension. Meeting the needs of these students will be costly and time consuming but much less expensive than dealing with the social costs of illiteracy.

Teaching Tip 3.3 revisits the theme of focusing on the "big ideas" and teaching them well.

PROGRAMS TO REMEDIATE STRUGGLING SECONDARY STUDENTS

One of the most heartbreaking sights in American schools today is that of children—once so eager to read—discovering that they are not learning how. There comes over those sparkling eyes a glaze of listless despair. We are not talking about a few children and scattered schools. We are talking about millions of children and every school in the nation. And the toll in young spirits is the least of it. The toll in the learning and thinking potential of our citizenry is beyond measure.

—Sylvia Farnham-Diggory
(as quoted in Spalding & Spalding, 1957/1990, p. 10)

TEACHING FOR LEARNING TIP 3.3

Teach More About Less

How to Get Started

If barreling through the book and covering content are your primary goals, be prepared to have students who know very little about a lot. That unfortunate circumstance may translate to having students who know just enough to pass the test and then instantly forget the skills and concepts you "taught." If the forgotten material is prerequisite for new learning, someone (probably you) must inevitably reintroduce and "cover" the content once again. Rather than focusing on "mentioning," concentrate on mastery. See Learning Tip 1.1 for a way to organize for teaching more about less.

Do you sometimes get the feeling that your own brain just can't hold any more facts or concepts, especially after a long day of professional development on a new topic? Your students know the feeling well. Of course, your "expert" brain is well-suited to simultaneously process multiple topics, concepts, and ideas related to your discipline. You have well-developed schemata in your long-term memory that function as filing cabinets into which you can place related information.

For example, if you teach history and read an article about Lewis and Clark's exploration of the West, you can connect what you have read with what you already know to construct new knowledge for your long-term memory.

Psychologist George Miller (1956) advanced a theory of working memory that hypothesizes we can hold only about seven (plus or minus two) things in our working memories (the desktops of our minds) at once, before we begin to get confused or forget. Novices like your students have limited schemata in which to integrate what they hear in your classroom and read in textbooks. Because they often have little prior knowledge to which they can make connections, initially they need to work with fewer concepts and information at one time until they form solid concept maps in their long-term memories. Start slowly and then pick up speed!

Thomas Fuller (1642/1929), described the ideal teacher in his essay, "The Good Schoolmaster," this way: "He is able, diligent, and methodical in his teaching; not leading them rather in a circle than forwards. He minces his precepts for children to swallow, hanging clogs on the nimbleness of his own soul, that his scholars may go along with him" (p. 24).

A Resource to Help You

Jetton & Dole, 2004. *Adolescent Literacy Research and Practice.*

Research on Teaching More about Less

Graves, Juel, & Graves, 2004; Jetton & Alexander, 2005.

There are many outstanding programs that have the potential to meet the needs of adolescents with reading difficulties. Resource B contains descriptions of ten programs that have been validated by extensive program evaluations and are being used with success in schools around the country, particularly in challenging settings. These programs offer comprehensive professional development support and, in most cases, on-site facilitation and supervision. All of the programs will meet the needs of adolescent nonreaders or students reading below the fourth-grade level.

There are many educators who resist the adoption of a "packaged" remedial program, believing an eclectic program developed by a gifted teacher with the ability to combine a variety of methods and programs can more effectively meet the needs of their students. In the first edition of this book, readers met Linda Nielsen who developed such a program at Frontier Continuation High School, part of the Oxnard Union High School District north of Los Angeles. Linda worked with students referred from one of the district's six comprehensive high schools because of unsatisfactory attendance patterns, a troubled disciplinary history, lack of academic success, or the need for a more flexible schedule. Frontier was their last hope of staying in school and earning a regular high school diploma. Linda Nielsen taught five ability-grouped sections of reading at Frontier to students ranging in level from second grade to seventh grade. She relied on a variety of experiences and training to meet her students' needs (early childhood specialist, administrator, staff developer, ESL teacher), using research-based curricula and methods.

Linda had the expertise to develop an eclectic program that included all of the pieces of the reading puzzle, but there are few teachers who bring such a broad range of experience and training to the task. That's why when Linda left Frontier to take another assignment in the Oxnard District, there was no one who could replicate what she had been doing. This is often the case when a gifted teacher with an extensive knowledge base is no longer available.

There is, however, a solution to the problem of replication—the adoption of a research-based, field-tested program with a solid professional development component, *The REACH System* (Grossen, 1999). Teaching for Learning Tip 3.4 describes the importance of mastery learning: the focus of *REACH*. *REACH*'s curriculum is structured and scripted with the primary teaching methodology being direct instruction (a style of teaching in which the teacher uses a scripted presentation based on responses desired from students). *REACH* contains three components: *Corrective Reading (CR)*, *Reasoning and Writing*, and *Spelling Through Morphographs*. Although the three components are available in stand-alone form, taught

TEACHING FOR LEARNING TIP 3.4

Teach for Mastery

How to Get Started

Teaching for mastery is an easy enough process to understand. The difficult part is changing how you feel about doing it, shifting your paradigm. If you believe that your responsibility as a teacher is to prepare a smorgasbord of content and leave the picking and choosing of what to learn up to your students, teaching for mastery will be difficult at first. To serve up a mastery-learning meal, the teacher decides what specific dishes are on the menu and in exactly what order they must be eaten. In mastery learning, the teacher decides precisely what is important for *all* students to know and do, develops rubrics and assessments to determine if *all* students have mastered the critical content and skills, and then provides alternative instruction and more opportunities for learning until *all* students have arrived. At the same time (and this is where many teachers get frustrated), the teacher also decides how to extend and enrich the curriculum to afford higher-level learning opportunities and requirements for gifted and talented students.

For the purpose of assigning letter grades, all students *will* earn C's, because they will all master the basic concepts and skills; some students will earn B's, because they are motivated to extend their learning to a higher level by putting forth more effort; and some students will earn A's, because they are motivated to fulfill the requirements set forth in the rubric to receive an A. In a mastery-learning classroom, all students know precisely what the requirements are and how they will be evaluated in advance of each unit. You will be surprised, as have many teachers who try mastery learning, at the number of students who were previously thought to be unmotivated or disinterested who suddenly become eager learners when the rules of the game are spelled out in advance.

A Resource to Help You

Gentile & Lalley, 2003. *Standards and Mastery Learning: Aligning Teaching and Assessment so All Children Can Learn.*

Research on Mastery Learning

Block & Anderson, 1975; Block & Burns, 1977; Block, Efthim, & Burns, 1989; Bloom, 1971, 1976; Carroll, 1963; Gentile, Voelkl, Mt. Pleasant, & Monaco, 1995.

in tandem, they give students a solid foundation in all of the pieces of the reading-writing puzzle.

The Oxnard District adopted the *CR* component of *REACH* for remedial students in Reading 9 classes at its six comprehensive high schools, offering intensive training and coaching for teachers. Pacifica High School, with a large population of at-risk and Title I students, offers eight sections of *Corrective Reading* for ninth-grade students at various levels of difficulty. Linda uses the first three components of *REACH*, combined with the regular English 9 curriculum, to teach the twenty lowest ninth-grade students at Pacifica as identified by the Stanford Diagnostic Reading Test and *REACH*'s *CR* Placement test—students who by their own admission don't like school, don't like to read, and avoid homework—no matter what the consequence. To the average observer, these students might seem unmotivated and uncooperative, but their test scores demonstrate that they simply lack both the most basic reading skills and faith in themselves as learners.

Well below grade level high school students can't possibly catch up without intensive time on task, so Linda teaches all of the pieces of the reading puzzle for three periods every day. She generally spends one period per *REACH* component, but since essential concepts and skills are often repeated in the other components in a spiraling fashion, students are provided with several opportunities for mastery. Linda is ecstatic about *REACH*. What has turned this highly experienced teacher into a cheerleader for such a highly structured and scripted program? Results. She reports that although most of her students score at the second- or third-grade level in reading in the beginning of the year, with hard work in her class, a few are able to score at a post-high-school level in reading by the end of the year, with most improving by four or five grade levels. However, they *all* improve in their self-esteem.

"This is their last chance, and I refuse to let them fail," Linda says. Once they discover that they must do homework for Linda and that she won't let them fail, they begin coming in during their lunch hour to do extra work and talk with her about their hopes and dreams. In the beginning, the students do a lot of complaining: "Why does it have to be perfect? Nobody ever checked everything before. Just give me the grade."

Linda's response: "If I just gave you a grade, you wouldn't be learning." Her students often come back to visit after they've moved on, telling her, "You're my best teacher." Other teachers report that Linda's students can really write a sentence and a paragraph. The reason is no mystery to Linda. She has taught them explicitly, systematically, and supportively for three periods every single day—bell to bell.

"I have one student right now [mid-November] who came in reading at the third-grade level and scored 7.7 on the last assessment. He hated school at the beginning of the year, but it's starting to 'click' for him. He's seeing how parts of words fit together and how the English language works. He's beginning to read voluntarily, and I wouldn't be surprised if his scores were high enough at the end of the semester to exit my class" (L. Nielsen, personal communication, December 12, 2005).

FIND THE STUDENTS IN SPECIAL EDUCATION WHO CAN'T READ AND TEACH THEM TO READ

Despite the well-developed knowledge base supporting the value of interventions that have been demonstrated to have positive outcomes, these interventions are not widely employed in typical classroom instruction, and models of service delivery for students with reading and learning disabilities implemented in schools are often ineffective. Recent research has demonstrated that this need not be the case, but there are many obstacles to change.

—Denton, Vaughn, and Fletcher (2003)

Many of the students in your school who can't read are in special education (SPED), a placement that initially offered them specialized instruction to overcome their disabilities. Regrettably, most of these students have made little progress in learning to read since their initial placements, some as long ago as second grade. Why haven't they learned to read after five to six years of special instruction? Their failure may have more to do with their instruction than their disability. Here are some questions to ask regarding how "special" the instruction in your SPED classes really is:

1. Are SPED teachers focused on building self-esteem and making students feel good about themselves, rather than teaching them the knowledge and skills they need to be successful readers?

2. Are teachers overly patient and understanding, attributing students' inability to read to their disabilities, rather than finding research-based programs that get results, even for students with reading disabilities?

3. Are teachers more concerned with being creative than with using systematic, structured programs that get results (Heward & Dardig, 2001)?

4. Are SPED teachers trained to teach reading using a variety of explicit, systematic, supportive reading programs (e.g., Lindamood-Bell, Spalding, *Corrective Reading*)? (See Resource B for more research-based reading programs.)

5. Do teachers and administrators in the school or district pay more than lip service to students' IEPs that indicate a need to improve reading?

Research regarding the ability of SPED programs to deliver on their promises is not positive, and millions of children in special education are left behind when it comes to learning to read (McIntosh, Vaughn, Schumm, Haager, & Lee, 1993; Moody, Vaughn, Hughes, & Fischer, 2000; Vaughn, Moody, & Schumm, 1998). In a case study of three seventh graders with reading disabilities, Bresnahan (2001) described "an overwhelming influence of general education on the content, instruction, and context of reading for students with learning disabilities at the middle school level and a lack of research based practices in the implementation of reading instructional practices" (p. 266). Although research strongly indicates that adolescents who struggle with basic reading need explicit, systematic, supportive language and code focused reading instruction and fluency training, this was not observed in any of the three instructional settings she studied (self-contained, total inclusion in the general education classroom, and a combination of resource room and regular classroom).

Overall, in many secondary settings, the schedules, curricula and methodologies of the general education program are used almost exclusively for many SPED students at the expense of their individualized needs. Students' IEPs often play a minor, if not nonexistent, role in driving reading instruction for students with learning disabilities.

There are exceptions to this gloomy picture. Dana DiTomaso is a former SPED teacher (at both middle and high school levels) who is now a Lindamood-Bell (LB) Facilitator at East High School in Pueblo School District 60 in Colorado. Until Dana was introduced to the Lindamood-Bell programs (see a complete description of the programs in Resource B), she was frustrated by her inability to make a difference in the lives of her students. She reports, "I would usually have a class of fifteen middle or high school students, whose reading levels ranged from the first to the eighth grades, and there was no way I could possibly meet all of their needs. How can one teacher teach comprehension at all of those levels? So I spent most of my time making copies of packets at a reading level somewhere in the middle" (D. DiTomaso, personal communication, January 30, 2006).

At the same time that Dana was asking herself how she personally could be more effective with SPED students, Pueblo administrators made the decision to implement the Lindamood-Bell Learning Processes suite of programs across all of the elementary schools, which met with impressive success (Owen, 2004; Sadowski & Willson, 2006; Worthington, 2005). Beginning in 1997, over 1,000 of Pueblo's teachers were trained, and clinics serving the most challenging lowest readers were established in thirty-three schools staffed by an intensively trained facilitator to coach and support teachers as well as work with students.

Beginning in 1998, a phased implementation of the LB programs started in regular education middle and high schools; a specific emphasis on reaching SPED students began during the 2004–2005 and 2005–2006 school years. Dr. Keith Owen, a former elementary principal in the district and now the Reading/Lindamood-Bell Director, explains their decision this way: "Over one-third of the students who receive an "Unsatisfactory" rating in reading on our Colorado Student Assessment Program (CSAP) test are identified special education students. We designed the secondary model to deliver intensive research-based instruction at the students' specific instructional levels" (K. Owen, personal communication, January 23, 2006).

Although trained as a SPED teacher, after her initial LP training, Dana taught regular education students for one year. She felt strongly, however, that the program would be perfect for SPED students and urged her principal to let her try it. She began teaching twenty students in five sections, each one geared to the needs of the students. It was then that Dana discovered the missing piece of the reading puzzle for her SPED students: "I have never found anything that is this effective," she says. "At the end of that year, all of my students made statistically significant gains (Owen, 2005) but three of them actually tested out of special education (based on the results of the Woodcock Johnson test), and they had been in SPED for most of their elementary and middle school years. One of the three was both SPED and an English Language Learner (ELL), and now he's making plans to go to college. He told me that he would never have considered college as an option before he took my reading class" (D. DiTomaso, personal communication, January 30, 2006).

Dana's success and enthusiasm have propelled her into a new position—facilitator. She is supervising the LB clinic at East High School, teaching one regular education group, and coaching three teachers who are working with six groups of SPED students with various needs. Dana is thrilled with the progress of both her teachers and their students. "One of my teachers was very doubtful that any program could teach students with limited intellectual capacity to read. I convinced her to give it a try, and she is flipping out over their success" (D. DiTomaso, personal communication, January 30, 2006).

If you and your colleagues are serious about raising reading achievement overall, identify the students in your school who can't read and teach them to read using research-based programs like those used in Linda Nielsen's classroom and in Dana DiTomaso's clinic. The programs they use are described in Resource B.

Teaching for Learning Tip 3.5 explains precisely how to teach students the seven strategies of highly effective readers.

TEACHING FOR LEARNING TIP 3.5

Teach Cognitive Strategies Explicitly, Systematically, and Supportively

How to Get Started

First, you will need a clear understanding of three terms: *explicit, systematic,* and *supportive.*

- *Explicit instruction* is characterized by a distinctly expressed and clearly stated lesson objective or purpose. It is direct, clearly stated, and often, it is written out on the board. For example, if you were teaching students how to summarize, you would let them know that the purpose of the lesson is to teach them how to write two to three sentences *in their own words* about what they have read. A nonexample of explicit instruction would be telling students to write a summary of a reading assignment without showing and directly teaching them *how* to write one.
- *Systematic instruction* is characterized by the use of a method or plan and is driven by an organized and sequential curriculum and teaching methodology. If your goal is to have all students use cognitive strategies in their reading, all of the strategies must be explicitly taught and practiced over time. Without a system, it is easy to fall back on doing what you've always done in the past.
- *Supportive instruction* serves as a "scaffold" to uphold students and keep them from failing or declining. Supportive instruction never gives students an assignment for which they have not been fully prepared ahead of time with modeling, guided practice, and opportunities for questions and explanations.

Resources to Help You

McEwan, 2004. *7 Strategies of Highly Effective Readers.*
Wood, Woloshyn, & Willoughby, 1995. *Cognitive Strategy Instruction for Middle and High Schools.*

Research on Direct and Explicit Instruction to Teach Cognitive Strategies

Dole, 2000; Duffy, 2002. See also Figure 4.3, Research Evidence for Strategic Reading Instruction.

REFLECTION AND DISCUSSION QUESTIONS

1. What roadblocks are keeping you from identifying the students who can't read?

2. Reflect on the reading stages suggested by Jean Chall (1983/1986). Estimate the percentage of students in your school or classroom who fall into each of these categories. What can you personally do to move more students into more advanced levels?

3. What new knowledge did you acquire in this chapter and how will it change your practice?

4. What piece of the reading puzzle has been totally misplaced in your district, school, or classroom?

5. What is the status of special education and ELL instruction in your school and district currently? Are the needs of these students being met? What needs to be changed? What are the roadblocks to making these changes?

Teach Every Student How to Read to Learn

The idea is not that content-area teachers should become reading and writing teachers, but rather that they should emphasize the reading and writing practices that are specific to their subjects, so students are encouraged to read and write like historians, scientists, mathematicians, and other subject-area experts.

—Biancarosa and Snow (2004, p. 15).

Do you remember the last time you had a comprehension breakdown? I vividly remember mine. The occasion was the purchase of a scanner and text recognition software. It was as if the assembly directions and documentation were written in a foreign language. I had never heard of optical character recognition, scanner drivers, or drag-and-drop functionality. To navigate the unfamiliar text, I used the Monitoring-Clarifying strategy, one of seven cognitive processes that skilled readers employ during the reading of challenging text (McEwan, 2004, p. 37).

As I read, I monitored my comprehension to see if my brain was firing on all cylinders, or clunking badly, in need of repairs. When I didn't understand what I was reading, I drew on my repertoire of fix-up or clarifying tools shown in Figure 4.1. I reread parts of the text several times, used the dictionary, talked aloud to myself, visualized the steps in the process, and highlighted some key points with sticky arrows. Gradually, the text began to make sense—but only because I am a strategic reader.

Figure 4.1   Clarifying Tools

Is there something specific you don't understand—a word, phrase, concept, or idea?
- Ask someone: an adult, an expert, a classmate, the author, or your teacher.
- Look it up: in the dictionary, an encyclopedia, the index, the glossary, or the Internet.
- Make a prediction: "This must be what the author means. I'm going to keep on reading and see if I'm right."
- Predict word meaning based on context or on the word's structure.

Is the text poorly written, disorganized, or very long?
- Chunk it: divide the text into smaller sections and work on one section at a time.
- Draw a picture or diagram: make a graphic organizer.
- Outline it.

Are you confused about the meaning of the text?
- Read the back cover copy, the blurb on the inside front jacket, the preface, a chapter summary, the introduction, a review, or a critique for more clues.
- Connect what you have read to your own experience: "This reminds me of the time that . . ."
- Read the text again or even twice more, if necessary.
- Read the text more slowly.
- Stop and think aloud to yourself about what you have read.
- Talk to someone: think aloud to a friend, family member, or classmate.
- Ignore temporarily the parts you don't understand and keep reading.

Many middle and high school students are not so fortunate. They experience comprehension breakdowns constantly and have no idea how to prevent or fix them. They stare blankly at the printed page, hoping for a miracle, but it never comes. These students must be taught to read strategically by strategic teachers.

Reading has been defined in many ways since it first became the object of intense educational and psychological research at the turn of the century. In the 1970s, however, reading comprehension began to be thought of differently, not as a discrete skill but as "the interaction of text and the knowledge possessed by the reader to produce meaning" (National Academy of Education, 1985, p. 8). It was at that point that cognitive scientists turned their unique spotlight on the act of reading and showed us that meaning does not come without the involvement and engagement of the reader. Van den Broek & Kremer (2000) described what happens during reading comprehension: "Readers construct a mental 'picture' of the text: a representation in memory of the textual information and its interpretation" (p. 2).

Whether the goal of reading is defined as meaning or a mental picture, scholars now consider the act of reading to be intentional thinking (Durkin, 1993). Although the first step to gaining meaning from print is undeniably the ability to decode words rapidly and fluently, the skillful use of cognitive strategies—those mental processes used by skilled readers to extract and construct meaning from text during the act of reading—is essential. Some describe this ability as *strategic reading* or *strategic learning.* Others call it simply *reading to learn.*

All middle and high school students encounter challenging reading during their academic careers: a physics textbook, the ACT test, or a literary classic. The big question is, What will they do when the reading gets tough: give up or get strategic? At this point, far too many of them are giving up.

In the chapter ahead, we consider how the incorporation of strategic reading instruction (SRI) into the curriculum of your school can raise reading achievement. We'll look at what expert readers do during the act of reading, listen in on a strategic teacher modeling for his students, and explore ways to help teachers assist all students to acquire these skills. One of the cognitive processes routinely employed by skilled readers is *questioning.* Teaching for Learning Tip 4.1 describes how to teach students the importance of questioning while they read and exactly how to go about doing it.

READING TO LEARN AND COGNITIVE STRATEGIES

> *The best way to pursue meaning is through the conscious, controlled use of strategies.*
>
> —Duffy (1993, p. 223)

I began an in-depth study of reading strategies in 1999. My own experiences as a teacher teaching reading comprehension were not memorable, and as a principal, my faculty and I saw the potential for strategy instruction and dabbled in it but never achieved mastery. Over a period of several years, my investigation led in several directions. I first consulted all of the popular books and articles, looking for the "best" strategies and quickly became confused and frustrated. There were dozens of different so-called comprehension strategies, all enthusiastically described by their proponents as essential. How could the average teacher (particularly one who is responsible for teaching content) decide which approaches are most effective? It would be impossible to use them all, especially in the context of teaching science, social studies, or math. There was little if any research in the individual books to support the use of one particular "strategy" over another.

In the middle of one sleepless night, I had an educational epiphany: I concluded that what many educators called *strategies* were in reality *instructional activities—the plans and procedures that teachers make and follow*

TEACHING FOR LEARNING TIP 4.1

Teach Your Students How to Ask Questions

How to Get Started

Teach students how to answer and ask four kinds of questions after they have read an assigned piece of text:

1. Questions for which the answer can be found in one place in the text.

2. Questions for which students must synthesize information from various parts of the text to come up with an answer.

3. Inferential questions for which students must combine what they know with what is stated in the text to find an answer.

4. Questions for which students must draw on their own experiences to answer.

After students have been taught the four types of questions, using the I Do It (the teacher demonstrates, models or thinks-aloud for students), We Do It (the teacher guides students in practice), You Do It (the students work in pairs or alone to demonstrate mastery) Lesson Plan, expect them to bring a question to class each day to use in quizzing their classmates or to make up a question as they exit from the classroom at the end of a period to be used during the following class period.

Students of any age (especially teachers and principals in my workshops) are reluctant to ask questions until I offer incentives to those who will write their questions on a sticky note and post it on the board in front of the classroom. At the end of the day, I hold a drawing for prizes for those who were willing to write questions about concepts they did not understand. I answer the questions individually or group them in categories and use them as a way to shift my instructional focus.

A Resource to Help You

McEwan, 2004. *7 Strategies of Highly Effective Readers.*
Schoenbach, Greenleaf, Cziko, & Hurwitz, 1999. *Reading for Understanding.*

Research on the Power of Questioning

Davey, 1983; Davey & McBride, 1986; King, 1990, 1992; King, Biggs, & Lipsky, 1984; Nolte & Singer, 1985; Raphael, 1984; Rosenshine, Meister, & Chapman, 1996.

for the purpose of cognitive strategy instruction. Instructional activities use a variety of props and prompts to *support* and *enhance* cognitive strategy instruction. Props are the physical objects that enable teachers and students to more readily understand and focus on the utilization of cognitive strategies. Props consist of items like colored pencils or highlighters; sticky notes, flags, and arrows; posters and charts; models; realia; and software. Prompts are sets of words or statements (e.g., questions, key words, or acronyms) that remind students of actions to take or processing activities to initiate.

Cognitive strategies, on the other hand, are the actual mental processes used by readers during the act of reading. Because cognitive processing occurs in the brains of readers, it cannot be observed by teachers or students, per se. The evidence of strategy usage is found in that hard-to-define and harder-still-to-teach concept called *comprehension.*

Even though I had made a critical distinction between instructional activities and cognitive strategies, I still was no closer to figuring out which strategies were actually used by skilled readers and therefore essential to teach to students. Psychologist George Miller theorized that our working memories can hold no more than about seven (plus or minus two) ideas at one time, and so my goal became to formulate a list of seven strategies that were research based and could easily be remembered by teachers and students in the beginning stages of strategic reading instruction (1956).

I decided to consult a body of work describing what goes on in the minds of skilled readers as they process text—*verbal protocols.* Verbal protocols are verbatim self-reports that people make regarding what is happening in their minds as they think and read (Pressley & Afflerbach, 1995). These transcripts are subsequently analyzed to answer specific research questions, such as, "What is the influence of prior knowledge on expert readers' strategies as they determine the main idea of a text?" (Afflerbach, 1990b).

As subjective as verbal protocols may seem to be, they provide a valid and highly useful tool for capturing "snapshots" and even "videos" of the ever-changing mental landscape that expert readers construct during reading. Pressley and Afflerbach (1995) conclude, based on their extensive collection of verbal protocols from expert readers, that reading is "constructively responsive—that is, good readers are always changing their processing in response to the text they are reading" (p. 2). A specific set of cognitive strategies used by skilled readers soon began to emerge from my study. I call them the seven strategies of highly effective readers, and their definitions are shown in Figure 4.2.

The next questions I asked myself were the ones you are no doubt asking me at this very moment: "Can teachers really teach *all* students how to employ cognitive strategies to extract and construct meaning from text? Does strategy instruction work?" These questions are important ones that should always be asked by educators regarding any idea, program, or methodology that is being proposed for implementation in their schools and

Figure 4.2   Seven Strategies of Highly Effective Readers

Strategy	Description
Activating	"Priming the cognitive pump" to recall relevant prior knowledge and experiences from long-term memory in order to extract and construct meaning from text
Inferring	Bringing together what is spoken (written) in the text, what is unspoken (unwritten) in the text, and what is already known by the reader in order to extract and construct meaning from the text
Monitoring-Clarifying	Thinking about how and what one is reading, both during and after the act of reading, for purposes of determining if one is comprehending the text combined with the ability to clarify and fix up any mix-ups if necessary
Questioning	Engaging in learning dialogues with text (authors), peers, and teachers through self-questioning, question generation, and question answering
Searching-Selecting	Searching a variety of sources in order to select appropriate information to answer questions, define words and terms, clarify misunderstandings, solve problems, or gather information
Summarizing	Restating the meaning of text in one's own words—different words from those used in the original text
Visualizing-Organizing	Constructing a mental image or graphic organizer for the purpose of extracting and constructing meaning from text

classrooms. The answer, supported by high-quality experimental research, is a resounding *yes*. Figure 4.3 lists the research evidence for strategic reading instruction, the explicit, systematic, and supportive instruction of cognitive strategies by all teachers in all grade levels and content areas.

Details about precisely how to do it can be found in a vast body of research on cognitive strategy instruction derived from the discipline of cognitive science (NICHD, 2000; Pressley, 2000; Pressley & Woloshyn, 1995; Rosenshine, 1997b; Rosenshine & Meister, 1994; Trabasso & Bouchard, 2000, 2002). Based on more than 200 scientific research studies and reviews, here is what we currently know about the power that cognitive strategies, taught well and consistently, have to increase students' abilities to understand and retain what they read:

- Skilled or expert readers routinely draw from a repertoire of cognitive strategies while they are reading challenging text.
- Students of all ability levels benefit from strategy instruction, both as evidenced in increased understanding and retention and also in higher standardized test scores.

Figure 4.3   Research Evidence for Strategic Reading Instruction

Research Questions	Research
Which strategies do skilled readers use?	Afflerbach, 1990a, 1990b; Afflerbach & Johnston, 1984; Pressley & Afflerbach, 1995.
Which students benefit from strategy usage?	Anderson & Roit, 1993; Brown & Campione, 1994; NICHD, 2000; Pressley, Johnson, Symons, McGoldrick, & Kurita, 1989; Rosenshine & Meister, 1994; Rosenshine et al., 1996; Trabasso & Bouchard, 2000, 2002.
Which multiple strategy approaches work best?	Brown, Pressley, Van Meter, & Schuder, 1996; Lysynchuk, Pressley, & Nye, 1990; Palinscar & Brown, 1984; Rosenshine, 1997a; Rosenshine & Meister, 1994.
Which instructional methods are most effective for teaching cognitive strategies?	Brown et al., 1996; Duffy, 2002; Duffy et al., 1987; Gaskins & Elliot, 1991; Pressley, El-Dinary, Marks, & Stein, 1992; Rosenshine, 1986; Rosenshine, 1997a, 1997b; Taylor, Pearson, Clark, & Walpole, 1999.
What is the current status of cognitive strategy instruction?	Biancarosa & Snow, 2004; Jetton & Dole, 2004; Pearson, 1996; Pressley, 2004.

- The effectiveness of a variety of individual cognitive strategies in boosting student achievement is well supported by experimental research.
- The effectiveness of several multiple-strategy instructional approaches is well supported by experimental research.
- There are specific instructional methods to teach cognitive strategies to students that produce results.

Strategies have the power to enhance and enlarge the scope of learning by making it more efficient. Strategic students learn and remember more in shorter periods of time with far less frustration. They are able to tackle assignments with a higher level of organizational skill, and more important, they face challenging assignments with confidence.

What happens to the students who reach middle and high school unable to read strategically? How do they deal with multiple textbooks (some poorly organized and badly written), lectures, assignments, projects, and tests? What if their teachers assume that it's not *their* job to teach students how to read to learn? These unfortunate students are destined to become casualties of an academic "survival of the fittest" in which strategic learners survive academically and the rest struggle or fail. One of the most challenging cognitive strategies for students to routinely employ is summarizing. Teaching for Learning Tip 4.2 introduces an instructional activity called *The Summarizer's Five Cs*, designed to teach students one way to approach it.

TEACHING FOR LEARNING TIP 4.2

Teach Your Students How to Summarize

How to Get Started

Be sure to think aloud and model for students how *you* would summarize a key concept that was introduced during class by choosing a key word, drawing a picture, or constructing a mnemonic device. Then write one or two sentences on the board or overhead explaining the key word. After you have modeled summarizing for students during two or three class periods, pair students to come up with key words and sentences together. Only after struggling readers have seen you model it and subsequently had multiple opportunities to work with partners to choose key words and write summarizing sentences should you expect them to select words and write sentences independently.

To prepare students to write summaries of what they have read in their own words (an important activity to get ready for writing research reports), model and explicitly teach The Summarizer's Five Cs (McEwan, 2004, pp. 112–116): (a) comprehend, (b) chunk, (c) compact, (d) conceptualize, and (e) connect. See Figure 4.4, The Summarizer's Five Cs, a template for organizing one's thoughts in preparation for writing a summary of text.

The Mathematics Department at Alief Hastings High School uses what they call a GROK Sheet to help their students summarize what they understand as well as what they don't understand about a concept, assignment, or unit. See Exhibits 4.1 and 4.2 for a sample GROK Sheet and scoring rubric.

A Resource to Help

Saphier & Haley, 1993. *Summarizers: Activity Structures to Support Integration and Retention of New Learning.*

Research on Summarization

Afflerbach & Johnston, 1984; Afflerbach & Walker, 1992; Armbruster, Anderson, & Ostertag, 1987; Bean & Steenwyk, 1984; Brown & Day, 1983; Brown, Day, & Jones, 1983.

THE STRATEGIC TEACHER

> *I am convinced that if we are to take children into the upper reaches of comprehension, we have to have been there ourselves. How can we teach children to synthesize ideas if we won't do this with our own reading?*
>
> —Donald Graves
> (as quoted in Zimmerman & Keene, 1997, pp. x–xi)

Mature and skilled readers who use cognitive strategies regularly in their reading know how valuable they can be. Some readers were fortunate enough to inherit a genetic predisposition for organized and strategic

Figure 4.4 The Summarizer's Five Cs

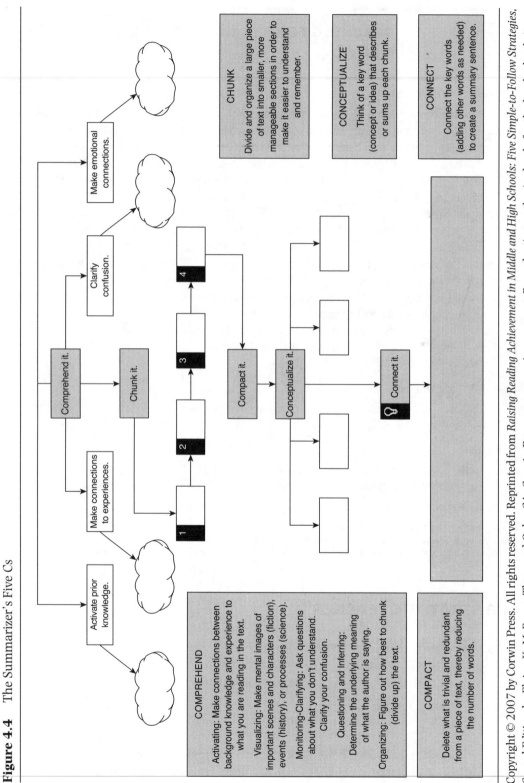

Exhibit 4.1 The GROK Sheet

Name: _____   Concept: _____

Date: _____

+

1. Answer the question.
   What did I understand?
   What is main idea?
2. Support (from lesson, article, problem)
3. What does this mean? Why is this important?

To grok (pronounced GRAHK) is to understand something so well that it is fully absorbed into oneself. In Robert Heinlein's (1961) science fiction novel, *Stranger in a Strange Land*, the word is Martian and literally means "to drink," but metaphorically means "to take it all in, to understand fully, or to be at one with." Today, grok sometimes is used to include acceptance as well as comprehension (Whatis.com, 2006).

1. What did I not understand about the lesson, problem, or article?
2. Why do I think I didn't understand it? Why am I confused?
3. What can I do to help myself?

−

SOURCE: Reprinted by permission of Raymond Lowery, associate principal, Alief Hastins High School, Alief ISD, Houston, TX.

Exhibit 4.2   Scoring Rubric for the GROK Sheet

+ Rubric	− Rubric
Scorepoint 0 • Nothing written or • Too vague • Too general	*Scorepoint 0* • Nothing written or • Too vague • Too general
Scorepoint 1 • Student attempts to answer the question/demonstrate an understanding	*Scorepoint 1* • Student attempts to answer the question/explain confusion
Scorepoint 2 • Student answers the question and supports the answer with information from the lesson, article or lecture	*Scorepoint 2* • Student explains his confusion or what led to the confusion and gives examples of and details about what he/she doesn't understand
Scorepoint 3 • Student clearly answers the question, supports the answer and extends/applies/explains the importance/relevance of the information/concept in complete sentences	*Scorepoint 3* • Student clearly explains confusion or what leads to confusion, gives examples of what he/she doesn't understand, and states goals/solutions/actions he will take to clear up his confusion in complete sentences

SOURCE: Reprinted by permission of Raymond Lowery, associate principal, Alief Hastings High School, Alief ISD, Houston, TX.

thought. Others received quality instruction at some point in their academic careers. Most of us, however, have refined our abilities to mentally process what we read the old-fashioned way—through trial and error. We wasted our energies and endured unnecessary frustration and often failure. Strategic learners do not spontaneously bloom in classrooms. They are taught, nurtured, and encouraged by strategic teachers, those individuals who are able to weave content and cognitive strategy instruction into a seamless whole.

In today's secondary schools, every teacher must be a strategic teacher. Attempting to teach content to students without simultaneously providing strategy instruction is like offering food to hungry diners but failing to provide them with the necessary dinnerware with which to eat. The skillful union of content and strategy instruction is a powerful aid to learning, a marriage that should delight all content area teachers who love their discipline and want every student to achieve content mastery. There is one catch, however. "Becoming an effective . . . strategies instruction teacher takes several years" (Brown, Pressley, Van Meter, & Schuder, 1996, p. 20). Figure 4.5 describes the variety of moves employed by strategic teachers

Figure 4.5   The Teaching Moves of Strategic Teachers

Move	Description
Explaining	Providing verbal input about what will happen in a lesson, what the goals and purpose are, how it will help students, and what the role of the teacher and the students will be during the lesson
Giving Direction	Providing unambiguous and concise verbal input that seeks to give students a way to get from where they are at the beginning of a lesson, task, or unit to the achievement of a specific task or outcome; providing wait time for students to process directions as well as time for students to respond and opportunities to ask clarifying questions
Modeling	Thinking aloud regarding cognitive processing (e.g., making connections with prior knowledge to something that is read in the text), demonstrating, acting out, or role-playing behaviors and actions (e.g., acting out different ways to receive a compliment given by a peer)
Reminding	Causing students to remember or think about something that has previously been taught; restating something that has been previously taught in a novel way to ensure remembering
Guiding Practice	Leading students through a supervised rehearsal of a skill, process, or 3R (routine, rule, or rubric) to ensure understanding, accuracy, and automaticity
Scaffolding	Providing instructional support (e.g., further explanation, modeling, coaching, or additional opportunities to learn) at students' independent learning levels that enable them to solve problems, carry out tasks, master content and skills, or achieve goals that would otherwise be impossible
Coaching	Asking students to think aloud, cueing them to choose strategies that have been taught (e.g., cognitive strategies for comprehension, problem-solving strategies in math, organizational, or social strategies), delivering mini-lessons when needed, and providing feedback to students
Atributing	Communicating to students that their accomplishments are the result of effort, wise decision making, attention to tasks, exercise of good judgment, and perseverance, rather than their intelligence or ability
Constructing Meaning	Working collaboratively with students to extract and construct multiple meanings from conversations, discussions, and the reading together of text
Motivating-Connecting	Generating interest, activating prior knowledge, and connecting instruction to the real world or the solution of real problems

(Continued)

Figure 4.5 (Continued)

Move	Description
Recapping	Summarizing what has been concluded, learned, or constructed during a given discussion or class period as well as providing statements regarding why it is important and where it can be applied or connected in the future
Annotating	Adding additional information during the course of reading or discussion, information that students do not have but need in order to make sense of the discussion or text
Assessing	Determining both formally (through testing) and informally (through questioning) what students have learned and where instruction needs to be adjusted and adapted to achieve mastery
Facilitating	Thinking along with students and helping them develop their own ideas rather than managing their thinking, explaining ideas, and telling them what and how to do something
Redirecting	Monitoring the level of student attention and engagement and using a variety of techniques, prompts, and signals to regain or redirect students' attention and focus on the learning task; transitioning students from one activity to another with minimal time loss
Affirming	Encouraging, praising, or rewarding students' actions, attitudes, thinking processes, verbal statements, and work products

while Figure 4.6 illustrates what those moves actually look and sound like in classrooms.

Facilitating the development of strategic teachers who automatically incorporate strategic teaching moves requires a considerable investment of human and monetary resources. Teaching reading strategies is a vastly different undertaking from teaching the "skills" as we did in the 1960s and 1970s. Skills are "procedures readers over-learn through repetition so that speed and accuracy are assured every time the response is called for" (Duffy & Roehler, 1987, p. 415), whereas strategies tap higher-order thinking skills in response to the demands of unique reading tasks. Strategies are used situationally. Teaching students how and when to use them is a completely different enterprise than drilling students on a discrete skill or serving up a smorgasbord of content and expecting students to help themselves. "Helping teachers [become good strategy teachers] will require a significant change in how teacher educators and staff developers work

Figure 4.6   What Strategic Teachers Say and Do

Direct Instructing Explaining	We'll be doing four different things in class every day. I call it a routine. Each activity has a special purpose designed to help you learn a foreign language. (Susan Graham)	The first activity is called *bell work*. This is a quiet time at the beginning of class for you to transition into Spanish. It will be a short, easy activity that everyone will be able to do. (Susan Graham)	The second activity is a song. We'll learn one song per week, put some motions or moves with it, and on Friday, we'll sing it along with some slides. (Susan Graham)	The third activity is the lesson. I'll present new material, and then we'll practice together, correct homework, ask questions, do some pair-and-share activities, and play games. (Susan Graham)	The fourth activity is quiet time for you to work on your own to figure out if you know what you're doing. If you don't, you'll have a chance to ask questions of me or your classmates. (Susan Graham)
Modeling	Watch me as I demonstrate what to do in the event of a fire while we're doing a lab experiment.	I'm going to show you how I go about brainstorming a list of topics for a writing assignment.	When I can't figure out what I'm being asked to do in a word problem, I follow this three-step process. Let me demonstrate it for you.		When I first get my test booklet, I skim through it to see how many questions there are so I can pace myself. I'm going to read and think aloud from this sample text booklet to demonstrate what you should be doing when you take a test.
Giving Directions	This morning I'm going to give you directions for how to set up your math homework. I've posted a large piece of notebook paper set up exactly the way I want you to set up your papers for every math homework assignment. (Hoedeman)	The assignment number is in a highlighted circle in the upper right-hand corner. That's important so that when I'm looking at your paper, I know which assignment it is, and I can log it in my grade book. (Hoedeman)	Your name and the date must be written on the top lines on the right and the name of the assignment should be written on the left. For the first couple of weeks, I'll have a model posted for you every day. (Hoedeman)		After that, I expect your homework to have these informational items every day. Are there any questions? Please set up your papers as if you were beginning a homework assignment. (Hoedeman)
Scaffolding	I've posted the vocabulary from our unit on the bulletin board. Notice that I've divided the words into syllables, just like you'd find if you looked the word up in the dictionary. I find that when I encounter a new word or an especially long word, it helps me to look at its individual parts, figure out each part and then blend them all together quickly.	I've also written what I call a "student-friendly" definition of the word next to it. Sometimes I find that dictionary definitions aren't always "friendly."			To help us all get more familiar with these words and be able to read them and use them in talking about the ideas in our unit and writing answers on tests, I'm going to point to the word and run my hand underneath it from left to right to help you pronounce it, read it, and write it with its correct meaning and spelling.
Attributing	You are the most strategic class I've ever had. You figured out what the most important ideas were, took the time to make some notes about it, and wrote the best exams I have ever received on this unit. Good work!	You aced this test because you did your homework consistently!			You can accomplish anything you want to in life with that kind of an approach to school. You asked questions, took the time to review, and you got it!
Coaching	Jason, I can tell from the look on your face that you are very pleased with your answer. Actually, I am too. But I want you to tell me precisely how you arrived at that answer.	I know you can do this. We talked about this kind of situation yesterday.			As you look at this problem, tell me what you think the unimportant information is. The author of the textbook put it in there to confuse you.

with teachers and what they count as important about learning to be a teacher" (Duffy, 1993, pp. 244–245). The process will take far more than a day or two of casual professional development because most teachers did not experience this kind of instruction themselves. Irene Gaskins, the founder and director of The Benchmark School, says it takes teachers at least three years to become strategic teachers (I. Gaskins, personal communication, July 5, 2000). Part of being a strategic teacher is helping students to make connections between concepts to gain the "big picture" of a unit of study or a topic. Teaching for Learning Tip 4.3 describes what concept maps are and how they differ from other graphic organizers.

TEACHING FOR LEARNING TIP 4.3

Use and Teach Concept Maps

How to Get Started

Graphic organizers are very popular and, when constructed by students themselves as they reach challenging text, they are highly effective in helping students to make sense of challenging or poorly organized text. Less appreciated for its power in helping students to construct long-lasting knowledge is a concept map: a graphic representation that identifies key concepts and joins them with connecting words showing the nature of their relationships. Concept maps differ from traditional graphic organizers in that they require students to specify how concepts are related rather than merely filling in blank boxes with words from the text. Figure 4.7 displays a simple concept map illustrating ways in which teachers can close the achievement gap.

It's relatively easy to fill in the blanks of a generic graphic organizer. However, constructing concept maps requires a deeper understanding of the relationships between the concepts, the ability to choose meaningful connecting words, and an understanding of the directionality of the relationship. For example, in Figure 4.7, note that connecting arrows go in both directions between some concepts, signifying different types of relationships. *Scaffolding struggling readers requires that teachers make no assumptions about students' prior knowledge.* Cooperative learning *is a methodology that uses collaborative processing to close the achievement gap.*

A Resource to Help You

Novak, 1998. *Learning, Creating, and Using Knowledge: Concept Maps as Facilitative Tools in Schools and Corporations.*

Research on the Power of Constructing Concept Maps

Novak & Gowin, 1984.

Figure 4.7 Closing the Achievement Gap Concept Map

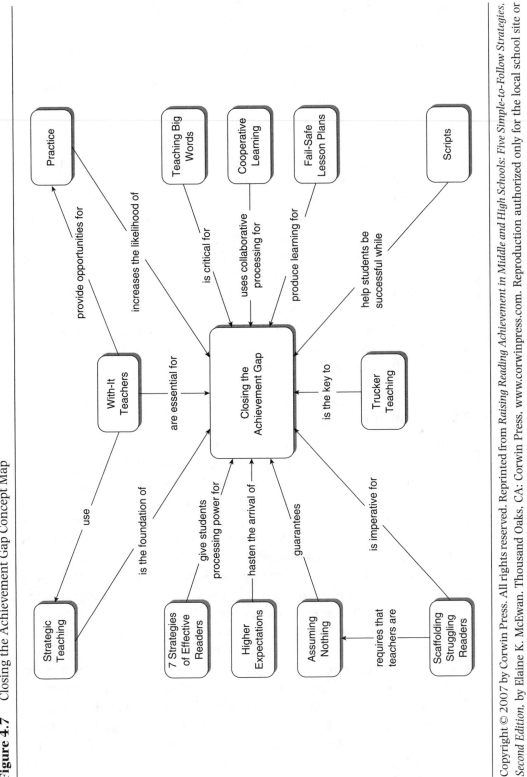

HOW TO TEACH COGNITIVE STRATEGIES

Despite a significant body of research in the 1980s suggesting the effectiveness of strategy instruction, especially for lower-achieving readers, strategy instruction has not been implemented in many American classrooms.

—Dole (2000, p. 62)

Cognitive strategy instruction as a field of study and research has become increasingly more sophisticated during the past twenty years. Researchers, intrigued with the success of a single strategy to improve comprehension, have gone on to combine several strategies to produce even more powerful results. The National Reading Panel (NICHD, 2000) concurs with Rosenshine, Meister, and Chapman (1996) that "the data suggests that students at all skill levels would benefit from being taught these strategies [e.g., prediction, clarification, question generation, and summarization]" (p. 201). In addition to the aforementioned cognitive strategies, students benefit greatly from being explicitly taught how to graphically organize text or teacher lectures. Teaching for Learning Tip 4.4 describes how you can teach this process to students.

Reciprocal Teaching

Reciprocal teaching was the first multiple-strategy intervention that was shown to promote reading comprehension (Palincsar & Brown, 1986). This approach when taught to students enables them to (a) make predictions about what is going to be in the text, (b) generate questions about the text content, (c) seek clarification of points that are not well understood or confusing, and (d) summarize what has been read (Pressley et al., 1990, p. 84). Students then discuss the text as they apply the strategies, with one student playing the role of discussion facilitator. Because of its relative ease of implementation, it has been a popular strategy package.

The biggest challenge for administrators and staff developers with regard to strategy instruction is that being strategic is much more than knowing a few or even a great many individual strategies. Strategy use is not a "paint by the numbers" activity. "When faced with a comprehension problem, strategic readers coordinate and shift strategies as appropriate. They constantly alter, adjust, modify, and test until they construct meaning and the problem is solved" (NICHD, 2000, sec. 4, p. 47). What is needed is a model that (a) allows for the ambiguity and messiness that occurs during "real" reading, (b) helps teachers deal with constant decision making and unanticipated actions and reactions, (c) encourages

TEACHING FOR LEARNING TIP 4.4

Teach Students How to Graphically Organize Content

How to Get Started

If you have not yet discovered the power of organizing content graphically to improve student achievement, here are some reasons to begin using organizers in your classroom today:

- Effective comprehension and thinking require a coherent understanding of the *organizing* principles in any subject matter; understanding the essential features of the problems of various school subjects will lead to better reasoning and problem solving.
- Transfer and wide application of learning are most likely to occur when learners achieve an *organized* and coherent understanding of the material.
- Learning and understanding can be facilitated in learning by emphasizing *organized*, coherent bodies of knowledge (in which specific facts and details are embedded).
- In-depth understanding requires detailed knowledge of the facts within a domain. The key attribute of expertise is a detailed and *organized* understanding of the important facts within a specific domain (Bransford, Brown, & Cocking, 2000, pp. 238-239).

Make a brief list of the organizers that are most suited to your discipline, and then teach your students how to use them. Figure 4.8 displays a list of graphic organizers categorized in three sections: nonfiction (expository text), fiction (narrative text), and mathematics. Model for students how you construct organizers to help you learn new material, get the big picture, and summarize large quantities of new material.

Remember that the individual who constructs the organizer realizes the learning benefits. You can model your own thinking for students, but unless they process the text and build their own organizers (using templates you have taught them), the learning benefits are minimal, if any.

A Resource to Help

Hyerle, 2004. *Student Successes With Thinking Maps.*

Research on the Power of Organization

Alvermann & Boothby, 1983, 1986; Armbruster, Anderson, & Meyer, 1991; Berkowitz, 1986; Borduin, Borduin, & Manley, 1994; Gambrell & Bales, 1986; Jones, Pierce, & Hunter, 1988/1989; Shriberg, Levin, McCormick, & Pressley, 1982; Sinatra, Stahl-Gemake, & Berg, 1984.

Figure 4.8 Graphic Organizers for Content Instruction

Organizers for Nonfiction (Expository Text)	Organizers for Fiction (Narrative Text)
Analogy organizer	Matrix
Cause-effect organizer	Network tree
Chain of command organizer	Picture
Chain of events organizer	Problem-solution outline
Historical figure character map	Puzzle
Chart	Relay summary
Compare-contrast matrix	Spider map
Concept map	Story frame
Concept wheel	Story grammar
Continuum	Story map
Crossword puzzle	Talking drawings
Cycle	Time line
Diagram	Venn diagram
Entailment mesh	Web
Fishbone diagram	Why-because pursuit chart
Flow chart	Semantic word map
Frayer model	Semantic features analysis
Grid	Concept map
Hierarchy organizer	
Semantic word map	
Semantic features analysis	
Human interaction outline	
List	

Organizers for Mathematics

Picture
Image
Diagram
Equation
Chart
Matrix
Semantic word map
Semantic features analysis

teachers to become strategic readers themselves in the "each one teach one" tradition, and (d) allows time for them to become expert. Transactional strategies instruction provides such a model.

Transactional Strategies Instruction

Transactional strategies instruction (TSI) had its genesis in three educator-developed programs: The Benchmark School, described in Resource B, and two public school programs. A transaction is commonly thought of as an exchange of money for goods or a business deal between two people, but the transactions that occur in transactional strategies instruction have to do with members of a group (including the teacher) using strategies to exchange ideas and jointly construct meaning from a text.

The long-term goal of transactional strategies instruction is the internalization and consistently adaptive use of strategic comprehension processes whenever students encounter demanding text. The short-term goal is deep understanding of the current reading assignment through the joint construction of text interpretations by group members (Pressley et al., 1990, p. 85).

Here are the teaching behaviors associated with TSI (Pressley et al., 1990):

• Strategy instruction is a long-term affair, with effective strategies instructors offering it in their classroom throughout the school year; the ideal is for high-quality process instruction to occur across multiple school years (e.g., throughout a middle or high school at all levels and in all departments).

• Teachers explain and model effective comprehension strategies. Typically, a few powerful strategies are emphasized. Teacher explanations and modeling include the following teacher behaviors:
   o Use of strategy terms, including defining such terms when necessary
   o Modeling of strategies by thinking aloud as teachers apply strategies during reading, including explaining the reasoning for applying particular strategies to particular parts of text—as well as how to apply the strategy to that part of text
   o Emphasizing that strategies are coordinated with one another before, during, after reading a text, with different strategies appropriate at different points in a text
   o Telling students the purpose of the strategies lesson (e.g., to understand stories by using the imagery strategy along with other strategies)
   o Telling students how they benefit from strategies use (i.e., how strategies help their comprehension), emphasizing that strategies are a means for obtaining comprehension and learning goals

• Teachers coach students to use strategies, on an as-needed basis, providing hints to students about potential strategic choices they might make. There are many mini-lessons about when it is appropriate to use particular strategies. Coaching includes the following:
   o Encouraging students to use strategy terms
   o Prompting students to think aloud as they apply strategies to text

  o Cueing students to choose one of the strategies they know for application at a particular point in text, sometimes going so far as to suggest a particular strategy
  o Explicitly reminding students to use bulletin board displays, posters, and cue cards summarizing strategies that can be applied during reading, with these prompts emphasizing that students should choose an appropriate strategy from ones they know
  o Prompting students to evaluate how well they read and to evaluate the impact of strategy use on their reading

• Teachers provide students with immediate feedback about their strategy application attempts. Such responses include the following teacher reactions:

  o Asking students to explain reasoning behind their use of a particular strategy
  o Restating students' strategic or interpretive responses
  o Praising students for using strategies
  o Pointing out when students are using strategies
  o Using teachable moments to discuss strategies—that is, using an occasion when a particular strategy might be profitably applied as an occasion for a mini-lesson on that strategy
  o Encouraging other students to make strategy use suggestions to a student experiencing difficulties processing a text strategically

• Throughout instruction, the usefulness of strategies is emphasized, with students reminded frequently about the comprehension gains that accompany strategy use. In addition to providing information about strategy benefits directly, sometimes teachers ask students whether the use of a particular strategy helped them to understand or enjoy text—that is, prompting students to reflect on strategy benefits. Sometimes, they explain how the student's use of strategy is probably benefiting him or her.

• Information about when and where various strategies can be applied is commonly discussed. Teachers consistently model flexible application of strategies in situations where the strategies can be appropriately applied; students explain to one another how they adapt strategies for use with particular texts.

• The strategies are used as a vehicle for coordinating dialogue about text. Thus a great deal of discussion of text content occurs as teachers interact with students, reacting to students' use of strategies and prompting additional strategic processing (see especially Gaskins, Satlow, Hyson, Ostertag, & Six, 1994). In particular, when students relate text to their prior knowledge, construct summaries of text meaning, visualize relations covered in a text, and predict what might transpire in a story, they engage in personal interpretation of text, with these personal interpretations varying from child to child and from reading group to reading group (Brown & Coy-Ogan, 1993).

- A variety of conventional teaching behaviors are coordinated with the teaching of strategies; for example, use of "wait time" (i.e., waiting for students to respond to questions that are posed as part of strategically mediated discussions of text).

SOURCE: Pressley et al. (1990, pp. 86–87). Reprinted by permission of Brookline Books.

READING TO LEARN AND VOCABULARY DEVELOPMENT

The importance of vocabulary is daily demonstrated in schools and out. In the classroom, the achieving students possess the most adequate vocabularies. Because of the verbal nature of most classroom activities, knowledge of words and ability to use language are essential to success in these activities. After schooling has ended, adequacy of vocabulary is almost equally essential for achievement in vocations and in society.

—Petty, Herold, and Stoll (1967, p. 7)

In spite of an almost universal recognition that knowing the meanings of lots of words is essential to gaining meaning and understanding during reading, teachers don't do very much teaching of vocabulary, and what little they do is poorly designed (Blachowicz, 1986). Having a literate vocabulary has even become cause for criticism, as I recently discovered. I was taken to task by a "reviewer" of one of my manuscripts; she didn't like the number of "big" words I used and specifically pointed out the ones she didn't know—all without a hint of embarrassment.

How many words do your students know? There are a variety of educated opinions to answer that question:

- The average high school senior knows 45,000 words (Nagy & Anderson, 1984).
- The average high school senior knows 17,000 words (D'Anna, Zechmeister, & Hall, 1991).
- The average high school senior knows 5,000 words (Hirsh & Nation, 1992).

Regardless of how many words adolescents know, they obviously don't know enough "big words," or their test scores would be going up instead of down. There are three basic ways for students to learn new words: (a) by being read to, (b) by reading themselves, or (c) from direct instruction in word meanings.

There is no doubt about the benefits of reading aloud to young children (and even older ones) with regard to their acquisition of vocabulary. The research regarding this assertion is compelling (Dickinson & Smith, 1994; Robbins & Ehri, 1994). Once students can read on their own, however, their vocabularies expand exponentially if they continue to read more challenging and well-written materials independently (Stanovich & Cunningham, 1993). In fact, there is much evidence to support the notion that learning vocabulary incidentally through reading is absolutely essential. There are far too many words that must be learned to teach them directly in the classroom (Sternberg, 1987). We simply do not have the time.

One author claims that by the middle grades, if students are to make grade-level progress (i.e., learning 3,000 to 5,000 new words per year), they should be reading more than 1.1 million words a year of outside school reading (twenty-five to thirty-five books or the equivalent) and about 1.7 million words in school texts (Honig, 1996, p. 103). Are your students reading this much? If students are to acquire the word meanings they need to read with understanding, they must not only read a lot, but they must learn how to become independent word learners much as they learn to become strategic readers. Carr and Wixon (1986) suggest that students must be taught how to (a) acquire word meanings (i.e., from context, structural analysis, and activating prior knowledge), (b) monitor their own understanding of new vocabulary (i.e., be ready to look up words they don't know), and (c) gain the capacity to change or modify strategies for understanding in the event of a comprehension failure.

Unfortunately, struggling readers are way behind in the vocabulary race before they even start kindergarten and will never catch up unless they receive daily direct vocabulary instruction from their teachers. Students from literacy-rich environments know the meanings of close to 20,000 words in first grade while students from literacy-poor environments know the meanings of only about 5,000 words (Hart & Risely, 1995). With limited vocabulary knowledge, struggling readers cannot access the content and are unable to use the context to predict the meanings of unknown words (Beck et al., 1997). They fall farther and farther behind their advantaged classmates. Even when struggling students acquire the skills and desire to read independently, they still need three types of intensive vocabulary instruction indirect, direct, and strategic.

Indirect vocabulary instruction takes place when teachers intentionally introduce "big" words (see Teaching for Learning Tip 5.3) in classroom conversations. Direct vocabulary instruction takes places when content teachers intentionally teach key vocabulary from each unit to students, building concepts and connections (Biemiller, 2003; Moats, 2004). Strategic vocabulary instruction includes teaching prefixes, suffixes, and word bases; directly teaching how to use context to tease out the meanings of words; and directly teaching students how to find words in the dictionary and then select the correct meaning (Archer et al., 2003; Carnine et al., 2004; Moats, 2004).

READING TO LEARN AND KNOWLEDGE ACQUISITION

Perhaps you have heard that rather tired argument about knowledge being irrelevant. We have all been stuffed with statistics about the exponential rate at which knowledge is growing and how impossible it is to contain it all in any one brain, much less the brain of a child who may not be "developmentally ready" to handle the cognitive demands. The idea that knowledge is somehow suspect has been around for close to a century (Cubberly, 1909). It enjoyed a healthy revival in the 1960s (Holt, 1964; Neill, 1960/1995) and is still going strong, albeit presently cloaked in the antistandards and antitesting movements (Kohn, 2000). Contemporary educators who downplay the role of knowledge in schooling usually point out that they can't possibly teach children everything there is to know, so a far better use of instructional time is to teach students ways to access and acquire information on their own. The persons who pontificate about the futility of cluttering kids' minds with facts are unable to tell you *when* children will actually become literate—knowing about art, literature, politics, science, history, religion, philosophy, or geography. Then again, perhaps it really *isn't* important in their grand scheme of things for students to know about the Holocaust, the countries that fought in World War II, the continents of the world, the books of the Bible, the Civil War, DNA, Shakespeare, Greek mythology, or the chemical elements.

The major problem with the denigration of knowledge per se is that knowledge is thought by most laypersons to be a byproduct of education, *and* the lack of knowledge is often a major contributor to poor reading comprehension (Perfetti, 1995). Some researchers have argued for a concept of comprehension that is unaffected by the reader's domain knowledge (Perfetti, 1989), but it is difficult to make a case that sports illiteracy will not impact one's ability to enjoy an article in *Sports Illustrated* or that ignorance regarding the vocabulary of science won't affect one's understanding of an article in *Scientific American*.

I heartily concur with E. D. Hirsch (1989), who wrote in his preface to *A First Dictionary of Cultural Literacy,* "Our schools' emphasis on skills rather than knowledge has . . . had the unintended effect of injuring disadvantaged students more than advantaged ones. Since more so-called skills are really based upon specific knowledge, those who have already received literate knowledge from their homes are better able to understand what teachers and textbooks are saying and are therefore better able to learn new things than are children from non-literate backgrounds. Consequently when schools emphasize skills over knowledge, they consistently widen the gap between the haves and have-nots instead of narrowing it" (p. xi).

HOW WE CAN ENGAGE MORE
STUDENTS IN READING TO LEARN

> *Without diminishing the importance of good early reading instruction or the difficulties children with disabilities face when reading, I would like to assert that many "poor readers" are actually lazy readers. This is not a reflection on their character. It's simply that no one ever told these children that reading was going to be work. Students turn on their stereos, kick back on their beds, and expect the book to transfer information from its pages to their brains.*
>
> —Jago (2000, p. 50)

We develop curricula, build schedules, and train teachers, meanwhile often forgetting that without the commitment of our students to the task, we are wasting our time and talents. The relationship of motivation to reading achievement is a relatively new topic of study, but for those who work with adolescents, it is highly relevant and very instructive (Borokowski et al., 1990).

That trite aphorism about leading a horse to water was never truer than it is in middle and high school. Teachers can "teach" cognitive strategies, assign interesting reading materials, activate prior knowledge, preteach key vocabulary, and hand out organizational and concept guides, but how can they get the proverbial horse to drink? How can teachers generate enthusiasm and excitement for learning when so many students either believe they are not capable of doing it because of past failures (learned helplessness) or are not willing to put forth the effort that strategic reading takes. Not only must we intentionally and systematically provide strategic instruction, we must also find ways to "energize the self-regulating executive skills necessary for strategy selection, implementation, and monitoring" (Chan, 1994, p. 319) in adolescent readers—a tall order, to be sure.

The cognitive apprenticeship model, referred to earlier in the book, is a powerful way to engage students and transmit cognitive strategies (Collins et al., 1991). In a traditional apprenticeship (e.g., one in trades such as plumbing or carpentry), the expert shows the apprentice how to do a task and then gradually gives over more and more of the responsibility for the task to the apprentice. In a cognitive apprenticeship, it is the teacher's thinking that is made visible to the students (e.g., Larry Snyder). The teacher situates what is being learned (i.e., the strategies) in the context of content instruction and then helps students see the worth of transferring what they have learned to new situations Strategic teachers are able to help students who believe they are not competent at performing a task become energized and motivated. Teaching students how to read to learn is like growing cotton or wheat or any other crop. One must cultivate, fertilize, irrigate, and then repeat the cycle. The seed will not germinate in just a day or two. It will take a full growing season to harvest the first crop. There may even be temporary setbacks due to "climate" beyond your control. Producing strategic readers can take as many as three to four growing seasons, but the results, both in standardized achievement test results and the confidence and success of your students, will be worth your investment.

COGNITIVE STRATEGY INSTRUCTION AT ALIEF HASTINGS HIGH SCHOOL

Alief Hastings High School (AHHS) in Houston, Texas, part of the Alief Independent School District (AISD), is a comprehensive high school of over 3,500 students. Dave Holmquist, Coordinating Principal, came up through the ranks at AHHS and was described by his faculty as compassionate, concerned, and involved. (Regretfully, he died this past spring. He was injured in an accidental fall during a graduation ceremony practice and, while recuperating from surgery, died of complications.) He was a strong and steady leader who knew the importance of delegating to his Associate Principals for Instruction, Kaye Arnold and Raymond Lowery. The demographics at AHHS are undeniably challenging: (a) a student population with a 20 percent mobility rate, (b) a high percentage of students who are economically disadvantaged (54 percent) or are designated at risk (66 percent), and (c) a veritable United Nations of languages (more than 50) and ethnic groups (more than 60). In spite of these obstacles to student achievement, AHHS's scores on the Exit Level Texas Assessment of Knowledge and Skills, given during the junior year, are among the highest in the district in all four content areas:

English/Language Arts, Science, Social Studies, and Math. However, teachers are unwilling to rest on past achievements. Twenty-two faculty members known as The Textpert Committee are moving deliberately and collaboratively toward the integration of cognitive strategy instruction into their classrooms. They are led by a trio of strong instructional leaders—Associate Principal Kaye Arnold, social studies department chair, Wendy Warren, and Title 1 Interventionist Allyson Burnett—with a vision to have all teachers teaching all students how to read to learn in their disciplines.

Shared leadership, professional learning communities, and collaboration are the hallmarks of the reading culture at AHHS. Allyson is the go-to support person for literacy at AHHS, providing leadership, motivation, coaching, and professional development for teachers. Her title belies her on-the-job performance—one part cheerleader, one part literacy expert, and one part troubleshooter. Allyson combines a solid literacy background with secondary content knowledge. She is able to model strategy instruction for teachers and then sit down and plan lessons together with them.

Allyson credits social studies department chairperson and Textpert Committee chair Wendy Warren with stepping up to show her colleagues that they could do it. "She picked up the gauntlet," says Allyson, "and because of who she is, people listened to her and followed her. She has made the process risk free and stress free for them" (A. Burnett, personal communication, October 4, 2005).

Associate Principal Kaye Arnold has a clear vision for what needs to happen, the power to procure whatever resources are needed, and the administrative authority that is essential to making things happen. However, she knows that administrators can never make it happen without talented and committed staff.

Literacy at the high school level had been a districtwide goal in AISD for several years: Resources and training had been provided for all faculty members, but the buy-in from many teachers was nominal. However, with the district commitment to hire interventionists at each building and the hiring of Allyson in 2004, the literacy committee enlarged its membership to twenty-two, renamed themselves as The Textpert Committee, and began to seriously examine how they could infuse strategy instruction into content classrooms. Kaye says, "All of the pieces of the literacy puzzle at AHHS are finally coming together. When Allyson arrived, the campus was primed for professional sharing and learning because the culture was operating informally in that mode with teacher leaders. We've always had a grassroots approach to using teacher leaders that supported district and campus instructional initiatives, and when the district adopted the professional learning community model three years ago, it further strengthened our culture of collaboration. The textperts are building on this foundation" (K. Arnold, personal communication, October 11, 2005).

In order to back up the claim inherent in their clever name, The Textperts did their homework first. They considered Douglas Reeves's (2004) research on 90-90-90 schools (these are campuses where in spite of the fact that 90 percent of the students are ethnic minorities and 90 percent of the students are eligible for free and reduced lunch, 90 percent of the students met or achieved high academic standards according to independently conducted tests of academic achievement). Reeves's research identified five characteristics that were common to all 90-90-90 schools: (a) a focus on academic achievement, (b) clear curriculum choices, (c) frequent assessment of student progress and multiple opportunities for improvement, (d) an emphasis on nonfiction writing, and (e) collaborative scoring of student work (p. 187).

Although research regarding the power of strategy instruction to raise achievement was solid, the big question for the textperts was how best to convince their colleagues that this wasn't just "one more thing to do." Staff members knew a great deal about strategy instruction, and many had participated in district training sessions, but the missing piece was the willingness to change. "The textperts had to find a way to help their colleagues overcome their fear of letting go of the curriculum," says Associate Principal Raymond Lowery. "Teachers were justifiably afraid that if they included strategy instruction, they wouldn't have time to adequately teach their content. The job of the textperts was to convince teachers through modeling and professional sharing that any time that they 'borrowed' from content instruction to build in strategy instruction would be returned to them many times over in the form of improved student achievement" (R. Lowery, personal communication, January 23, 2006). According to Allyson, Raymond's active involvement on The Textpert Committee was a big factor in gaining buy-in from the math and science teachers he supervises. "Raymond really endorsed what we were doing and sent a message to his teachers that literacy was essential in every classroom" (A. Burnett, personal communication, January 25, 2006).

The textperts chose a model that would allow them to develop their own expertise—expertise they did not yet have. However, Kaye Arnold worked with the central office secondary reading coordinator, Dianne Lee, to arrange for an intensive summer training opportunity for six committee members. It was at this training with Cris Tovani that the textperts began to strengthen their understandings of cognitive strategy instruction. The Textperts Committee decided to focus their efforts in three areas:

(a) direct instruction in specific cognitive strategies, (b) regularly scheduled writing-to-learn activities in every content area, and (c) expectations that students would learn how and regularly employ various text-marking processes in which students indicate their thinking about the text by using highlighters or sticky notes (Tovani, 2004).

Textperts are aware of the time needed for teachers to integrate strategy instruction into their teaching repertoires: They are only a few small steps ahead of their colleagues. But they are also enjoying the small successes that are becoming routine. Chemistry teacher and textpert Tila Hidalgo explains, "When my students got excited about a lesson in which I integrated reading and writing strategies, I told my fellow science teachers about it. There's nothing like success to pull people in to trying new things" (T. Hidalgo, personal communication, December 01, 2005).

Wendy Warren is delighted with the way teachers are moving from making comments like, "Why can't the English department do this?" to developing lessons collaboratively. The English department at AHHS has been teaching students how to use cognitive strategies to read literature for quite some time. However, without direct instruction in the reading of nonfiction, students are unlikely to make the transfer independently (W. Warren, personal communication, November 29, 2005).

Social studies teacher Barbara Guidry believes that the big reason this initiative is taking hold has to do with its "grassroots" nature. "The textperts are teachers coming up with ideas, people who are in classrooms right now." Barbara sees indications that students are applying cognitive strategies across the curriculum. "I was walking down the hall and ran into Teri Fleming, the science teacher. She had given her students a writing prompt [see the science rubric to evaluate writing in science, Exhibit 2.1, in Chapter 2] about Typhoid Mary and got a response from a student that made both of us feel fabulous. In the second paragraph of her response, the student had written that what happened with Typhoid Mary reminded her of what Jean Jacques Rousseau wrote about freedom, and she then quoted Rousseau [a Social Studies discussion from the prior week]. When I hear examples like this, I know we're on the right track. We [teachers *and* kids] are like roses just beginning to bloom. All we need is a little watering from Allyson and the textperts to grow another crop of roses next year" (B. Guidry, personal communication, January 23, 2006).

To celebrate their "blooming," The Textpert Committee held a two-day "Textpo" near the end of the school year. They invited staff to take a portion of their conference period (the time of day reserved for teacher planning and conferencing with colleagues) to celebrate the progress the committee made during the year, and they invited parents and central office administrators as well. Four kiosks were set up around the library with multiple examples of lesson plans, student work products, and videos of classroom lessons. Of course, food was featured prominently, but the real purpose of Textpo was to give those teachers who were not yet "blooming" an opportunity to view what their colleagues had been doing during the school year and for all teachers to provide feedback to the textperts about what kind of professional development and support they needed for the coming year.

Allyson is excited about the changes she sees happening in social studies, math, and science classrooms. "Kids who have often just gone through the motions in school are being asked to think on a deeper level. The use of various strategies involves the students in ways they haven't experienced before. And when it happens in all of their classes, they realize that their teachers are serious.

"As teachers we are all trapped within our own development—prisoners of our own background knowledge and experience. We know collaboration is powerful. But we learned through our participation in developing professional learning communities at AHHS that what is needed for a group to be successful is at least one person who knows what they're doing and is willing to share that knowledge along with sharing ownership and credit for the accomplishments of the group. That's what the textperts have done" (A. Burnett, personal communication, March 15, 2006).

REFLECTION AND DISCUSSION QUESTIONS

1. What can you personally do to engage more of your students in reading the text of your discipline?

2. Evaluate where you, your colleagues, and your school are in terms of strategic reading instruction.

3. What is your biggest comprehension problem and how might you solve it using cognitive strategies?

4. What is thinking aloud, and why is it one of the most critical components of strategic reading instruction?

5. Can *you* teach all students to read to learn? What do you need to do first?

Motivate Every Student to Read in the Zone

The percentage of adult Americans reading literature has dropped dramatically over the past 20 years. The decline in literary reading parallels a decline in total book reading. Literary reading is declining among all education levels and age groups. The steepest decline in literary reading is in the youngest age groups. The decline in literary reading foreshadows an erosion in cultural and civic participation.

—National Endowment for the Arts (2004)

Vinh came to the United States from Vietnam in 1975. He was nine years old and knew very little English. His fourth-grade teacher didn't waste a day of instructional time and immediately began teaching Vinh the sound-spelling correspondences. Then he was introduced to the school library, and the seemingly endless shelves of beautiful books on every imaginable subject fascinated him. No such place had existed in Vinh's Vietnamese school. He couldn't wait to read them all: Greek mythology, world history, botany, fairy tales, and fabulous stories like *The Lion, the Witch and the Wardrobe* (Lewis, 1994).

He started with the easy books that matched his reading level but quickly began devouring more difficult texts. He read about the Civil War, the Old West, and the New Deal. Soon, he knew more U.S. history than his teacher. He carried a well-thumbed pocket dictionary and looked up every word he didn't know. He lived in the library, checking out books by the dozens. His teacher wisely realized that to deny Vinh the daily library privileges he needed to satisfy his craving for books would be akin to denying food to the malnourished. Vinh was feeding his growing mind. What Vinh saw in the looking glass of the hundreds of books he read was an educated and literate citizen of the United States, someone who could be and do anything he desired. Through the stories he read, Vinh acquired not only literacy but possibilities, options, and a vision for who he could become. Vinh received his degree from the University of West Florida in 1991 and is now a successful business owner, husband, and father. He reads aloud to his young daughters every night, sharing stories like *The Lion, the Witch and the Wardrobe* with them. He is passionate about instilling a love for the stories and books that changed his life in his daughters (V. Rocker, personal communication, May/June, 2000).

Vinh is an example of what inevitably happens when a student gets hooked on reading in elementary school, reads voraciously, reads increasingly more challenging texts, and uses cognitive strategies to gain meaning. The more you read with understanding and retention, the more you know. The more you know, the smarter you get. The student who doesn't have or easily acquire vocabulary and background knowledge at the outset of his or her schooling career often falls farther and farther behind as the words and concepts of grade-level texts become increasingly difficult to understand. The voracious reader, who reads increasingly more challenging books as reading abilities improve, acquires new knowledge and vocabulary from every book that is read, thus making further reading an even more enjoyable and instructive exercise (Stanovich, 1986).

THE VALUE OF READING A LOT

> *The great gift is the passion for reading. It is cheap, it consoles, it distracts, it excites. It gives you knowledge of the world and experience of a wide kind. It is a moral illumination.*
>
> —Hardwick (1990, p. 24)

There is an abundance of conventional wisdom and correlational evidence regarding the benefits of reading a lot. See Figure 5.1. Even though elementary educators have been arguing on and off since the turn of the century about which methodology is best for teaching students to read (phonics vs. whole language), they have agreed that reading is learned through reading.

Figure 5.1   Research Support for Reading a Lot

Type of Research	Correlational Research Findings
Differences in the amount of reading done by high- and low-achieving students	Higher-achieving students do more reading in school than their lower-achieving counterparts (Allington, 1977, 1980, 1983, 1984).
	Higher-achieving students read more outside of school (Anderson, Wilson, & Fielding, 1988; Nagy & Anderson, 1984). Anderson and his colleagues found that students achieving at the 90th percentile read 40 minutes per day, which amounted to well over 2 million words per year, while students achieving at the 50th percentile read only 12.9 minutes per day for a total of 601,000 words per year; and students achieving at the 10th percentile read a scant 1.6 minutes per day for an appallingly low 51,000 words per year.
Research showing a relationship between amount of reading both in and out of school and reading achievement	The most extensive correlational study showing a relationship between reading a lot and achievement is the 1998 National Assessment of Educational Progress. At Grades 4, 8, and 12, students who reported reading more pages daily in school and for homework had higher average scale scores than students who reported reading fewer pages daily (Donahue, Voelkl, Campbell, & Mazzeo, 1999).
Acquisition of second languages through reading a lot	Reading a lot makes a huge impact on the acquisition of a second language when the learners are beyond the beginning reading level. There is a wide body of literature that makes one wonder why we aren't more proactive about motivating our ESL students to read a lot in English (Pilgreen & Krashen, 1993). Language and literacy development around the world has been stimulated by reading a lot: United States (Krashen, 1993), England (Hafiz & Tudor, 1989), Japan (Mason & Krashen, 1997), the Fiji Islands (Elley & Mangubhai, 1983), South Africa (Elley, 1999), Sri Lanka (Elley, 1999), Ireland (Greaney & Clarke, 1973), and Hong Kong (Tsang, 1996).
Relationship of academic learning time and student achievement	When students are actually engaged in learning tasks with a high level of success, their achievement goes up (Berliner, 1981; Fisher & Berliner, 1985). A logical conclusion one can draw from this literature is that time spent reading at a high level of success will result in reading achievement.

Our deep and abiding belief in the benefits of reading has created a mini-industry around the concept of motivating students to read more books. Programs such as Scholastic's Reading Counts and Renaissance Learning's Accelerated Reader are based on this premise. Millions of pizzas have been donated to the cause of getting kids to read more. I've met principals who've shaved their heads, eaten fried worms, and kissed pigs—all for the cause of motivating their students to read more. I even had the temerity to jog around my school in a 1920s bathing suit to celebrate the number of books my students had read.

So it came as a bit of a surprise to those of us, myself included, who have been preaching that reading a lot will result in increased achievement, to find no solid empirical research to back up this assertion. Oh, there are some so-called experimental studies evaluating motivational programs, but unfortunately, researchers did not use control groups, were sloppy about collecting data, and used different achievement tests to determine differences between experimental and control groups (McEwan & McEwan, 2003; NICHD, 2000). The sales brochures for Accelerated Reader and Reading Counts contain glowing reports, and it salves our consciences regarding low-achieving readers to believe that purchasing a "canned" program will solve reading problems. However, the National Reading Panel (NICHD, 2000) found that

> Despite widespread acceptance of the idea that schools can successfully encourage students to read more and that these increases in reading practice will be translated into better fluency and higher reading achievement, there is not adequate evidence to sustain this claim. (sec. 3, p. 28)

Studies have not shown that motivating students to read more *doesn't* work; the practice just hasn't been shown by any high-quality experimental research studies to be effective in raising achievement overall on standardized tests.

What are educators to do with this information? Cancel SSR (sustained silent reading), DEAR (drop everything and read), and SQUIRT (super quiet reading time)? There is some evidence to suggest that simply turning students loose to grab any book off the library shelves with no monitoring as to its reading level or without accountability for gaining meaning (i.e., through discussion or written assignments) is not a particularly wise use of precious allocated time. I have walked through classrooms and stopped to ask students about books they were reading and received blank stares. On the other hand, in some classrooms, SSR is alive and well. It may provide a relaxing and enjoyable break in the school day, and it may even be beneficial for some groups of students. But for many students, this time could be used more effectively. The panel did not suggest that we stop encouraging students to read. It did call, however, for more rigorous research to illuminate the question.

We have already discussed the critical importance of teaching decoding, developing fluency, and increasing the use of cognitive strategies to raise reading achievement. The research is solid in these three areas. Secondary school students who do not have these prerequisite skills would be better served to spend their instructional time with skilled teachers acquiring skills and strategies and then practicing in reading materials geared to their specific reading levels far away from the prying eyes of their peers. Staring at just any printed page during SSR will not transform low achievers into high-achieving readers. Very-low-achieving readers will make gains in achievement only if they spend their time with proven programs. Low-achieving students need focused, direct instruction along with reading a lot in leveled materials to improve their achievement. Conversely, if good readers are not held accountable while reading challenging, well-written, and varied text during SSR, their reading may be just another example of activity without achievement. Many students miss the delights to be found in silent reading because of a bad habit they have acquired—guessing. Teaching for Learning Tip 5.1 describes the symptoms of the guessing syndrome and offers some suggestions for eliminating it among your students.

READING IN THE ZONE

I was deeply depressed when I first read what the National Reading Panel (NICHD, 2000) had to say about motivational reading programs, but as I reflected on what practices associated with reading a lot might actually result in higher achievement, two variables emerged: (a) accountability while reading and (b) reading increasingly challenging text. When students are voraciously reading appropriately challenging text with accountability, they are in what I call the *zone.* For the time that students spend reading to affect their achievement, it is essential that they be reading in the zone. Figure 5.2 is a Venn Diagram that illustrates exactly where the zone is located. It is the area where voracious reading, challenging text, and accountability overlap to produce fluency, meaning, knowledge, vocabulary, and flow.

Sometimes, however, teachers work too hard at taking the work out of schooling, denying students the satisfaction that comes from mastering a challenging assignment or understanding a piece of text that at first glance appeared too difficult. All students will have unique reading zones, depending on their current reading levels, the difficulty of the text, and

TEACHING FOR LEARNING TIP 5.1

Eliminate Random Guessing During Silent Reading

How to Get Started

Guessing is a strategy that is rampant in many classrooms. It is widely used by secondary students in response to the challenge of reading connected text when they have not mastered the sound-spelling correspondences needed to decode the text. In the absence of decoding skills, elementary school students are encouraged by teachers to make a guess, based on the context. This strategy, used repeatedly over time, often results in a guessing habit. Guessing may work when the text is simple and there are pictures to give clues, but in the upper grades, it severely inhibits comprehension and takes away the enjoyment and flow of reading.

Here are some symptoms of the guessing syndrome you may observe in your students:

- They read a word one day and then seem to forget it the next
- They often miss details and even main ideas
- They frequently misread simple words
- They frequently misread two-syllable words
- They have serious problems with spelling

When presented with the letter portions of the forty-four sound-spelling correspondences, students with the guessing syndrome are unable to quickly identify which sounds they represent, hence their extreme difficulty with both spelling the words when the sounds are pronounced (encoding) and producing and blending the sounds when the letters are presented (decoding). The only cure for the guessing syndrome is explicit, systematic phonics instruction in those specific sound-spelling correspondences that students have not mastered. Often students in this category are able to catch up very quickly. Their comprehension difficulties are due completely to their inability to identify the words correctly, thereby creating total confusion regarding what the text is really about.

A Resource to Help You

McGuinness & McGuinness, 1998. *Reading Reflex.*

Research About the Importance of Decoding

Adams, 1990; Chall, 1967/1983; NICHD, 2000; Snow, Burns, & Griffin, 1998.

their backgrounds and vocabulary knowledge, but the experience of reading in the zone is nothing like a daydream or a mini-vacation. It's more akin to what Walt Whitman (as quoted in Gilbar, 1990) describes as an "exercise [or] a gymnast's struggle; [something] that the reader is to do for himself, [he or she] must be on the alert [and] must himself or herself construct . . . the poem, argument, history, metaphysical essay—the text

Figure 5.2   Reading in the Zone

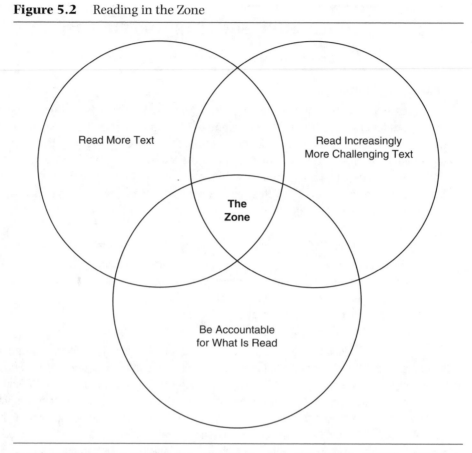

furnishing the hints, the clue, the start or [the] framework" (p. 39). Careful, thoughtful strategic reading demands engagement. This kind of reading is nearly as exhausting as physical exercise. To suggest to students that mental effort is other than work is to mislead them. Although reading difficult text is admittedly a challenging undertaking, teachers can help to reduce the cognitive load by designing more student-friendly instruction. Teaching for Learning Tip 5.2 describes the process.

THE IMPORTANCE OF READING CHALLENGING FICTION *AND* NONFICTION

Reading books is good, reading good books is better.

—L. C. Powell (as quoted in Gilbar, 1990, p. 55)

TEACHING FOR LEARNING TIP 5.2

Reduce the Cognitive Load for Students

How to Get Started

Cognitive load refers to the total amount of mental activity imposed on working memory at an instance in time (e.g., a classroom period or a lesson). The major factor in cognitive load is the number of elements that need to be attended to. Students (and teachers) do not automatically remember what they hear or read as if capturing it on videotape in their minds. What they remember depends more on what they already know than on what is actually presented. If the capacity of our working memory (about seven plus or minus two different elements) is exceeded during instruction, some if not all of the information will be lost.

- Present just one important concept or idea at a time.
- Write only the most critical concept on the board or overhead at one time.
- Carefully design handouts so that all of the information needed to complete a page is on that page.
- Pass out only one handout at a time.
- Give only one direction at a time or chunk directions into smaller sections.
- Eliminate the working memory load associated with asking your students to mentally integrate several sources of information by physically integrating and summarizing the sources for them.

An example of cognitive overload substantiated by research relates to animated Power-Point and video presentations (Mayer, Hegarty, Mayer, & Campbell, 2005). Researchers showed that paper-based textbooks in which students can control the rate at which they process the text and illustrations lead to better understanding and retention than computer-based animation and narration. Some reasons for the superiority of paper-based learning materials are that information is presented in a more segmented and meaningful order and students can go back and forth in the printed text to find answers to questions.

A Resource to Help You

Paas, Renkl, & Sweller, 2003. *Cognitive Load Theory: A Special Issue of Educational Psychologist.*

Research on the Power of Reducing Cognitive Load

Cooper, 1990; Miller, 1956; Pollock, Chandler, & Sweller, 2002; Sweller, 1994.

I received a question from a parent to answer in my newspaper column asking about a book her eighth-grade daughter was reading for her language arts class. Usually, parents complain about some aspect of content (e.g., profanity or sexually explicit material), but this parent questioned the difficulty of the book and the worth of spending nearly two months of class time doing dioramas, discussions, and dramatizations based on the book. The title in question was *Who Put That Hair in My Toothbrush?* (Spinelli, 1994). I obtained a copy of this young adult novel by Newbery-Award-winning author Spinelli (*Maniac Magee*, 1990) to check it out for myself. The plot is an appealing one to adolescents, with its offbeat humor and theme of sibling rivalry. The only problem is the suitability of this book for in-depth study in an eighth-grade language arts class.

I applied the Dale-Chall readability formula to the text (Chall & Dale, 1995) and discovered that reading levels in the book ranged from a low of first grade (based on a passage containing sixteen sentences and no unfamiliar words) to a high of fourth grade. The eighth-grade students who spent over six weeks of instructional time "studying" this book didn't learn one new word they shouldn't have mastered by fourth grade or earlier nor were they exposed to any worthy themes or new information that might result in increased reading achievement in the future. The entertainment value probably even began to wear thin for most students after the first week. Merely reading is not enough. For able students, the text must be challenging for them to mature into literate adults.

Not only must students read ample amounts of challenging text, they must read both expository and narrative texts. The early childhood emphasis on picture books and fairy tales plus the literature-based instruction that has dominated the reading diets of most elementary students has not prepared most middle and high school students for reading expository text. They can deal with plots, settings, and characters. But they are baffled by comparison and contrast, cause and effect, or a sequence of historical events.

With the advent of the Readers' Workshop (Atwell, 1998) and literature-based instruction, nonfiction has even fallen on hard times in middle and high schools. ACT, the nation's largest provider of tests for college-bound students, periodically surveys middle, high school, and college teachers regarding the types of skills thought to be needed by students to succeed in college, as well as the type of reading that should consume the majority of students' reading time. Teachers across the levels were in agreement about the skills needed for success in college, with drawing conclusions and making inferences from the text rated as the top two skills. They differed, however, on the most important type of reading needed for college success.

Secondary teachers ranked prose fiction as the most important type of reading, ahead of text from the social sciences, humanities, and sciences. College teachers, on the other hand, ranked social science reading as being most important, with the humanities second, and prose fiction third (ACT, 2000, p. 10). "There should be greater use of multiple texts in reading instruction, and most especially, the texts studied should not only be narrative, but also expository" (Kibby, 1993, p. 38). Make sure that the Language Arts-English teachers in your school have not totally forsaken expository texts in favor of fiction, particularly young adult fiction (e.g., *Who Put That Hair in My Toothbrush?*) with watered-down vocabulary and simple syntax.

THE IMPORTANCE OF ACCOUNTABILITY

My daily contact with real live teenagers makes me absolutely certain that students need to be held accountable for their reading.

—C. Jago (2000, p. 63)

Without accountability, focus, and purpose, students will often "read" on automatic pilot. How do the best teachers hold students accountable for what they have read? There is no one right answer. But here's how one teacher does it.

Carol Jago (2000), an English teacher at Santa Monica High School, tells students what they will read—classics that she chooses—and then holds them accountable on a daily basis for what they have read. She believes that "all books are not created equal." She goes on to say, "Some [books] have the power to transport us to unexplored worlds and allow us—at least for as long as the book lasts—to become other than who we are. Others only attempt to offer us chicken soup for our teenage or middle-aged souls. While there is no question that it is easier to persuade students to pick up the second kind of novel, a critical reading of classical literature results in a deep literacy that I believe is an essential skill for anyone who wants to attempt to make sense of the world" (p. 7).

Carol holds her students accountable for reading the classics she assigns and explains her method of making sure they're reading their assignments:

> I select a key sentence or two from the end of the chapter that has been assigned and ask students to write for five minutes, placing this sentence within the context of the story. Rather than putting students on the spot to remember details, I ask them to reflect on how the novel is developing. If I choose the sentence carefully, students can't do this without having read the chapter. These short responses are also easy to read and evaluate—no small thing when you meet 150 students a day. I don't assign grades to the responses but simply give students credit or no credit for having done their homework. (Jago, 2000, pp. 63–64)

Students' enjoyment and understanding of what they read is greater when they have word knowledge—knowing the meanings of many words. Teaching for Learning Tip 5.3 sets forth a way to teach big words daily in content classrooms.

TEACHING FOR LEARNING TIP 5.3

Teach Big Words Daily

How to Get Started

Your goal in this Teaching for Learning Tip is to make the vocabulary of your discipline come to life for students. You can't do it by simply handing out a vocabulary list on Monday, assigning the definitions to be done by Wednesday, and giving a test on Friday. Students will, as you know, numbly copy the meanings from the dictionary or glossary with little or no conceptual understanding. Unless you personally bring those words to life and help your students take ownership of them, many of your students will memorize the meanings for the test and promptly forget them; others won't even be able to remember them for the test. Oh, some students may recognize them in their reading, but the solid understanding they need to comprehend the text of your discipline won't be there. If you are using the Teaching for Learning Tips 3.1 or 3.2 in which you develop fluency and teach students how to break your content words in syllables, combine your vocabulary instruction with those activities. The highest priority words to teach are those concepts and ideas that lay the foundation for entire units of study or for your discipline in general. Use these questions to help you formulate your priorities:

- What are the key concepts of your discipline?
- What words are indispensable to understanding the text?
- What words have multiple meanings?
- What are the common idioms?
- What words are needed to take tests? (See Teaching for Learning Tip 6.4)
- What words are essential in your classroom or discipline for ELL students?

Here's how to teach a word for mastery. (a) Provide a student-friendly definition of the word; (b) suggest synonyms or antonyms for the word; (c) put the new word into a context or connect it to a known concept; (d) use the new word on multiple occasions and in multiple contexts, such as sentence starters and in games; (e) place several new words into a shared context; (f) ask questions that contain the new word so students must process its meaning in multiple ways; (g) add the new word to an already existing classroom concept map or construct a new concept map using the new word as the foundational concept.

Resources to Help

Beck, McKeown, & Kucan, 2002. *Bringing Words to Life: Robust Vocabulary Instruction.*
Feldman & Kinsella, 2005. *Narrowing the Language Gap: The Case for Explicit Vocabulary Instruction.*

Research on Direct Vocabulary Instruction

Beck, Perfetti, & McKeown, 1982.

Resources to Help You Implement

McEwan, 2004. *7 Strategies of Highly Effective Readers.*

Research on Teacher Modeling During Strategy Instruction

Afflerbach, 2002; Duffy, 2002; Trabasso & Bouchard, 2000, 2002.

Traditional book reports have fallen on hard times lately, replaced by dioramas, brochures, mobiles, slide shows, and collages. Students can get credit for a "book report" without reading the book. There are, however, dozens of other ways to encourage students' creativity, personal response, and interpretation while still ensuring accountability. Here are a few of the most effective ways:

Portfolios

A portfolio is a collection of student work, connected to what has been read and studied, that reveals student progress. It might include items such as personal responses to reading assignments; self-assessments, teacher observations, attitude and interest surveys; writing samples (both complete and in progress); evidence that the student reads for enjoyment and information; and summaries (Educational Research Service, 1998, p. 5). It might also include a list of books read by the student, a summary of several books read during the school year, a listing of books read categorized by genre to illustrate the breadth of reading during a school year, a description of a favorite book, a list of books read at home or a list read at school, a brief description of the five books read most recently, or a list or descriptions of favorite authors.

Reading Journals

Reading journals contain daily written responses to what has been read during a silent reading period. Some teachers ask students to choose a quotation, copy it into the journal, and then explain its importance to the story. Others ask students to choose words they do not know and write their meanings. Another approach asks students a specific question to which they respond in their journals.

Book Reviews

Accountability could come in the form of a written review for an online bookseller. Acquaint your students with the review aspect of these Web sites and then offer them the option of writing an online review. Make sure that the written product is well edited before a student clicks the send command, however. Erasing the review is impossible once it's been published.

Here's another way to utilize students' affinity for sharing their thoughts online: At Billings Senior High School in Montana, reading teacher TerraBeth Jochems envisioned a schoolwide Web site devoted to book reviews and recommendations by students and faculty. She was inspired by the concept of the movie *Pay It Forward*, in which the movie's main character, a middle schooler, comes up with a plan to change the world—spread good will and happiness by doing a good thing for three other people and encouraging each of them to pass along an act of kindness to three others. TerraBeth's idea was called Read It Forward and encouraged students and teachers to post reviews of good books they would recommend to someone else. She enlisted the help of technology teacher Vince Long to design a Web site. Read It Forward has been moving reading forward at Billings Senior High School for four years. You can check out the latest reviews at http://broncgeeks.billings.k12.mt.us/readitforward/.

Essays

Essay assignments that call only for formal analysis of a text are far more common than those that call on the reader to include a personal response (Applebee, 1993, p. 171). However, these two types of assignments are comparable in their effects on reading comprehension (Marshall, 1987). In Marshall's study, students reported that they sometimes perceived formal analytic writing as merely "an exercise in fulfilling their teacher's expectations rather than an occasion for thinking through the literature," whereas personal essays provided an opportunity to begin the process of independent analysis (Educational Research Service, 1998, p. 5).

Personal Anthologies

Students create personal anthologies by acting as editor: They search for works of literature that best connect with their interests and tastes, develop a theme, and then compile these works into an anthology (Sullivan, 1988).

This process can motivate learners to read more widely and to make connections between the different works they read (Educational Research Service, 1998, p. 5).

Every-Pupil Response Activities

After reading a portion of text, either in class or for a homework assignment, every student completes a brief written response to the text. They then participate in a discussion with a partner. The writing assignment might include a brief explanation of a specific situation, problem, or question as a way of assessing the students' understanding of the concepts about which they were reading. These are self-assessments, rarely collected and never graded. The goal is to reach consensus with their partner regarding the question that was posed by supporting their responses with text evidence and good reasoning, as well as by considering the evidence and rationale presented by their partner (Gaskins, Satlow, Hyson, Ostertag, & Six, 1994, pp. 559–560). There are dozens of additional alternative evaluation methods that include (a) rewriting the end of a story, (b) writing newspaper articles about events in the text, (c) writing a modern-day version of a piece of historical fiction, (d) rewriting the text as a play or poem, (e) writing up an interview with a character in the book, or (f) writing a letter to a character in the book.

MOTIVATING STUDENTS TO READ A LOT

A study by the National Endowment for the Arts (2004) reported some depressing news about lower reading rates in the United States, especially among young adult readers. The study concluded, "Reading is at risk, foreshadowing an erosion in cultural and civic participation" (p. 2). The hypothesized cause of this decline?—increased participation in a variety of electronic media, including the Internet, video games, and portable digital devices.

The majority of students are not "hooked on books" anymore. The closest most come to a meaningful encounter with text is the love affair all adolescents seem to have with hypertext and text messaging. A news story reported that literary classics are now being abbreviated as text messages—the technological version of CliffsNotes. Milton's *Paradise Lost* has been translated: "Devl kikd outa hevn coz jelus of jesus & strts war. [The devil is kicked out of heaven because he is jealous of Jesus and starts a war.]" (Ananova, 2005). If you're looking for a novel way to teach summarizing, this may well be an engaging lesson plan. But if reading the text message precedes the actual processing of Milton's text and students are unable to write the translation using standard English, the picture is an even bleaker one than originally painted.

It has been said that students who are personally motivated by their own needs and interests will invest time in reading (Guthrie et al., 1996), but teachers are finding it increasingly difficult to motivate even the best students to read. For reading to result in increased understanding and retention of meaning, students must be *personally motivated* to read and be *engaged* in reading. They must be tuned in, on task, and cognitively processing text. They must be reading in the zone, the intersection or overlapping of reading a lot, reading at an appropriate level of difficulty, and reading with accountability.

Steve Gardiner has managed to keep his students in the zone in his high school journalism and English classes with his personal version of SSR. He believes that if students don't learn to enjoy reading and look forward to periods of time when they can read for enjoyment, they won't be ready to sit down and take a high-stakes test in a positive frame of mind. Steve says, "Reading itself has to mean something to a student before he will be able to test successfully on literacy skills" (S. Gardiner as quoted in ASCD, 2005, p. 1).

ENGAGING STUDENTS IN READING

Identifying and nurturing the context variables that genuinely motivate students to become engaged readers, rather than students who merely pretend to read, is a critical task for educators. These variables include (a) the right kind of teachers, (b) the skills to read with confidence and success, (c) the right kind of books, (d) opportunities for directed and focused silent reading in text that students can read independently during the school day, (e) the promotion of books by every classroom teacher, and (f) superior library and media services.

The Right Kind of Teachers

> *Now we come to the nub of the matter. Non-reading children are made by non-reading adults. Our resources may be poor, our stocks battered and too thin, we may be subject to all manner of difficulty, but one fact overrides all. The adult who reads for him or herself with conviction and who is knowledgeable about what is available for children is indispensable in literary education. Indeed, such a person is so important that his or her active presence can succeed in the face of enormous problems to a point far in excess of a school that has much better facilities but lacks a reading adult. The evidence for this is now legion.*

> —Chambers (1985, p.12)

The teachers at Griffin Middle School in Tallahassee, Florida, are the right kind of teachers. They devote fifteen minutes of their homeroom period several days each week to building interest and excitement about reading. On Monday, the school's TV station broadcasts a reading-related short feature produced by students. On Tuesday, all of the teachers read the same selection from *Chicken Soup for the Preteen Soul* (Canfield, Hansen, Hansen, & Dunlap, 2000). Library copies of the book are routinely all checked out as students follow along, read ahead, or reread a selection they particularly enjoyed. On Thursday, silent reading is on the menu, and teachers are expected to monitor by walking around and tapping students on their shoulders and requesting a one-minute whisper read to make sure that they are reading a "just-right" book on their reading level.

SKILLS TO READ WITH CONFIDENCE AND SUCCESS

High self-direction and student expertise should not be viewed as an attribute of a child; rather, the process of self-direction depends on the "fit" between the demands of the situation and the ability and interests of the student.

—Meichenbaum and Biemiller (1998, p. 54)

When one reads comments like the following from interviews with school administrators, counselors, and teachers, one can easily see why their students aren't successful:

- "By the time students get to high school, it is all over as to who will achieve."
- "Once students get to high school, they are either intrinsically motivated or not, and this cannot change."
- "Below-average and average students lack the discipline and motivation to succeed."
- "Because of the way below-average students were brought up, they do not want to learn. They view school as something to get away from" (Oakes & Guiton, 1995, pp. 15–17).

Students must experience success if they are to progress in reading proficiency. Therefore, teachers must structure learning situations that ensure success. Success increases the willingness of students to work harder and to endure some frustration. Teachers can control a student's success in three ways: (a) selection and sequencing of instructional objectives, (b) grouping of students for instruction, and (c) instructional procedures and activities (Marliave & Filby, 1985, p. 230). The material selected for instructional use must be at an appropriate level of difficulty for the student. If a high school student has a fifth-grade reading level, asking that student to read material written at a high school level will result in frustration for both student and teacher. Placing students who are not reading on grade level into smaller ability-based groups increases the likelihood that they will experience success.

The Right Kind of Books

Ample Choices in Classrooms and the Library-Media Center

Students are often unaware of the vast variety of materials and services available in the library—pamphlets, booklets, historical documents, microfilm, microfiche, books, and magazines. They often read in a rut, failing to discover science fiction, fantasy, biography, history, science, art, psychology, or poetry. They need to be introduced and then expected to read from a variety of sources. Every classroom needs books, magazines, and newspapers. The school as a whole must be serviced by a well-stocked library-media center.

Materials at Appropriate Reading Levels

My biggest challenge as a media specialist was helping reluctant readers find the right book. First of all, it had to be interesting and appealing to the reader. Then it had to be on the right reading level—not too babyish or the student would be embarrassed and refuse to read the book but not too hard or the student couldn't read the book. Now there's an answer to leveling books with almost pinpoint accuracy: the Lexile Framework (MetaMetrics, 1998). It is a tool that makes it possible to place readers and text on the same scale and eliminate the guesswork from helping readers choose books. The difference between a reader's Lexile and the Lexile of the text can be used to forecast the degree of understanding a reader will experience with the text. The Lexile Framework was developed under the auspices of the National Institute of Health and Human Development and includes a software program called the Lexile Analyzer that measures the difficulty of text by analyzing the vocabulary. When a reader has the same Lexile measure as a text, the reader should read that text with 75% comprehension. When the reader's measure exceeds the text Lexile, comprehension goes up to 90%, and the reader experiences total control and automaticity. The Lexile Framework has the potential for reducing the risk of frustrating readers and turning them off with text that is too difficult. "In reality, there are no poor readers—only mistargeted readers who are being challenged inappropriately" (Stenner, 1996).

Opportunities for Directed and Focused Silent Reading During the School Day

Free to Read

The administrators, teachers, students, and parents of Central Middle School in Omaha, Nebraska, are "free to read" during homeroom period every Thursday for twenty-three minutes. The school's literacy team is out to promote the enjoyment of reading as well as conversations between teachers and students about books, particularly those teachers who in the students' minds have nothing to do with reading (e.g., art, PE, and math teachers). Free to Read also involves parents who are invited to come to school and join in the reading *and* the conversations about books.

Teaching Tip 5.4 explains a unique way to help students visualize the meanings and pronunciations of new vocabulary, whether in English or another language.

Individualized Reading Classes

Pervasive reading—reading in every subject, in every physical space, reading just about anything, just about all the time—is the key to reading success. A book is a piece of technology best used by the individual, not by the group. Try to liberate readers from the group, and capture the intimate pleasures of reading, as often as possible.

—P. Temes, Director of the Great Books Foundation,
(personal communication, April, 2000)

TEACHING FOR LEARNING TIP 5.4

*Teach Students How to Visualize for
Vocabulary and Concept Acquisition*

How to Get Started

Ask students to draw pictures to help them master the meanings of new content vocabulary. This technique is equally effective for students who are acquiring a second language, either English or another language. For foreign language learning, in addition to asking students to draw a picture to match a word's meaning, also require them to come up with a smaller picture clue to the word's pronunciation. See, for example, Figure 5.3 in which Spanish teacher Susan Graham has used pictures for both word meanings and pronunciations.

A Resource to Help You

Rose & Nicholl, 1998. *Accelerated Learning for the 21st Century.*
This book contains dozens of ideas for helping students improve their learning and retention.

Research on Learning

Bransford, Brown, & Cocking, 2000.

Figure 5.3   Visualize the Meaning and the Pronunciation

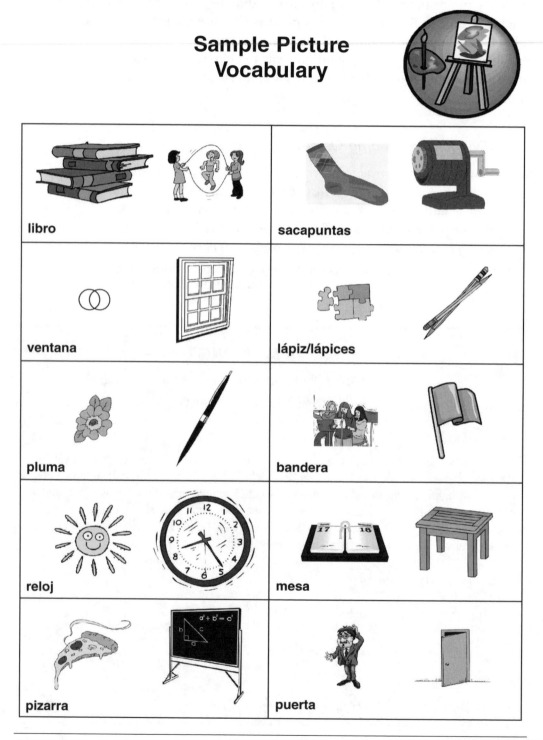

SOURCE: Adapted with permission of Susan Graham.

Individualized reading classes have been around since the 1930s, and they enjoyed a brief resurgence in the 1970s (Blow, 1976). Perhaps the time has come to reinvent the wheel or at least polish it up a bit in the new millennium. The individualized class offers at least four advantages: (a) the time students need to read without other content pressures, (b) opportunities to talk about books with peers and a teacher, (c) accountability for what is read, and (d) choice. In the past, individualized reading classes focused primarily on reading literature, and that is certainly one option. However, an individualized reading program could also be structured as an independent study for credit in which a student and teacher might develop a reading list based on a topic (e.g., genetics, the Civil War), a genre (e.g., science fiction), an author (e.g., Charles Dickens), or a specific individual (e.g., Charles Lindbergh or Hillary Clinton) and meet periodically to talk about what has been read.

The individualized reading class or independent study is not remedial in nature nor does it directly teach cognitive strategies. Its sole purpose is to give students opportunity (and credit) during the school day to read more widely than they would have time for otherwise. The following guidelines are taken from one individualized reading program at Cedar Falls High School in Iowa, directed by Barbara Blow:

- Students can read any books they choose, and nearly all class time is reserved for reading.
- When students register for the course, a note goes home to parents explaining that the choice of books is up to the student and his or her parents. The note invites parent participation and includes testimonials from parents of previous students who have enjoyed recommending books and talking with their children about them.
- When students finish reading each book, they have a ten- to fifteen-minute individual conference in which they discuss the book with the teacher. The teacher may make suggestions for other books that students might enjoy.
- The teacher reads each book (or at least skims it) prior to the discussion. To enable teachers to build up a sufficiently large background of reading so that they can talk knowledgeably about the books, most programs have the same teacher handle several sections over an extended period of time. This contrasts with some unstructured (and usually unsuccessful) programs in which the course is seen more or less as a free-reading study hall with little or no preparation required from the teacher. (Blow, 1976)

Reader's Workshop

When I finish a book, I have in some way finished a chapter in a relationship that I will continue to nurture. There are always two or three more books awaiting that I have already started, and another pile near my bed that have aroused my interest from their former place on a friend's bookshelf, the library, or a bookstore. I carry a book with me everywhere, just in case a train comes by or I'm stuck in a waiting room. I cannot imagine a day of my life without reading.

—Wilhelm (1997, p. 5)

Nancie Atwell (1998) is generally acknowledged to be the founding mother of The Reading Workshop, an approach to literature-based instruction in which adolescent readers generally choose the books they will read.

Here are some of the rules for the workshop as it is structured in Nancie's classes:

1. You must read a book. Magazines, newspapers, and comic books don't have the chunks of text you need to develop fluency, and they won't help you discover who you are as a reader of literature.

2. Don't read a book you don't like. Don't waste time with a book you don't love when there are so many great ones out there waiting for you.

3. If you don't like your book, find another one. Browse, ask me or a friend for a recommendation, or check the "Favorite Books" list or display.

4. It's all right to reread a book you love. This is what readers do.

5. It's okay to skim or skip parts if you get bored or stuck; readers do this, too.

6. Record every book you finish or abandon on the form in your reading folder. Collect data about yourself as a reader, look for patterns, and take satisfaction in your accomplishments over time.

7. Read as well and as much as you can. (Atwell, 1998, pp. 116–117)

Harder isn't always better. Teaching for Learning Tip 5.5 encourages teachers to use easier reading books to build background knowledge before introducing students to the textbook treatment of a topic.

TEACHING FOR LEARNING TIP 5.5

Assign Easier Books to Build Background Knowledge

How to Get Started

Help all students, both struggling readers and gifted students, to let go of the idea that reading easy books is embarrassing. Where do *you* go when you're looking for information about an unfamiliar idea or topic? To a 400-page textbook written by experts or to an easy-reading *World Book* article that summarizes the key concepts? Background knowledge is essential to the comprehension of more difficult text, and reading easy nonfiction books that explain the big ideas and central concepts of a topic is an ideal way to expose all students to the essential background knowledge they need to have before they can understand their textbooks.

The next time you introduce a topic for which all students, even your best and brightest, typically lack background knowledge, work with your librarian or media specialist to assemble a collection of easy-reading books. Make sure you have enough books on various reading levels to meet the needs of all of your students, and plan a cooperative learning activity. "For struggling readers, the suggestion to read an easy book, as a way to gather background information, is not filled with fear of failure or dread that the reading will take a very long time and great effort as might be the case if the assignment were to read a more difficult book" (Pressley, Gaskins, Solic, & Collins, 2005).

A Resource to Help You

You will need the help of your librarian or media specialist to acquire or borrow the books you need for this activity. He or she will have access to a variety of tools to develop bibliographies of easier-to-read books on your specific topics.

Research on the Acquisition and Importance of Background Knowledge

Afflerbach, 1990a, 1990b; Bransford, 1983; Dole, Valencia, Greer, & Wardrop, 1991; Palinscar & Brown, 1984; Pearson, Roehler, Dole, & Duffy, 1992; Pressley, Gaskins, Solic, & Collins, 2005.

In-Class Reading

Carol Jago (2000) has finally come to grips with the reality of the high school schedule and the lives of contemporary teenagers. She wishes she could assign thirty pages for homework and that everyone would read it without fail, but such is not the case. So she allocates 75 minutes of her 275-instructional-minute week to silent reading of the texts under consideration. This is how it works:

For example, when I think that students will find a chapter particularly difficult to get through, I ask them to read a page silently and then we talk about what we have read together. After a few minutes of discussion, we read another two pages. We talk some more. With each break, I extend the length of the passage to be read. This is far from a foolproof system because the very slowest readers have trouble keeping up whatever pace I set, but if I'm sensitive about putting these individuals on the spot to respond to what they haven't yet read, students tell me that the exercise helps them keep going. (pp. 73–74)

The Promotion of Books by Every Teacher

Just as every teacher is a reading teacher, every teacher should also be a book specialist—not a book generalist, as is the school librarian, but a specialist. That is, science teachers should know the books in the school library that pertain to his or her discipline and be ready to recommend them or read them aloud to students as appropriate during the school year. They should also be recommending science titles to the librarian for possible purchase.

Superior Library-Media Services

When I . . . discovered libraries, it was like having Christmas every day.
—J. Fritz (as quoted in Gilbar, 1990, p. 154)

A gifted media specialist who knows students, teachers, and the content of middle and high schools is essential to engaging students in reading. Hire an individual whose first priority is service to students and teachers, whose second priority is putting materials and people together, and whose third priority is making sure that the library is humming every single minute of the day. Look for an individual who is warm, inviting, doesn't mind noise and messes, and can always be interrupted.

REFLECTION AND DISCUSSION QUESTIONS

1. TerraBeth Jochems thought "outside the box" to come up with a way to get students "reading in the zone." What ideas have occurred to you while reading this chapter?

2. Are you a voracious reader? Think about the reasons why or why not, and use that information to motivate your students to "read in the zone."

3. What is the role of reading aloud in the secondary classroom? What other ways can you think of besides the traditional round-robin reading method that often embarrasses struggling readers?

4. List the reasons for reading you might give to students to motivate them to read more.

5. Steve Gardiner (2005) is sold on the concept of SSR. In fact, he wrote a book about his success. How can teachers balance this concept with the importance of having students read at their own instructional level?

Create a Reading Culture in Your School

[A reading culture is] the collective attitudes, beliefs, and behaviors of all of the stakeholders in a school regarding the activities associated with enabling all students to read at the highest level of attainment possible for both their academic and personal gain.

—McEwan (2004, p. 181)

Building a reading culture in secondary schools is not an assignment for the faint of heart, but neither is it an impossible undertaking. This chapter contains practical advice to help you instill and nurture the beliefs and values that support a reading culture while you develop and implement a plan to raise reading achievement in your school. The advice comes from four sources: (a) my own personal experience in raising achievement in a failing school, (b) the lessons I have learned consulting with low- and under-performing schools and districts around the country, (c) wisdom I have gleaned from highly effective principals and teachers who have turned around their low-performing schools (McEwan, 2003), and (d) reviews and descriptions of schools that have histories of producing educational success with students who have failed to learn to read in a regular education setting (Pressley et al., 2004; Pressley et al., 2005). You will hear the story of one such school, Griffin Middle School in Tallahassee, Florida, later in the chapter. Here's what successful practitioners do:

- Pay attention to the basic beliefs and core values held by stakeholders
- Determine what needs to be changed
- Identify the roadblocks to change
- Make sure the principal is an assertive instructional leader
- Hold everyone accountable
- Make a plan
- Don't forget the parents and the kids
- Assess for learning
- Play "the achievement game" with academic press and instructional tenacity

PAY ATTENTION TO THE BASIC BELIEFS AND CORE VALUES OF STAKEHOLDERS

Determine whether you and your team members are operating under the old paradigm, the new paradigm, or somewhere in between. See the discussion in Chapter 2 if you need a refresher regarding the major differences between the old and new paradigms. The big questions are these: How do people feel about the fact that literacy is not yet a high priority in your school? Are the stakeholders eager to get started, recognizing that literacy is the foundation of every discipline in the school? Are they somewhat neutral or even apathetic regarding a literacy initiative? Do they feel that they (and everyone else) are doing just fine and have no need to change? Do they excuse low student achievement by blaming the students and parents? Or are they just plain resentful that anyone would presume to think that raising reading achievement is a job for secondary educators?

Principal Dave Owen and his staff at Kamiakin High School (KHS) in Kennewick, Washington, are living examples of a new paradigm. Their paradigm can be summed up in one word: personalization. Five core personalization beliefs drive everything they do as a team to raise the achievement of academically deficient students, including decisions about instruction, placement, scheduling, teaching assignments, and resource allocation. Following each core belief is an italicized statement of how it impacts daily practice at KHS.

- Every student needs some level of personalization, but the students with academic deficiencies need to be the primary focus of personalization efforts. *Students with academic deficiencies rarely fall through the cracks at Kamiakin. They are front and center.*
- Students with academic deficiencies must remain in classes with students who are progressing normally so that they have good

models of what good students do and the kind of work that good students produce. *Students with academic deficiencies receive personalized instruction, but they are always included in a regular math or reading class where expectations are high. Scaffolding is provided in the form of a reading teacher who also teaches their "elective" reading class and consults frequently with their science or social studies teachers.*

- Students with academic deficiencies need additional time and extra instruction so that they can achieve the same learning targets that other students are achieving. *Students with academic deficiencies may receive two periods of instruction in English and reading and two periods of math instruction, in addition to science and social studies classes. The extra periods of instruction in reading and math are the "electives" for academically deficient students.*

- There must be coordination among the teachers of students with academic deficiencies. *At Kamiakin, students with academic deficiencies are hand scheduled first by the principal. One group of teachers works with one group of students so there is constant communication between them. The coordinating reading teacher never has more than one science or one social studies teacher with whom to coordinate.*

- The best teachers must work with the students with academic deficiencies. *Every teacher, regardless of tenure or specialty, teaches at least one section of students with academic deficiencies. It's part of being a faculty member at Kamiakin.* (D. Bond, personal communication, February 2, 2006).

The first step to raising reading achievement is to find out how people feel about achievement, the students with whom they work, and their ability to make a difference in the academic lives of their students. Once you know where people stand, the assignment then becomes to provide experiences and professional development opportunities that will help to change people's beliefs, values, attitudes, and inappropriate behaviors. Exhibit 6.1 contains a sample set of basic beliefs and core values to guide your discussion, or you could choose to use the KHS core personalization beliefs to frame your discussion. Resource C contains a sample process called Sample Set of Basic Beliefs and Core Vales to help you get started.

DETERMINE WHAT NEEDS TO BE CHANGED

In order to raise reading achievement in your school, the attention of all individuals who work in, attend, or send their children to the school must be focused on literacy. This is the defining quality of a *pervasive* reading

Exhibit 6.1   Sample Set of Basic Beliefs and Core Values

The teaching of strategic reading is the responsibility of every teacher.

We can teach every student in our school how to read.

Every student can learn.

Learners should be treated with respect, even if they are behaving inappropriately.

Teachers make a difference in how, what, when, and why students learn.

Good teaching involves creating as many opportunities as possible for students to achieve mastery.

We must model and then teach strategic reading to our students.

We will support and encourage each other through mentoring, coaching, sharing, and cooperating.

Effective two-way communication is the responsibility of every student, teacher, parent, and administrator.

Important decisions must be made collegially.

Time to teach and learn must be protected.

If students work hard, they will achieve.

We have high expectations for every student.

We have high expectations for ourselves as teachers and administrators.

Every teacher shares the responsibility for the behavior and learning of every student in our school.

We respect, value, and welcome the ideas, input, and concerns of parents.

culture. See the definition at the beginning of this chapter. Newcomers to the school community will immediately be made aware of the commitment of all of the stakeholders to literacy for every student and soon find that they have been enlisted in the cause as well. Pervasive and persuasive reading cultures are characterized by the twelve benchmarks found in Form 6.1. Use this instrument to determine the perceptions of administrators, teachers, and parents regarding the viability of each of these variables (benchmarks) and then decide what needs to be changed and how. Simultaneously, take an inventory or audit the various components of literacy currently in place at your school:

- Reading classes for students currently being taught
- Implementation of reading in the content areas; cognitive strategy instruction
- Data gathering and assessment tools being used
- Availability of reading materials for all students at their independent reading levels

Form 6.1   Reading Culture Benchmarks Scale

	Never	Seldom	Sometimes	Usually	Always
Benchmark 1	1	2	3	4	5

Strong instructional leadership by both administrators and teachers to include shared decision making regarding vital curricular and instructional issues

Benchmark 2	1	2	3	4	5

High expectations and accountability for students, teachers, and parents as evidenced by a sense of academic press that is shared by the entire school community

Benchmark 3	1	2	3	4	5

A relentless commitment to results driven by meaningful and measurable short- and long-term goals

Benchmark 4	1	2	3	4	5

Research-based curricula designed to teach all students to read and to teach all students to read to learn

Benchmark 5	1	2	3	4	5

A well-designed instructional delivery system that offers coordinated and differentiated instructional interventions for a full range of learners

Benchmark 6	1	2	3	4	5

Comprehensive assessment of student progress that includes early identification and frequent monitoring of students at risk of reading failure

Benchmark 7	1	2	3	4	5

The scrupulous use of allocated instructional time (before and after vacations) and the creative marshalling of extracurricular instructional time (e.g., before and after school)

Benchmark 8	1	2	3	4	5

The integration and coordination of special services (e.g., special education, Title I, remedial reading, and speech)

Benchmark 9	1	2	3	4	5

Constant communication and coordination between and among teachers regarding curriculum and instruction

Benchmark 10	1	2	3	4	5

Embedded, ongoing, and meaningful professional development

Benchmark 11	1	2	3	4	5

The support of parents and the community for literacy

Benchmark 12	1	2	3	4	5

The availability and allocation of adequate resources at both the building and district levels

- Remedial interventions available for a range of struggling readers
- Motivational programs
- Parental involvement

Exhibit 6.2 shows the literacy components in place at Millard Central Middle School in Nebraska. You can take stock of the components in place at your school by filling in a similar graphic organizer (Form 6.2) with the literacy components currently in place in your school.

IDENTIFY THE ROADBLOCKS TO CHANGE

How can you determine the facilitating forces currently working in your favor to create or sustain a reading culture in your school while at the same time identifying the restraining forces that must be addressed in order to move forward? Do a force field analysis.

Force field analysis is a problem-solving process developed by Kurt Lewin in the 1940s. Participants identify a problem or define a goal and then describe the driving forces that push toward a solution of the problem or completion of the goal and the restraining forces that work against success. The process helps group members to verbalize both positive and negative feelings about a problem, a proposed solution, or a goal statement.

The identification of positive forces enables group members to harness and strengthen those forces, while the articulation of the negatives illuminates erroneous information and issues that may be hindering the accomplishment of goals. Force field analysis always works best when it involves the group members who are most resistant to change and enlists them in solving a problem or setting a goal (McEwan, 1997, pp. 100–102).

Without student involvement and engagement, the most carefully planned lessons can be exercises in futility. Teaching for Learning Tip 6.1 offers suggestions for planning high-involvement lessons.

Before you, as a principal or teacher leader, do the process with the entire faculty, complete the process by yourself or with a small leadership team. Reflect on your personal feelings about the goal and what you think could hinder or help you and your colleagues to reach it. Make a copy of Form 6.3, Force Field Analysis Worksheet, on which to record your ideas. At the top of the form, write the vision, mission, or specific goal to which your school aspires: (e.g., to become a school in which all students read with confidence and enthusiasm and in which all teachers model strategic reading and teaching). On the left-hand side of the form, write all of the facilitating (positive or driving) forces that contribute to the achievement of the stated goal. If a force appears to be complex, break it down

Exhibit 6.2 Student Literacy Components at Millard Central Middle School (Omaha, Nebraska)

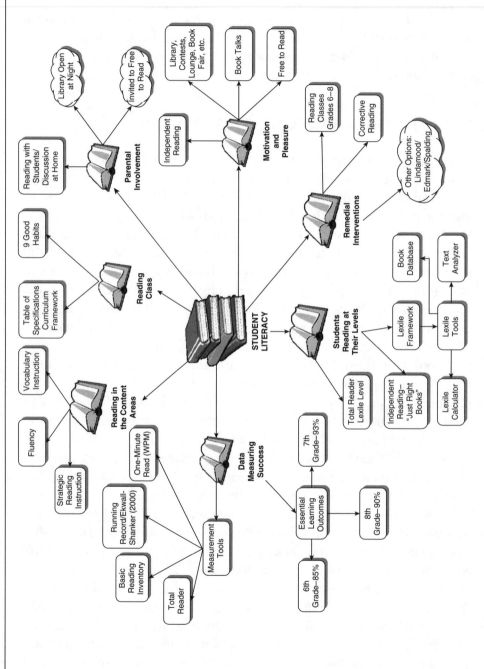

SOURCE: Reprinted by permission of Beth Balkus, assistant principal, Millard Middle School, Omaha, NE.

Form 6.2 Student Literacy Components at My School

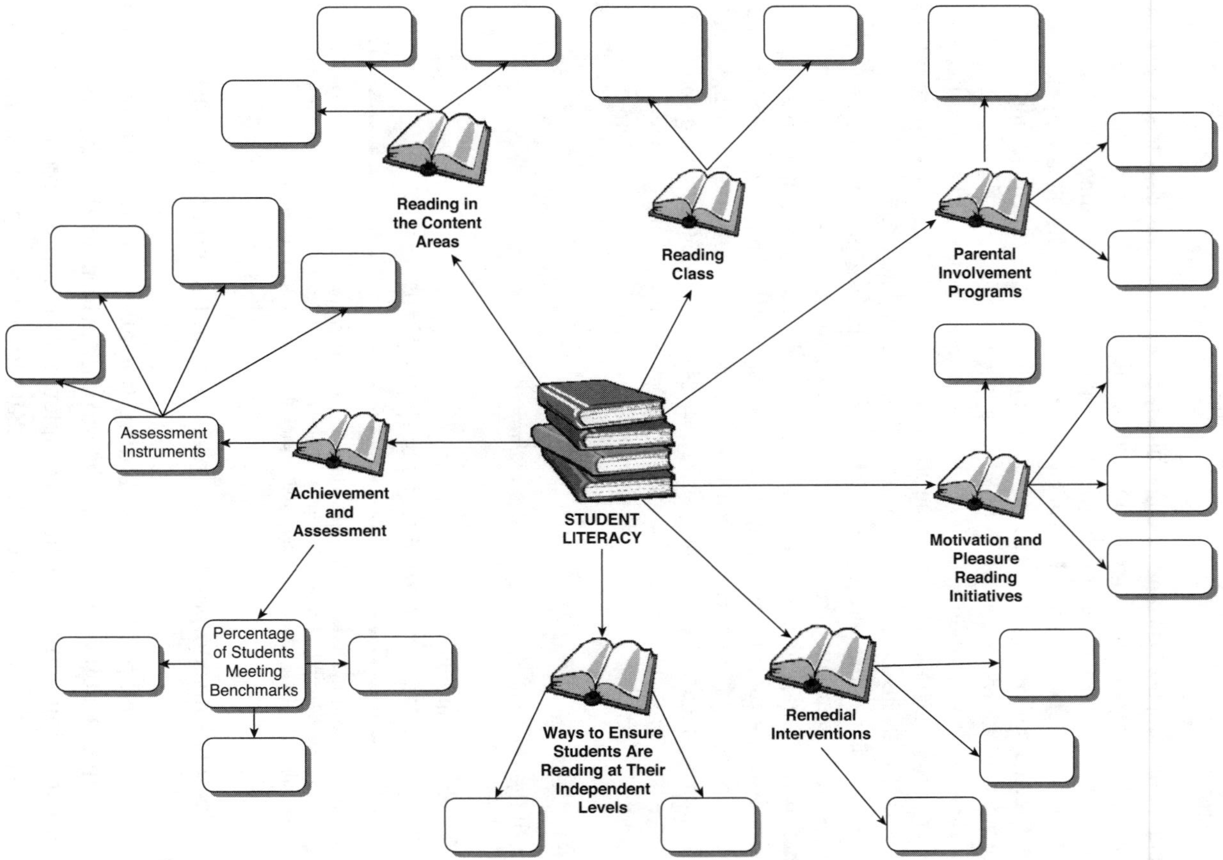

Reading in the Content Areas
Reading Class
Parental Involvement Programs
Assessment Instruments
Achievement and Assessment
STUDENT LITERACY
Motivation and Pleasure Reading Initiatives
Percentage of Students Meeting Benchmarks
Ways to Ensure Students Are Reading at Their Independent Levels
Remedial Interventions

TEACHING FOR LEARNING TIP 6.1

Plan High-Involvement Lessons

How to Get Started

Planning lessons that are well organized and briskly paced is a challenge—especially when you are teaching four periods in a row or teaching more than one course. The suggested resource for this tip contains a variety of ideas for developing academic routines. Here's my version of the Write-Share-Learn plan that I use in my all-day workshops. After I teach participants a brief routine regarding how to return to their seats quietly after we've been talking in small groups, they are ready for what I call a PTA (a Personal Think-Aloud).

Everyone is expected to jot down their thoughts about two or three questions that activate their prior knowledge on a topic. There are no right answers, and papers are not corrected, but I monitor and gently insist that everyone get their thoughts down. Before using the structured think-aloud, I found that many participants were unfocused during discussion, even though they had received a written copy of the questions. However, requiring that they respond in writing has improved participation and motivation 100 percent. After writing, participants pair up and exchange ideas. I then give them a signal, and in less than three seconds, 100 people are back in their seats and ready to move on. I encourage those who finish first to find someone else who is on the same time line. This keeps fast finishers from becoming bored and gives them more time for sharing. Meanwhile, the more thoughtful students feel some pressure to move forward.

A Resource to Help You

Harmin, 1994. *Inspiring Active Learners: A Handbook for Teachers.*

Research on Student Engagement

Dillon, 1988; Gabbert, Johnson, & Johnson, 1986; Gall, 1970.

into its separate components. Do not worry at this point about prioritizing the forces.

Then develop a list of restraining (negative) forces that are holding back student achievement. Again, do not prioritize the results of your brainstorming. Once you have completed a personal force field analysis, engage your faculty, department, or team in the same process. After everyone completes their own copies of Form 6.3, collate the results. Exhibit 6.3 is an example of one faculty's completed force field analysis. It is a compilation of the facilitating and restraining forces identified by the entire group.

Form 6.3   Force Field Analysis Worksheet

Facilitating Forces	Goal/Problem	Restraining Forces

When collating the responses made by group members, pay attention to the number of times a particular restraining force is mentioned. A problem that is singled out by only one staff member is never as crucial as one that is mentioned by the majority. When your group has identified all of the possible facilitating and restraining forces, cross off the restraining forces that cannot be changed (e.g., student demographics). Rank the remaining forces for their solvability and then list some possible action steps that might reduce the effect of a specific force or eliminate it completely. This part of the process could take several meetings.

Force field analysis is a powerful tool to identify where change needs to occur in order to create a reading culture in your school. The status quo is only one powerful impediment to change; there are many others. Knowing what these forces are, as well as how ingrained they may be in your school's current culture, will help you to prioritize and then plan for

Exhibit 6.3 Sample Force Field Analysis

Goal/Problem	
To become a school in which all students read with confidence and enthusiasm and all teachers model strategic reading and teaching.	
Facilitating Forces	**Restraining Forces**
⟶	⟵
Dedicated, caring, hardworking, and knowledgeable faculty	Too many students below grade level when they enroll at our school
Well-organized professional development	Lack of parental support
Core group of high-achieving students and parents	School not high priority for students—extracurricular activities and work interfere
People wanting to improve	Don't know anything about reading instruction—we're content teachers
Supportive administration	Students not reading enough
Resources available in form of grants and budget allocations	Students not liking to read
Good climate and culture in school	Low expectations regarding what we can realistically accomplish with low-achieving students
	Too much on our plates already
	Lack of time
	Scheduling problems

change. Encourage every faculty member to be brutally honest about which of the alterable variables they believe are creating the most serious roadblocks to achievement (e.g., low expectations, lack of a common set of values with regard for grades and homework, lack of consistent routines and rules throughout the school, or inconsistent instruction across a grade level or department).

The most daunting assignment, however, will be changing negative beliefs or values regarding the importance of teaching reading and the ability of teachers to make a difference. Values permeate an organization in subtle and often unseen ways. They drive behavior and govern decision making. What beliefs and behaviors would you like to see exhibited on a daily basis? As a teacher leader or administrator, model them yourself in visible and authentic ways. Think about how the various values might be evident as they are acted on in classrooms, the library, faculty meetings, through grouping practices, curricula, traditions and ceremonies, student council, in how people are affirmed and rewarded for their accomplishments, and even in the hundreds of spontaneous personal contacts that take place daily in a school. Decide what you believe must be changed in your school if it is to become an organization that values, supports, and is successful with regard to reading.

Teaching for Learning Tip 6.2 explores a variety of ways to motivate students to read—reasons for reading. You will no doubt have several of your own to add to the list.

TEACHING FOR LEARNING TIP 6.2
Give Reasons for Reading

How to Get Started

There are dozens of reasons to read. Just ask Robert, the student you met in Chapter 1. He could tell you that because he learned to read, he won a citizenship award, met a wonderful woman who became his wife, can read aloud to his toddler, and got the job of his dreams. If these reasons seem too far removed from the lives of your students, consider these reasons offered by Kelly Gallagher (2003):

- Reading is rewarding.
- Reading builds a mature vocabulary.
- Reading makes you a better writer.
- Reading is hard and "hard" is necessary.
- Reading makes you smarter.
- Reading prepares you for the world of work.
- Reading well is financially rewarding.
- Reading opens the doors to college and beyond.
- Reading arms you against oppression (p. 39).

Build motivational "reading reason" mini-lessons into your content instruction weekly. Once you've used a few of the ideas suggested in this resource, begin to think of reasons to read science (to figure out if global warming is really a big problem), social studies (to find out just what did start the Civil War), mathematics (to master algebra so you can get into the college of your choice), literature (to "live" other lives and go other places through the pages of a book), or computer manuals (to get a better job).

A Resource to Help You

Gallagher, 2003. *Reading Reasons: Motivational Mini-Lessons for Middle and High School.*

Research on Reasons for Reading

Graves, Juel, & Graves, 2004; Guthrie & Wigfield, 2000.

HIRE A STRONG (ASSERTIVE) INSTRUCTIONAL LEADER

> *An instructional leader has a sense of purpose, broad knowledge of the educational process and knows learning theory. He or she is a risk taker, has people skills, and unlimited energy.*
>
> —McEwan (1998, p. 7)

The daily instructional leadership behaviors of principals make a difference in the quality and equity in student learning (Andrews & Soder, 1987; Heck, Larson, & Marcoulides, 1990; Heck, Marcoulides, & Lang, 1991; Sillins, 1994). Principals' abilities to successfully respond to the organizational and environmental contexts in which they work and to communicate powerful visions for their schools directly influences their teachers' expectations for students, students' opportunities to learn, and the level of reading achievement. When teachers perceive their principals as strong instructional leaders, students achieve more.

What Does It Take to Be an Assertive Leader?

Strong leaders are assertive leaders. Assertiveness is a mindset or attitude that impacts the way principals communicate (words) and behave (deeds) in their everyday (habitual) interactions with teachers, students, and parents. It is a positive, forthright approach to leadership that stands in stark contrast to less effective leadership styles characterized by either aggressiveness or hesitancy. Aggressive administrators dictate, dominate, and direct. Hesitant administrators, on the other hand, are unable to make decisions, say "no," and maintain appropriate boundaries between themselves, teachers, parents, and students.

How can principals (or their teachers) determine if they are assertive? Complete the Assertive Administrator Self-Assessment, Form 6.4, for administrators, or the Assertive Administrator Teacher Perception, Form 6.5, for teachers.

Assess the Principal's Instructional Leadership

Assertiveness is not enough, however. Principals who get results use their assertive skills to accomplish goals in seven areas of instructional leadership. They are committed to the daily practice of the seven steps listed on page 135.

Form 6.4   The Assertive Administrator Self-Assessment Form

	Never	*Seldom*	*Sometimes*	*Usually*	*Always*
Indicator 1	1	2	3	4	5

I recognize the importance of boundaries and am able to stay connected to others while at the same time maintaining a sense of self and individuality.

Indicator 2	1	2	3	4	5

I have positive feelings regarding myself and am thus able to create positive feelings in others.

Indicator 3	1	2	3	4	5

I am willing to take risks, recognizing that mistakes and failures are part of the learning process.

Indicator 4	1	2	3	4	5

I am able to acknowledge and learn from my successes as well as my failures.

Indicator 5	1	2	3	4	5

I am able to give and receive both compliments and constructive criticism from others.

Indicator 6	1	2	3	4	5

I make realistic promises and commitments and am able to keep them.

Indicator 7	1	2	3	4	5

I genuinely respect the ideas and feelings of those I work with.

Indicator 8	1	2	3	4	5

I am willing to compromise and negotiate in good faith.

Indicator 9	1	2	3	4	5

I am capable of saying no and sticking to a position, but I do not need to have my own way at all costs.

Indicator 10	1	2	3	4	5

I am capable of dealing forthrightly with those whose behavior and attitudes are interfering with building a positive school culture.

Indicator 11	1	2	3	4	5

I am capable of dealing forthrightly with teachers whose ineffective teaching is holding back individual and schoolwide student achievement.

Indicator 12	1	2	3	4	5

I am capable of advocating for my school with central office administrators and the school board when central office programs and mandates are interfering with individual and schoolwide student achievement.

Form 6.5   The Assertive Administrator Teacher Perception Form

	Never	*Seldom*	*Sometimes*	*Usually*	*Always*
Indicator 1	1	2	3	4	5

The principal recognizes the importance of boundaries and is able to stay connected to others while at the same time maintaining a sense of self and individuality.

Indicator 2	1	2	3	4	5

The principal has positive feelings regarding himself or herself and is thus able to create positive feelings in teachers.

Indicator 3	1	2	3	4	5

The principal is willing to take risks but recognize that mistakes and failures are part of the learning process.

Indicator 4	1	2	3	4	5

The principal is able to acknowledge and learn from his or her successes as well as his or her failures.

Indicator 5	1	2	3	4	5

The principal is able to give and receive both compliments and constructive criticism from others.

Indicator 6	1	2	3	4	5

The principal makes realistic promises and commitments and is able to keep them.

Indicator 7	1	2	3	4	5

The principal genuinely respects the ideas and feelings of teachers and others.

Indicator 8	1	2	3	4	5

The principal is willing to compromise and negotiate in good faith.

Indicator 9	1	2	3	4	5

The principal is capable and willing to say no to teachers and sticking to a position, but he or she does not need to have his or her own way at all costs.

Indicator 10	1	2	3	4	5

The principal is capable of dealing forthrightly with those whose behavior and attitudes are interfering with building or maintaining a positive school culture.

Indicator 11	1	2	3	4	5

The principal is capable of dealing forthrightly with teachers whose ineffective teaching is holding back individual students and schoolwide student achievement.

Indicator 12	1	2	3	4	5

The principal is capable of advocating for our school with central office administrators and the school board when programs and mandates are interfering with individual and schoolwide student achievement.

1. Establish, implement, and achieve academic standards.

2. Be an instructional resource for your staff.

3. Create a school culture and climate conducive to learning.

4. Communicate the vision and mission of your school.

5. Set high expectations for staff and yourself.

6. Develop teacher leaders.

7. Establish and maintain positive attitudes toward students, staff, and parents. (McEwan, 2003, p. 15)

One powerful way in which principals can demonstrate instructional leadership is through their daily presence in the classrooms of their schools. The percentage of classrooms that can reasonably be visited every school day depends on the size of the school. Principals should set goals, however, and try to reach those goals every day. I developed a checklist of my faculty's names and systematically made my way through the list at least every third to fifth day. If the school is engaged in a building-wide initiative to raise reading achievement, principals and teachers should have a checklist or set of goals to keep them focused on specific teacher and student behaviors that give evidence of outstanding reading instruction.

Writing to learn is one of the most powerful ways to raise reading achievement. Teaching for Learning Tip 6.3 explains.

HOLD EVERYONE ACCOUNTABLE

A group of people is not a team. A team is a group of people with a high degree of interdependence geared toward the achievement of a goal or completion of a task. In other words, they agree on a goal and agree that the only way to achieve the goal is to work together.

—Parker (1990, p.16)

Lest you feel overwhelmed by the responsibility of single-handedly raising reading achievement in your school, be assured that you don't have to do it alone. My training for the principalship included some passing references to participatory management and group decision making, but my job description led me to believe that I was personally responsible for doing it all. Fortunately, I was rescued from that mind-set when the concept of building leadership teams was introduced to our district.

TEACHING FOR LEARNING TIP 6.3

Write to Learn

How to Get Started

Expect all students to write in response to reading every day for a C grade. Expect students who want an A or B to write a longer "research" paper. I'll never forget the research paper I wrote for Mr. Norgrove's American History class when I was in high school. I spent hours in the library perusing dusty newspapers reading about President Warren G. Harding's scandalous administration. There is nothing like writing to improve learning. That project was my first "real" writing experience, and it changed my life. If you don't provide challenges like this to your students, they may never know the excitement and satisfaction that comes from writing to learn. Although writing to learn may not change your students' lives like it did mine, you'll never know unless you incorporate it in your content class.

You may think that giving reading assignments to students is enough to create learning, and that may well be the case for some students. But lasting and deep learning only comes when students have to process the text they read by producing a piece of writing (two sentences to twenty pages) that answers questions, infers, and summarizes.

Expand your students' horizons and expect them to write to learn. Begin with just writing a few sentences every day in response to content text they have read. See Exhibit 6.4. Many students think only of writing as something they do in a journal or a short answer response they provide on a test. Of course students can't write a major paper in every discipline every year in high school, but perhaps departments could rotate the responsibility. During a four-year cycle, students would write one research report for English, social sciences, science, and math or foreign language.

If this idea sounds too daunting, incorporate at least one shorter writing-to-learn assignment into each grading quarter. See Exhibit 2.1 for a rubric to score writing in science. Exhibits 6.4 through 6.6 contain forms and rubrics for writing in the disciplines of math and social studies.

A Resource to Help You

Benjamin, 2003. *Writing in the Content Areas.*

Research on the Benefits of Regular Writing

Reeves, 2004; Shanahan, 2004.

After the training period, our team met one full afternoon per month charting a course for school improvement and tackling the substantive issues related to teaching and learning. My staff members were definitely more committed to implementation when they were involved from the beginning in making important decisions about how to reach our goals. Shared decision making has been shown to increase job satisfaction (Ashton & Webb, 1986, pp. 95–97), create ownership leading to a more

Exhibit 6.4 Rubric for Social Studies Writing

Scorepoint 5

A—Excellent.

In this type of response, the student . . .

- Gives a clear answer to the question
- Clearly and accurately explains or analyzes the answer
- Supports the explanation or analysis with evidence from the text that is clearly connected to the answer
- Shows a deep understanding of the event or topic throughout the answer and gives a thoughtful response when providing his or her "insight" (which answers "so what?") that is well-written, focused, and cohesive.

Scorepoint 4

B—Good.

In this type of response, the student . . .

- Gives a clear answer to the question
- Clearly and accurately explains/analyzes the answer
- Supports the explanation/analysis with evidence from the text that is clearly connected to the answer
- Shows a definite understanding of the event/topic when providing his/her "insight."

Scorepoint 3

C—Good Enough.

In this type of response, the student . . .

- Answers the question
- Provides an explanation/analysis
- Supports answer with evidence from the text that relates to the answer, but may not be specific
- Shows a basic understanding of the event/topic when providing his/her "insight."

Scorepoint 2

D—Almost.

In this type of response, the student . . .

- Answers the question
- Provides vague explanation/analysis
- Supports with evidence that is too general, or vague, or doesn't clearly connect to the answer
- Shows little understanding of the event/topic; merely summarizes what he/she has already written; or simply restates his/her answer.

Scorepoint 1

F—Not Quite.

In this type of response, the student . . .

- Answers the question in a vague or general way that shows a lack of understanding
- Provides explanation/analysis that is too general or vague
- Supports with evidence that is too general or vague and doesn't relate to the event/topic
- Shows no evidence of understanding.

(Continued)

Exhibit 6.4 (Continued)

Scorepoint 0
F—Nope.
In this type of response, the student . . .
• Offers little attempt to answer the question, or no response at all.

Grading Scale and Point Conversions for Written Responses

Scorepoint	10-Point Scale	15-Point Scale	20-Point Scale	25-Point Scale	33-Point Scale	50-Point Scale	100-Point Scale	Letter Grade
5	9–10	14–15	18–20	23–25	30–33	45–50	90–100	A
4	7–8	12–13	16–17	20–22	27–29	40–44	80–89	B
3	7	11	15	19	25–26	37–39	75–79	C
2	6	10	14	18	23–24	35–36	70–74	D
1	5	7–9	10–13	12–17	17–22	25–34	50–69	F
0	< 5	< 7	< 10	< 12	< 17	< 25	< 50	0

SOURCE: Reprinted by permission of Andy McBurney, Social Studies Specialist, and Allyson Burnett, Interventionist, Alief Hastings High School, Alief ISD, Houston, TX.

positive attitude toward the organization (Beers, 1984), and engender a more professional environment within the school (Apelman, 1986). After your team is formed, get training to help the group become cohesive and productive. You cannot expect a team to develop a collaborative working relationship instantaneously. If necessary, use a consultant or other resources to help your team develop the skills and trust it needs to be successful.

MAKE A PLAN

> *Problems are our friends because only through immersing ourselves in problems can we come up with creative solutions. Problems are the route to deeper change and deeper satisfaction. In this sense, effective organizations embrace problems rather than avoid them.*
>
> —Fullan and Miles (1992, p. 750)

As you work with your reading task force or school improvement team to plan for change, consider the process from several perspectives. First,

Exhibit 6.5   How to Write a Paragraph

GETTING STARTED

Each paragraph expresses one main thought or idea and discusses it.

Each paragraph should begin with your **answer to the question** that expresses your main point.

At the end of your **answer**, ask "why?" Your **explanation** will answer the question "why."

Remember—write in complete sentences!

ANSWER TO THE QUESTION

This is your main point—you don't need to offer any words of justification for it—just state it.

Example:
- British Prime Minister Neville Chamberlain made the wrong decision at the Munich Conference.

EXPLANATION(S)

Each explanation provides justification for your answer. It is with these sentences that you begin to answer the question, **"why?"**

Example (continued):
- The naïve decision to let Hitler annex the Sudetenland encouraged Hitler to take over more countries.

EVIDENCE/PROOF

For each explanation, you must offer evidence or proof in order to be convincing. It is with these sentences that you answer the question, **"how do you know?"**

Example (continued):
- In March of 1939, after making President Hacha of Czechoslovakia feel "threatened and bullied," Hitler had his troops seize what was left of Hacha's country.

INSIGHT

This is your opportunity to tell the reader what he/she should learn from what you have written. Your insight will answer the question, **"so what?"**

Example (continued):
- Chamberlain, blinded by his desire for "peace with honor," should have known that giving in to a power-hungry dictator would just encourage more aggression.

SAMPLE PARAGRAPH STRUCTURE

- ❖ Answer to the Question
- ❖ Explanation
- ❖ Evidence/Proof
- ❖ Insight

REMEMBER TO:

Write in Complete Sentences!

Check Your Spelling!

Use Third Person!

Write Legibly and Neatly!

SOURCE: Reprinted by permission of Andy McBurney, Social Studies Specialist, and Allyson Burnett, Interventionist, Alief Hastings High School, Alief ISD, Houston, TX.

Exhibit 6.6   Paragraph Writing Worksheet

Assignment

- Each paragraph expresses one main thought or idea and discusses it.
- Each paragraph should begin with your **answer to the question** that expresses your main point.
- At the end of your **answer**, ask "why?" Your **explanation** will answer the question "why."
- Remember—write in complete sentences!

Answer to the Question

This is your main point—you don't need to offer any words of justification for it—just state it.

_____
_____
_____

Explanation(s) and Evidence/Proof

Each explanation provides justification for your answer. It is with these sentences that you begin to answer the question, **"why?"**

For each explanation, you must offer evidence or proof in order to be convincing. It is with these sentences that you answer the question, **"how do you know?"**

Explanation _____
_____
_____
_____
_____
_____

Evidence/Proof _____
_____
_____
_____
_____
_____
_____
_____

Insight

This is your opportunity to tell the reader what he/she should learn from what you have written. Your insight will answer the question, **"so what?"**

_____
_____
_____

SOURCE: Reprinted by permission of Andy McBurney, Social Studies Specialist, and Allyson Burnett, Interventionist, Alief Hastings High School, Alief ISD, Houston, TX.

provide plenty of research and resource materials, speakers, and site visits so that team members can make decisions from a sound knowledge base. Don't reinvent the wheel, but don't rush out to duplicate what someone else has done, either. Consider your student body, faculty, and parent community before you make change. For example, if you decide that new textbooks or a new program need to be chosen, leave no stone unturned in gathering resource materials and research studies. Do not rush to judgment.

In addition to content vocabulary, students also need to know the meanings of academic words used to give directions and explanations. Teaching for Learning Tip 6.4 gives examples and suggestions.

Planning for change involves setting goals. Goals that are too numerous or too vague will frustrate teachers. A good goal statement must include the following five elements:

- *The Baseline:* Where your students are currently performing (e.g., 80 percent of students are reading below grade level as measured by the Stanford 9 Achievement Test)
- *The Goal:* What you want to have happen (e.g., increase by 25 percent the number of students who are reading at or above grade level)
- *The Outcome Indicator:* The measure that will be used to demonstrate success (e.g., the Benchmark tests given annually in Grades 6–12)
- *The Standard or Performance Level:* The level of success that shows substantial progress (e.g., grade-level reading achievement will be defined as a rating of Proficient on the state assessment that is annually given in seventh grade)
- *The Time Frame:* The time line for accomplishing the goals, indicating how much progress you hope to achieve after one year, two years, and three years (e.g., 10 percent increase in number of students in Year 1, 10 percent increase in Year 2, and 10 percent increase by Year 3; Policy Studies Associates, 1998, p. 54).

There are many excellent and inexpensive resources to guide your schoolwide improvement efforts (Educational Testing Service, 1996; RMC Research Corporation, 1995; WestEd, 1997). Which one you use is less important than that you choose a specific framework and stick to it.

DON'T FORGET THE PARENTS AND KIDS

When a process makes people feel that they have a voice in matters that affect them, they will have a greater commitment to the overall enterprise and will take greater responsibility for what happens to the enterprise. The absence of such a process insures that no one feels

TEACHING FOR LEARNING TIP 6.4

Teach Academic Vocabulary

How to Get Started

Teachers often assume that students fully comprehend the subtleties of academic vocabulary. But do they know precisely what to do when given a direction or asked a question containing academic vocabulary? Not only do students need a working knowledge of the essential concepts in your discipline, they also need a solid understanding of what terms like *evaluate, discuss, explain, analyze, classify, compare, contrast, assess, outline, summarize, infer, predict, support, trace, interpret,* and *illustrate* mean as well as the responses that these terms require from them. For example, consider the term *important.* Students hear the word hundreds of times in a given day at school. But do they know its precise meaning, and furthermore, do they know how to respond when they hear you say, "This is important?" Exactly what do you mean and what student response do you expect? One teacher says, "I expect, when I say 'It's important,' that my students will highlight it in their notes, underline it in their text (if appropriate), put a Post-it note in the margin, write it down in a notebook or journal where 'important' ideas are stored for further reference, and make sure to study it before the test." Only you can define what the term means in your classroom, but unless you explicitly teach it to your students, they will never give your statement a second thought.

Or consider how your students respond to directions on a test that direct them to *Trace the events leading up to the Civil War.* They may have a sound understanding of the Civil War but be unaware of the precise academic meaning of the term *trace,* thinking of another meaning (and there are at least a dozen in the dictionary). Or when they are asked to *illustrate* how poverty affects the lives of students, they may fall back on the meaning they learned in kindergarten and draw a picture.

The same caveats about teaching vocabulary that were suggested in Learning Tip 5.3, Teach Big Words Daily, apply in the teaching of academic terms. Give student-friendly definitions, and when you give directions or assignments that contain the terms, always model and give specific examples and nonexamples to help students make the term their own.

Resources to Help You

Coxhead, 2005. *The Academic Word List.*
Marzano, 2004. *Building Background Knowledge for Academic Achievement: Research on What Works in Schools.*
Marzano & Pickering, 2005. *Building Academic Vocabulary: Teacher's Manual.*

Research on Academic Background Knowledge

Marzano, 2004.

responsible, that blame will always be directed externally, that adversarialism will be a notable feature of school life.

—Sarason (1990, p. 61)

Parental involvement and support are crucial to raising reading achievement in your school. One way in which we garnered parental support and involvement was through publishing an *I Can Learn* booklet that set forth the outcomes in reading, writing, and mathematics for all grade levels so parents knew what we expected their children to learn. We also included a set of teacher expectations (e.g., "the teacher is expected to provide quality instruction for all students, hold students accountable for following school rules and completing assignments, and evaluating and communicating student progress to parents and students") as well as expectations for parents and students. This document sent the message to parents that we were serious about learning and that we all (teachers, parents, and students) had to be accountable if we were to reach our goals. I believe that when parents observe the following evidence in your school, they will back you 100 percent:

- Evidence of students' (both their own and others) learning that is validated through both formative testing made available to individual parents and published summative evaluations made available to the community
- Evidence of teaching effectiveness as observed by parents when they are participating in the life of the school as volunteers or visitors (e.g., frequent planned events that bring parents into classrooms to observe)
- Evidence of educators' desires to make parents a part of the learning team through advisory groups, inclusion on the building leadership team, and through periodic surveys requesting parental input

There are five important things that parents can do to assist in your achievement initiative:

- Read at home and talk with their children about what they are reading at school; have a wide variety of books, newspapers, and magazines in the home
- Visit their children's teachers to find out how their children are learning and how they can help; this requires that teachers have an open-door policy and are able to explain what they are doing in lay language—educational jargon is not an acceptable means of communication

- Insist that their children learn how to read and read regularly with and to them at home
- Help their children understand the importance of planning for college by visiting campuses, familiarizing them with college requirements, and exploring financial aid options available to students
- Show the importance of reading for every career choice by talking with their children about the use of reading in their work or the work of adults they know

When parents are unable for whatever the reasons to do some or all of these things, offer assistance through the guidance or counseling offices. Raising expectations for students and giving them opportunities to expand their horizons is a critical responsibility of every teacher, in cooperation with the guidance counselors.

ASSESS FOR LEARNING

We strongly recommend that school districts [and schools] clearly define their understanding of the desired end result early in the change process.

> —Harrison, Killion, and Mitchell (1989, p. 56)

If you want to lead your school toward excellence in reading achievement, every teacher and administrator must be evaluation minded (Nevo, 1991). The following components must be evaluated regularly: the instructional leadership effectiveness of all administrators, the teaching effectiveness of the staff, the reading proficiency of your students, and the overall effectiveness of programs. Evaluation in each of these areas must be both summative and formative (Scriven, 1967). Summative evaluation offers a final determination of the worth of a program or an individual's performance in a role. It is not designed to be constructive; rather it is designed to be ultimately judgmental and primarily used by those stakeholders who will make some decision about a program's worth. Formative evaluation, on the other hand, is conceptualized as constructive. In both roles, evaluation serves to inform decision making (Goldring & Rallis, 1993, pp. 96–97.)

How will you and your team determine your student body's level of literacy? That decision should be made before you launch into your reading improvement plan. If you're going to use a different measure of student achievement than you have presently been using, administer a pretest to all of the students to gather baseline data. If testing is to be meaningful and helpful to classroom teachers, it must track the performance and progress of each individual student in your school over a several-year period. The tests should be standardized and administered yearly to every student.

As noted in Chapter 1, many states are excluding larger numbers of students each year, and not surprisingly, achievement scores rise. This is not the kind of improvement to which you should aspire. Although my state and district offered testing exemptions to these populations, as a principal, I wanted to know how effective our efforts were at helping diverse learners join the mainstream. To know that an individual student has made substantial gains in achievement, even if he or she is still below grade level, is far more instructive than knowing that the composite reading score of a particular grade level or of the school as a whole is reasonably high.

We examined the longitudinal test data of each of our students to determine their progress over time. We tracked the type of teachers with whom they experienced the most success. We expected our target students (those who were well below grade level) to overcome huge deficits in performance through our interventions, and seeing those results in black and white was highly motivating to teachers. Gains in reading achievement are made one student at a time. We also disaggregated our data to determine how well we were serving the students in various subpopulations.

Overall improvement in reading achievement that is based only on the achievement of students in the top quartile means that you are achieving quality without equity, a condition that discriminates against students in the bottom quartile. At the same time that you are planning how to summatively evaluate the results of your implementation, don't overlook the importance of formative evaluation, the ongoing monitoring of a program that will help you determine if any students or teachers are falling through the cracks. The purpose of formative testing is to provide information to the learner and to the teacher about what the learner knows.

Assessment is essential to improvement. Without continuous monitoring of progress, you will be unable to answer questions about specific individuals or groups of students. It is the action around assessment—the discussions, meetings, revisions, arguments, and opportunities to continually create new directions for teaching, learning, curriculum, and assessment—that ultimately have consequence. The "things" of assessment are essentially useful as dynamic supports for reflection and action, rather than as static products with value in and of themselves (Darling-Hammond, Ancess, & Falk, 1995, p. 18).

PRESS ACADEMICALLY AND BE
INSTRUCTIONALLY TENACIOUS

In the first edition, I was far more relaxed about the time lines for implementing your reading plan. I've changed my thinking about that. Knowing what I know now about the numbers of students who are struggling in their secondary content classes and doing poorly on reading tests, I believe there is no time to waste. We need the kind of assertive instructional leadership and instructional tenacity demonstrated by Michelle Jones-Gayle and her teachers in the case study found at the end of the chapter. The longer you delay, the more students you will lose.

Do take time for goal setting, planning, training, implementation, fine tuning, and evaluation. However, if you take too long, your stakeholders will realize that the goal was only about developing a plan—not raising reading achievement. Do listen to teachers who may have reasonable and helpful questions or concerns. But if you spend too much time handholding the naysayers and the "yes-butters," more students will drop out. Teachers do go through a variety of stages on their way to successfully implementing a new program, but keep them moving through the stages with high expectations for change and improvement.

GETTING THE JOB DONE AT
GRIFFIN MIDDLE SCHOOL

It is no simple matter to reform teaching, learning, and the supporting conditions that fuel and refuel the moral purpose of teaching.

—Fullan (1994, p. 79)

What does it take to create a reading culture? There is an abundance of literature describing and summarizing the qualities, characteristics, attributes, and conditions to be found in schools where students at risk of failure have experienced success (Bryk & Schneider, 2002; Pressley et al., 2004; Pressley et al., 2005; Raphael, Pressley, & Mohan, 2004; Teddlie & Reynolds, 2000; Teddlie & Stringfield, 1993). However, for school leaders who are just beginning to explore the idea of raising reading achievement, an example is far more instructive than a checklist of characteristics. As you read about Griffin Middle School in Tallahassee, Florida, remember the twelve benchmarks of a reading culture. They will be noted parenthetically as they relate to what is going on in our case study. Principal Dr. Michelle Jones-Gayle and her energetic and talented faculty show us how they built a reading culture starting from the ground up.

Nearly half of Griffin Middle School's 725 students are eligible for free and reduced lunch. But when she was hired, Michelle was absolutely certain that demographics would not determine the destiny of her students. The year before Michelle came aboard as principal (2000–2001), Griffin had received a grade of C on the Florida State Grading System. Michelle has never been satisfied with mediocrity and let her faculty know in no uncertain terms that a group of teachers as smart and talented as they obviously were could be getting an A. Michelle's defining attribute is *dissatisfaction.* "She always wants more," her teachers say. Michelle puts it this way, "I know we can achieve more. If you become satisfied, you slip backwards."

She didn't sit around waiting for things to happen. She immediately began sitting down with teachers and looking over their lesson plans and samples of their students' work. She discovered that expectations were low, many assignments were meaningless, and standards and benchmarks were virtually ignored. She communicated her expectations to teachers: Focus on what's important, and throw the rest "out to the curb." **(Benchmarks 1, 2, and 3: Strong instructional leadership coupled with high expectations, accountability, and a relentless commitment to results)**

Their joint efforts paid off, and Griffin received an A for their achievements during Year 1 of Michelle's tenure. In some schools, once spring testing is over, teachers and students breathe a collective sigh and take the rest of the year off. Not at Griffin. "I had a clear idea of where we needed to sharpen our focus for Year 2," Michelle explains. "We sat down and looked at the needs of various groups of students and talked about building a rigorous program for all students that all teachers could support." **(Benchmark 6: Comprehensive assessment of student progress that includes early identification and frequent monitoring of at-risk students)**

Michelle wasn't really satisfied with the A rating that Griffin received. It wasn't a solid A, and she knew that with the rising standards and increased achievement around the state, more work would be needed to maintain their standing. She signed up Griffin for the Florida Reading Initiative—sixty hours of training to build the knowledge base of teachers about reading instruction and to provide strategies they could adapt to their content instruction. Although teachers were paid a small stipend, it did not begin to cover their time commitment. But they wisely realized the need for a shared knowledge base and common language. **(Benchmark 9: Constant communication and coordination between and among teachers regarding curriculum and instruction)** Michelle explained, "Secondary schools really miss the boat when they try to give teachers training that doesn't pay respect to their disciplines. This training zeroed in on exactly what we needed" (Jones-Gayle, 2006). **(Benchmark 10: Embedded, ongoing, and meaningful professional development)**

At the end of Year 2, Griffin received a solid A—twenty-four points above their first-year A grade. There was cause for celebration, but the good feelings didn't last long. During that summer, Michelle and Griffin Middle School experienced a setback. A medical emergency during the summer break put Michelle in the hospital with a serious eye condition that necessitated half a dozen surgeries over the course of the year. Her assistants kept the school running, but Michelle's instructional relentlessness and academic press were sorely missed. When the Year 3 grade was published in the newspaper, it was a solid C. Michelle was devastated. She said, "I didn't want my teachers to be discouraged. I knew they had worked so hard. I felt as though I had let my community down. I permitted myself to feel the public humiliation that Griffin had gone from an A to C for just one day. Then I picked myself up and determined to build our momentum back up again." Notice the servant leadership attitude of Michelle. Even though she pushes and presses and is relentless, when the news was bad, she assumed the blame. When the news is good, her faculty and students receive the credit. **(Benchmark 1: Strong instructional leadership)** Michelle realized it was time for what Michael Fullan (2001) called "refueling." Here's how she did it.

"I chose a theme for Year 3: *C-ing our way back to an A.* I thought of a list of C words to help us focus: collaboration, communication, etc. I did shirts. I did bags. If I could have paid for skywriting, I would have. We continued with the Florida Reading Initiative and began holding strategic learning camps in reading for students. We held Saturday and afterschool academies to provide remediation in specific areas where students were deficient. **(Benchmark 7: The scrupulous use of allocated instructional time and the creative marshalling of extracurricular instructional time)** I surveyed students before the academies to find out their attitudes about effort and grades, and we involved parents in our efforts to raise expectations for their children." **(Benchmark 11: The support of parents and community for literacy)**

"At the end of Year 3, our grade went up to a B—just 7 points from an A. The standards were going up around the state. We celebrated that achievement and then began to systematically look at every aspect of our school improvement plan. What allowed us to be successful? What was a total waste of time? We became action researchers, all the while remaining focused on student achievement. **(Benchmark 1: Shared decision making regarding vital curricular and instructional issues)** The teachers became more skilled at using data to determine student needs, and they became far more open to differentiated instruction. They knew better than to tell me, "We can't do this." **(Benchmark 5: A well-designed instructional delivery system offering coordinated and differentiated instructional interventions for a full range of learners)**

In Year 4, the mantra at Griffin became "Aiming for Excellence," and the graphic representation was a target. The bull's eye for Michelle was professional development. She described what was happening: "Conversations in the faculty lounge evolved from 'That kid is driving me crazy,' to 'It's driving me crazy that I can't come up with a strategy that will work with this group of kids.' Our professional conversations have focused on higher-order thinking. **(Benchmark 3: A relentless commitment to results driven by meaningful and measurable short- and long-term goals)** We've developed a pre-AP program for a group of students identified before they enter Griffin" **(Benchmark 5: Differentiated instructional interventions)**

As you have seen, Michelle is always pushing the limits, but her teachers have definitely learned to appreciate her relentless push for academic excellence at Griffin. She says, "Sometimes I've thought, 'I push 'em too hard. I ask too many questions.'" Given Michelle's continually growing expectations for what teachers and students can do, you might expect her teachers to have a degree of dissatisfaction themselves. They, however, are thrilled with their success and empowered with a renewed sense of efficacy. They nominated Michelle for the district's outstanding administrator award sponsored by the teachers' union. Michelle said, "I didn't care whether I won the district award (which she did), but to have that kind of trust and respect from my faculty will keep me happy for the next ten years." Notice that Michelle said "happy," not "satisfied!"

REFLECTION AND DISCUSSION QUESTIONS

1. What are the biggest challenges to creating embedded, ongoing, and meaningful professional development? What can you do to overcome those challenges?

2. What are some of the ways that principals can be instructionally relentless and still be humane and caring individuals?

3. In the light of Michelle's experience with achievement dropping when she was temporarily sidelined, how can principals build internal capacity to keep the momentum going without their physical presence?

4. Brainstorm the ways that secondary principals can engage students and parents in literacy initiatives.

5. What are some ways that the needs of both gifted *and* at-risk students can be met (in addition to those used by Michelle and her faculty at Griffin)?

Resource A

Assessment Tools

RESOURCE A.1

Prereading Assessment Form

Question 1   True   False

At least 20 percent of students in any given grade-level cohort have reading disabilities or other special needs that make it impossible for them to learn to read, no matter what methodology is used.

Question 2   True   False

The lack of phonemic awareness is a strong predictor of reading failure.

Question 3   True   False

Guessing based on context is a helpful strategy for identifying unknown words.

Question 4   True   False

Phonics is only helpful when teaching decoding to students in kindergarten and first grade.

Question 5   True   False

Overall reading achievement in the United States is excellent considering the number of students with special needs, limited English proficiency, and other at-risk characteristics.

Question 6   True   False

Comprehension cannot really be "taught" to students, especially those who have experienced reading failure in elementary school.

Question 7   True   False

Reading fluency is generally an accurate predictor of a student's ability to comprehend text.

Question 8   True   False

Struggling secondary school readers require at least three periods per day of intensive reading-spelling-writing instruction to make progress in their reading achievement.

Question 9   True   False

The most important things secondary teachers can do for struggling readers in their classrooms is to avoid embarrassing them.

Question 10   True   False

Content teachers should not be expected to teach struggling readers "how to read."

Question 11   True   False

The best teachers to teach students how to access and comprehend content text are the teachers who teach that content.

Question 12   True   False

The biggest roadblock to raising reading achievement in middle and high schools is student apathy.

Question 13   True   False

Motivational reading programs like Sustained Silent Reading, Accelerated Reader, and Reading Counts are very effective for raising student achievement.

Question 14   True   False

Without strong instructional leadership, raising reading achievement in secondary schools is unlikely.

RESOURCE A.2

Prereading Assessment Key

Question 1   True

At least 20 percent of students in any given grade level cohort have reading disabilities or other special needs that make it impossible for them to learn to read, no matter what methodology is used.

With early interventions that provide adequate time, research-based methodologies, and effective instruction, reading failure can be reduced to between 4–6 percent.

Question 2   True

The lack of phonemic awareness is a strong predictor of reading failure.

This statement is true of students in kindergarten as well as adults.

Question 3   False

Guessing based on context is a helpful strategy for identifying unknown words.

*Although this "strategy" has been popularized by the whole-language methodology, it does not work at all for older readers who do not have pictures and predictable text on which to rely. Guessing the **meaning** of words based on context is an excellent strategy. Guessing at the pronunciation of a word to identify it while reading is very time-consuming and gives students only a 1 in 4 chance of being the correct.*

Question 4   False

Phonics is only helpful when teaching decoding to students in kindergarten and first grade.

There is a substantial body of experimental research showing that phonics instruction is beneficial for anyone of any age who has not mastered the forty-four sound-spelling correspondences. Some struggling adolescent readers also need phonemic awareness, fluency, and cognitive strategy instruction to overcome their deficits.

Question 5   False

Overall reading achievement in the United States is excellent considering the number of students with special needs, limited English proficiency, and other at-risk characteristics.

Reading achievement in the United States is low among other student populations as well. Furthermore, students with special needs, limited English proficiency, and other at-risk characteristics can learn to read with research-based methods and early interventions.

Question 6   False

Comprehension cannot really be "taught" to students, especially those who have experienced reading failure in elementary school.

Cognitive science has produced a large body of research demonstrating that when students are directly taught cognitive strategies by skilled teachers, their comprehension improves.

Question 7   True

Reading fluency is generally an accurate predictor of a student's ability to comprehend text.

Fluency, the ability to read text automatically and accurately, thus freeing the working memory to focus on the meaning of text, is a strong predictor of comprehension, if the reader has the vocabulary and background knowledge to comprehend the decoded text.

Question 8   True

Struggling secondary school readers require at least three periods per day of intensive reading-spelling-writing instruction to make progress in their reading achievement.

Catching up below-grade-level adolescent readers is a very labor-intensive undertaking. Typically, middle and high school students do not even make one year of reading progress during one year, and struggling readers may take even longer.

Question 9   False

The most important things secondary teachers can do for struggling readers in their classrooms is to avoid embarrassing them.

The most important thing secondary teachers can do for struggling readers in their classrooms is to scaffold instruction to make the concepts and text of the discipline as accessible as possible.

Question 10   True

Content teachers should not be expected to teach struggling readers "how to read."

*Content teachers do not have the training and background to teach students **how to read**. That assignment calls for a skilled reading teacher who understands the components of reading instruction like phonemic awareness, phonics, and fluency. Content teachers must, however, teach their students how to read to learn in the text of their discipline.*

Question 11   True

The best teachers to teach students how to access and comprehend content text are the teachers who teach that content.

There is no one better suited to teach students how to read chemistry, physics, and biology than science teachers. The same principle is true for social studies, literature, art, music, and technology teachers.

Question 12   False

The biggest roadblock to raising reading achievement in middle and high schools is student apathy.

While motivating adolescents to read is a challenging task, the biggest roadblock is the belief that it can't be done.

Question 13   False

Motivational reading programs like Sustained Silent Reading, Accelerated Reader, and Reading Counts are very effective for raising student achievement.

There is no solid research base showing that these programs are more effective for raising reading achievement than any other program taught by an effective teacher. There is solid correlational research regarding the benefits of reading a lot, but much is unknown about how the variables interact.

Question 14   True

Without strong instructional leadership, raising reading achievement in secondary schools is unlikely.

In order to bring about and sustain meaningful change, a strong instructional leader who is committed to literacy is essential. Teachers need instructional support, resources, and someone to protect their teaching time and energies if they are to be successful.

RESOURCE A.3

Postreading Assessment Form

Question 1   True   False

With appropriate instructional interventions, no more than 5 percent of students will have crippling reading deficits.

Question 2   True   False

Phonemic awareness, the ability to hear and manipulate sounds, can only be acquired in two ways: genetically or through language-rich early literacy experiences.

Question 3   True   False

All readers have comprehension difficulties when they encounter text for which they lack background and vocabulary knowledge.

Question 4   True   False

The most effective way to accurately and automatically identify words is to memorize them.

Question 5   True   False

It doesn't matter what students are reading during SSR as long as they are reading.

Question 6   True   False

One of the most effective ways to teach comprehension to students is through modeling one's own cognitive processing of text.

Question 7   True   False

Gifted students almost never have comprehension difficulties.

Question 8   True   False

Research shows that comprehension will be improved if content teachers teach cognitive strategies in their classes.

Question 9   True   False

Covering the content is an effective method for raising achievement in secondary schools.

Question 10   True   False

All teachers need to teach all students how to read to learn.

Question 11   True   False

Building a reading culture is the principal's job. Teachers should tend to teaching.

Question 12   True   False

The biggest roadblock to raising reading achievement in middle and high schools is lack of money in the budget.

Question 13   True   False

Raising student expectations is an effective way to raise student achievement.

Question 14   True   False

Teaching more about less is more effective than teaching less about more.

RESOURCE A.4

Postreading Assessment Key

Question 1   True

With appropriate instructional interventions, no more than 5 percent of students will have crippling reading deficits.

The presence of a strong, research-based elementary school reading program is essential to high achievement in middle and high school. Remediation is time-consuming, expensive, and requires highly trained teachers. Doing it right in kindergarten is also time-consuming, expensive, and requires highly trained teachers. But doing it right in the first place reduces failure, behavior problems, special education referrals, parental problems, and high school drop outs.

Question 2   False

Phonemic awareness, the ability to hear and manipulate sounds, can only be acquired in two ways: genetically or through language-rich early literacy experiences.

Phonemic awareness can also be acquired from a highly trained and effective teacher using a research-based program.

Question 3   True

All readers have comprehension difficulties when they encounter text for which they lack background and vocabulary knowledge.

If you doubt the truth of this statement, pick up an academic journal in a discipline for which you have no training, background, or vocabulary knowledge.

Question 4   False

The most effective way to accurately and automatically identify words is to memorize them.

There are many words in the English language that must be memorized because they are spelled and pronounced in unpredictable ways. However, if students attempt to make every word a "sight" word and do not learn how to decode, they will soon find themselves on memory overload. Sight words that are memorized are stored in a different part of the brain than are the words that become automatic through the decoding process.

Question 5   False

It doesn't matter what students are reading during SSR as long as they are reading.

Students must be reading text at their independent reading levels (no more than 5 pronunciation errors per 100 words) to ensure adequate comprehension. Students who are pretending to read in text that is too difficult for them are wasting their time.

Question 6   True

One of the most effective ways to teach comprehension to students is through modeling one's own cognitive processing of text.

The role of the teacher is that of a cognitive master. Students become their cognitive apprentices as they watch and listen to the ways in which their teachers process the text of their disciplines.

Question 7   False

Gifted students almost never have comprehension difficulties.

*Anyone who is reading text for which they lack background and vocabulary knowledge will have comprehension difficulties. That is why cognitive strategy instruction is essential for **all** students.*

Question 8   True

Research shows that comprehension will be improved if content teachers teach cognitive strategies in their classes.

Those teachers most qualified to teach students how to understand the textbooks and primary sources of their disciplines are content specialists.

Question 9   False

Covering the content is an effective method for raising achievement in secondary schools.

Covering the content is similar to mentioning the content. No one will understand or remember it except the teacher.

Question 10   True

All teachers need to teach all students how to read to learn.

Content instruction and cognitive strategy instruction belong together!

Question 11   False

Building a reading culture is the principal's job. Teachers should tend to teaching.

Principals have a critical role to support and provide resources to teachers. However, decisions about literacy should be made with the involvement and input of all teachers.

Question 12   False

The biggest roadblock to raising reading achievement in middle and high schools is lack of money in the budget.

Money is rarely the biggest roadblock. The biggest roadblocks are lack of will and courage.

Question 13   True

Raising student expectations is an effective way to raise student achievement.

Expectations are difficult to measure and quantify. But you will see results if teachers work together to develop performance rubrics in reading and writing, communicate those expectations to students, and scaffold their attainment of those expectations.

Question 14   True

Teaching more about less is more effective than teaching less about more.

When students have mastered a solid foundation in a content area, their subsequent learning will be more efficient and effective.

Resource B

Programs for Learning to Read in Secondary School

The following informational reviews describe research-based reading programs for middle and high students. The programs are designed to help adolescents acquire proficiencies in various areas of reading. Some programs are geared to only one area of reading while others are more comprehensive. The specific features of each program are coded as follows: phonemic awareness (PA), phonics (PH), fluency (F), spelling (SP), cognitive strategy instruction (CS), and vocabulary (V). Where available, citations to research (experimental and quasi-experimental studies comparing the effects of the program with other treatments as well as qualitative studies) and program evaluation studies (results of before-and-after tests with selected groups of students) are included.

For additional information and program reviews, see the Florida Center for Reading Research Summary Table at www.fcrr.org/FCRR Reports/table.asp.

BENCHMARK PROGRAM

(CS)

The Benchmark School of Philadelphia, Pennsylvania, is a private school where students are bright but have reading difficulties. In regular school settings, many of the students would be classified as dyslexic or learning disabled. At the Benchmark School, founded and still led by Irene Gaskins, students master cognitive strategies that make them the envy of their classmates when they return to their public and private schools in ninth grade and earn highest honors in high school. The history of the Benchmark School must command the attention of any educators considering how to raise reading achievement. Opened with just one class of poor readers in 1970, the school has grown under the leadership of Gaskins to a student body of 188 students composed entirely of privately funded students whose primary referring problem is poor reading despite average or better intelligence (Gaskins & Elliott, 1991, p. 5). What distinguishes the Benchmark School from the majority of schools has been its development of a research-based cognitive-strategy instruction program that pervades every aspect of school life. Working with eminent reading researchers Richard Anderson, Jonathan Baron, and Michael Pressley, the staff of Benchmark has focused on teaching thinking skills while imparting knowledge. The eighty-three staff members (fifteen head teachers supported by coteachers and support teachers) teach a core group of seventeen strategies for meaning and remembering. In addition to the core strategies, two stand-alone courses on learning and thinking are required that teach students how the mind works. These courses provide students with a rationale for learning the strategies that are being taught in their other classes. Gaskins believes that teaching students about the inner workings of the mind gives staff and students a common language for discussing the processing of information (p. 99) and helps them to understand the "why" as well as the "what" of strategic learning. For example, middle school students "are regularly reminded that their goal is to become goal-driven, planful, strategic, self-assessing students. Regular discussions ensue regarding *why* they think this goal is important and *how* it can be accomplished" (p. 64).

Gaskins makes seven suggestions to principals contemplating the implementation of a reading strategies program: (a) Select innovations that meet demonstrated needs of students, (b) involve the staff, (c) help teachers acquire knowledge, (d) foster an attitude of becoming, (e) create a safe environment for expressing concerns, (f) expect change to take time and to require ongoing support, and (g) set aside time to reflect and renew (Gaskins & Elliott, 1991, pp. 189–203).

Resources

Gaskins & Elliot, 1991. *Implementing Cognitive Strategy Instruction Across The School: The Benchmark Manual For Teachers.*

Pressley, Burkell, Cariglia-Bull, Lysynchuk, McGoldrick, Schneider, Snyder, Symons, & Woloshyn, 1990. *Cognitive Instructional Strategies That Really Work.*

Pressley, Gaskins, Solic, Collins, 2005. *A Portrait of Benchmark School: How a School Produces High Achievement in Students Who Previously Failed.*

Wood, Woloshyn, & Willoughby, 1995. *Cognitive Strategy Instruction for Middle and High Schools.*

Professional Development

The Benchmark School offers summer professional development opportunities taught in the Philadelphia area. They do not provide onsite training.

Program Information

The Benchmark School
2107 N. Providence Road, Media, PA 19063
Attn: Irene Gaskins
(610) 565-3741
Benchmarkinfo@aol.com
www.Benchmarkschool.org

CORRECTIVE READING

(PH, CS)

Corrective Reading (Engelmann et al., 1999), a remedial program for students in Grades 4–12, is part of the Direct Instruction family of instructional materials that was developed at the University of Oregon under the direction of Siegfrid Engelmann. If you are unfamiliar with direct instruction, you may be wondering what makes it different from any other kind of instruction. In his review on teacher effectiveness, Rosenshine (1979) summarized it thusly:

> Direct instruction refers to high levels of student engagement within academically focused, teacher-directed classrooms using sequenced, structured materials. [It] refers to teaching activities focused on academic matters where goals are clear to students; time allocated for instruction is sufficient and continuous; content coverage is extensive; student performance is monitored; questions are at a low cognitive level and produce many correct responses; and feedback to students is immediate and academically oriented. In direct instruction, the teacher controls instructional goals, chooses material appropriate for the student's ability

level, and paces the instructional episode. Interaction is characterized as structured, but not authoritarian; rather, learning takes place in a convivial academic atmosphere. (p. 17)

Both *Corrective Reading* and its beginning reading program counterpart, *Reading Mastery,* are validated by an extensive research base (Adams & Engelmann, 1996; Stebbins, St. Pierre, Proper, Anderson, & Cerva, 1977). The goal of *Corrective Reading* is to accelerate learning in order that students who have fallen behind can catch up with their peers. The tightly sequenced, scripted lessons provide hard-to-teach students with the structure they need to learn, practice, and master the essential decoding and comprehension skills. Highly effective instructional behaviors, such as adequate amounts of repetition and active responding by students, are also hallmarks of the program.

Many secondary schools and districts around the country are using *Corrective Reading* for readers in the bottom 30 percent (See Chapters 2 and 3). There are four instructional levels in both the decoding and comprehension programs, and students are assigned to a level according to placement test performance (Grossen, 2000).

Resources

Carnine, Silbert, Kameenui, & Tarver, 2004. *Direct Instruction in Reading* (4th ed.).

Professional Development

Contact Dr. Bonnie Grossen at the University of Oregon for professional development options. She can be reached at bgrossen@oregon .uoregon.edu or (541) 686-9185.

Program Information

SRA-McGraw Hill
(888) SRA-4543
www.sra4kids.com

HIGHER-ORDER THINKING SKILLS (HOTS)

(CS)

The Higher-Order Thinking Skills (HOTS) Project is an alternative approach to Title I for Grades 4 through 8 in which the compensatory activities consist solely of systematically designed higher-order thinking activities (Pogrow, 1995). Traditional drill and practice activities and content instruction are eliminated. The thinking activities are designed to generate gains in basic skills expected from Title I programs, while also improving thinking ability and social confidence. By learning how to learn, students are then able to learn content the first time it is taught in the classroom. The program is conducted in a computer lab using a detailed curriculum taught by a teacher specially trained in Socratic dialogue techniques. The teacher is the most critical component of the program, and the program will not be successful without the right teacher. The curriculum is designed in accordance with information-processing theories of cognition. The program operates as a pull-out program for thirty-five minutes a day, four days a week, for two years. In the first part of the period, the teacher engages students in sophisticated conversations. Students are then given a challenge that they go to the computer to try to solve. They later discuss their findings and approaches and how they know whether their strategy for solving the problem did or did not work. HOTS is unique in its ability to produce significant gains in achievement in later grade levels (Darmer, 1995).

HOTS is the only remedial program that treats students as though they were gifted and relies strictly on activities that challenge them intellectually. There is no content remediation, and students do not receive work sheets. HOTS has been in use for over twenty years as a Title I–validated program, and schools in which it is used consistently raise student achievement.

Resources

Pogrow, 2004. The Missing Element in Reducing the Learning Gap: Eliminating the "Blank Stare." *Teachers College Record.*

Pogrow, 2005. HOTS Revisited: A Thinking Development Approach to Reducing the Learning Gap After Grade 3.

Pogrow, in press. Redesigning High Poverty Elementary Schools for Success: The Traditionalist and Progressive Approach of the Hi-Perform School Model.

Professional Development

A weeklong workshop is provided to HOTS teachers on how to use Socratic techniques while teaching the HOTS curriculum. Teachers are trained in how to maintain an active learning environment in which students are given the time and responsibility to think through problems and articulate their ideas. HOTS students show gains in reading (and mathematics) that are double the national Title I average. It is interesting that in some schools, HOTS students are identified as gifted students after graduating from the HOTS program.

Program Information

> Education Innovations
> Attn: Dr. Stanley Pogrow
> Professor of Educational Leadership
> San Francisco State University
> 1600 Holloway Avenue
> San Francisco, CA 94132
>
> HOTS Project
> PO Box 42620
> Tucson, AZ 85733
> (800) 999-0153
> www.HOTS.org

LANGUAGE!®

(PA, PH, SP, CS, V)

Language!® (Greene, 2004) is a comprehensive literacy curriculum that is appropriate as a middle or high school replacement for language arts or English classes. Placement in the program is based on students' mastery levels, not on their grade levels. The program is appropriately paced for ELL students, those with language learning disabilities, and the most severely at-risk students. It directly teaches word recognition and spelling, vocabulary and morphology, grammar and usage, and speaking and writing, along with listening and reading comprehension. In order to do justice to the comprehensive nature of the program, it should be taught for two to three periods per day, across two to three years.

Language!® does not incorporate any specific teaching routines, such as those found in *Corrective Reading,* but includes a wide range of activities from which teachers can choose. For these reasons, the program is most effective in the hands of highly skilled and experienced reading teachers who are able to select activities suited to their students' needs.

Resources

Sopris West. *Implementation Results With Language!*® *at the Middle and High School Grades.* Longmont, CO: Author. Retrieved January 19, 2006 from www.teachlanguage.com/PDFs/Implementation_Data_Middle&High_%20School.pdf.

Sopris West. *Research Base for Language!*® Longmont, CO: Author. Retrieved January 19, 2006 from www.teachlanguage.com/PDFs/Research_Base%20_for_LANGUAGE!.pdf.

Sopris West. *Implementation Results With Language!*® *of Students Who Are Limited English Proficient.* Retrieved January 19, 2006 from www.teachlanguage.com/PDFs/Implementation_Data_Limited_English_Proficiency.pdf.

Professional Development

Initial training from Sopris West prepares classroom teachers, reading specialists, ELL specialists, learning disability specialists, and other literacy professionals for implementation. Course credit is available from accredited universities.

Program Information

Sopris West
4093 Specialty Place
Longmont, CO 80504
(303) 651-2829
www.sopriswest.com

LINDAMOOD-BELL LEARNING PROCESSES

(PA, PH, SP CS)

Lindamood-Bell Learning Processes were originally developed for use in clinical settings but have more recently been adapted for schoolwide and district use. In 1997, Lindamood-Bell Learning Processes partnered with Pueblo School District 60 (PSD60) in Colorado to implement a theoretically based program to improve reading achievement on the Colorado Student Assessment Program (CSAP). PSD60 is a heavily minority urban district with many Title I schools. This study focused on Grades 3, 4 and 5 in which CSAP testing was conducted most years from 1997 to 2003. A series of repeated measures analyses of covariance—controlling for school size, minority student percentage, socioeconomic status, and the time a school was included in the intervention—were conducted between PSD60 schools and the statewide CSAP average. In both overall and Title 1 school analyses, statistically significant and increasing gains favoring the Lindamood-Bell Learning Processes reading intervention were found (Sadowski & Willson, 2006).

Patricia Lindamood, a speech pathologist, and her husband, Charles, a linguist, originally conceived the program. Nanci Bell, the other half of the Lindamood-Bell team, developed the spelling and comprehension components of the program. The Lindamood-Bell Learning Processes Company produces three programs to meet the needs of low-achieving or nonreaders: (a) *Lindamood Phoneme Sequencing* (LiPS), (b) *Seeing Stars: Symbol Imagery for Sight Words and Spelling,* and (c) *Visualizing and Verbalizing for Language Comprehension and Thinking.* The programs can be used singly or in combination.

Lindamood Phoneme Sequencing Program

The Lindamood-Bell group was a pioneer in the development of a pure phonemic awareness program, first called *Auditory Discrimination in Depth* and renamed *Lindamood Phoneme Sequencing Program* (LiPS; Lindamood & Lindamood, 1998). Although the program was developed for one-on-one treatment in a clinical setting, it has now been refined for use in a variety of school settings.

LiPS is a true linguistic program, meaning that it teaches sounds before letters. *LiPS* teaches the forty-four phonemes by a process of discovery, feeling movements of the mouth, and watching these movements in a mirror. The program incorporates a new vocabulary to talk about phonemes (e.g., *lip poppers:* /b/, /p/ or *nasals:* /m/, /n/, /ng/). It helps students analyze and track phonemes using colored blocks, and it constantly engages the student in Socratic questioning so as to enable the learner to become independent and self-correcting.

The LiPS program draws on the sciences of linguistics and speech pathology to develop awareness of the articulatory gestures that produce the phonemes. Rather than identifying some vowels as "long" and "short," which can seem arbitrary because each vowel can be said in a sustained "long" way or a brief "short way," the fifteen vowel sounds are categorized and classified in just four groups. Second, the oral-motor feedback for consonants and vowels is used to track and verify the identity, number, and order of phonemes in syllables and words (Lindamood, Bell & Lindamood, 1997, p. 154).

Seeing Stars: Symbol Imagery for Sight Words and Spelling

Seeing Stars (Bell, 1997) successfully develops symbol imagery. The program begins with visualizing individual letters and extends into multisyllables, contextual reading, and spelling. Teachers work with students to image letters in words and apply that imagery to phonetic processing, sight words, spelling, and reading fluency. Students who have learned phonics and can sound out words but who still have difficulties reading because of slow phonetic processing benefit from *Seeing Stars.* When word identification and reading fluency have not improved at the same rate as word attack skills, this program can often provide the missing piece in the learning-to-read puzzle.

Visualizing and Verbalizing for Language Comprehension and Thinking

This program (Bell, 1986) is designed to meet the needs of students who can read words accurately but cannot comprehend content. If words seemingly go in one ear and out the other, the student is probably having difficulty creating an imaged gestalt—a whole. This is the result of weak concept imagery. *Visualizing and Verbalizing* stimulates concept imagery. Individuals learn to image gestalts to improve their language comprehension, reasoning for critical thinking, and expressive language skills.

NOTE: The descriptions of the Lindamood-Bell processes have been adapted from advertising literature.

Resources

Lindamood, Bell, & Lindamood, 1997. Sensory-cognitive factors in the controversy over reading instruction. *Journal of Developmental and Learning Disorders.* Contact Lindamood-Bell for a free copy of this article.

Professional Development

Training workshops for teachers are offered at sites around the country. Call for information regarding workshops in your area. You can also contract with Lindamood-Bell to bring training to your school district.

Program Information

Lindamood-Bell Human Learning Processes
416 Higuera Street, San Luis Obispo, CA 93401
Paul Worthington, Director of Research
(800) 233-1819
www.lblp.com

READING IS FAME

(PH, CS, V, SP)

Reading Is FAME was designed by two outstanding Harvard-trained reading educators, Mary Beth Curtis and Ann Marie Longo, to meet the needs of the adolescents with reading difficulties who enroll at Father Flanagan's Boys Town in Nebraska. It is based on Jeanne Chall's (1983/1986) Stages of Reading Development. There are four courses in the curriculum. Course 1, Foundations of Reading, is designed for young adults reading below the fourth-grade level. The goals in this class are to teach the most common letter-sound correspondences and to provide opportunities to apply this knowledge while reading books aloud. About eight to ten students make up a Foundations class, taught by a teacher and assisted by a paraprofessional. For about ten minutes each day, students work in pairs on spelling software, which has been customized to teach up to six different syllable types as well as frequently used Latin suffixes found in the English language. Groups of students also spend about ten minutes each day playing a game (e.g., Concentration or Wheel of Fortune) with words that fit the rule they have been practicing. Students learn very quickly that time is limited, and they know that the more they are on-task, the more fun they will have.

The remainder of class each day is spent in a small group, four to five, with a teacher, reading aloud from a novel. Novels are at a high enough reading level to provide practice in applying the phonics rules being learned and interesting enough to make the effort it takes to do so worthwhile. The reading is done collaboratively, with students and teacher taking turns reading and passing back and forth at unexpected times. This technique requires that every student follow along and stay engaged in the reading. The teacher supplies unknown words when necessary, while at the same time encouraging students to identify unfamiliar words. Short, informal discussions about the novels help to maintain comprehension and interest as well. Homework assignments in the Foundations course include activities like syllable cloze activities, finding words that do and do not fit rules, and sentence writing.

Course 2, Adventures in Reading, is intended for adolescents and young adults reading between the fourth- and sixth-grade levels. The goals in this course are to improve students' ability to recognize words and their meanings and to increase oral reading fluency. As in the Foundations course, students work in pairs, for about ten minutes each day, on computer software customized to improve their reading vocabulary. Students also spend about ten minutes each day in small groups playing games that provide practice with the words (e.g., Password and Jeopardy). Oral reading is also included in Course 2, and the emphasis continues to be on application and enjoyment during reading. In Adventures, however, fluency rather than accuracy is the focus. Homework assignments in the Adventures course include crossword puzzles, cloze sentences, and analogies that provide additional practice on the same words used in the day's computer software and games.

Mastery of Meaning, Course 3, is designed for young adults reading between the sixth- and eighth-grade levels. The goal in Mastery is to build up knowledge of word meanings to improve comprehension. The classes contain anywhere from ten to fifteen students per teacher. The design of the activities and materials in Mastery are based on five principles of effective vocabulary instruction drawn from the research literature (McKeown & Curtis, 1987): (a) Students get numerous opportunities to learn words and meanings, (b) words are presented in a variety of contexts, (c) students are asked to process words in active and generative ways, (d) distinctions as well as similarities among words' meanings are stressed, and (e) improvement in students' ability to use words in speaking and writing as well as to recognize their meanings is emphasized. Students' independent reading in the Mastery course occurs mostly in informational texts. Because they are now making the transition from "learning to read" to "reading to learn," much of the reading is done silently. Homework assignments in the Mastery course include writing assignments using target vocabulary words along with cloze passages and sentence completions.

The fourth and final course, Explorations, is intended for young adults reading at the eighth-grade level and beyond. The goal in Explorations is to promote the ability to integrate information via both reading and writing. Students are taught study skills, such as note taking and summarizing, in the context of materials taken from a variety of content areas. As they work on problem-solving software, students practice using their study skills. Use of study skills is also required in an activity called the Explorations Board, where students are asked to respond in writing to short-answer and essay questions. Homework in Explorations provides additional practice in using reading and writing as tools for learning.

NOTE: This description of Reading Is FAME has been adapted by permission from Curtis and Longo (1997) and the Reading Is FAME promotional brochure.

Research and Evaluation Results

Students who take the Foundations course average one or more years of growth for one semester of instruction on individually administered basic reading measures. Oral reading rates and performance on an overall course spelling test also improve. Gains for students who take the Adventures course average one and a half or more years of growth for one semester of instruction on an individually administered measure of word recognition and vocabulary. Students also show improvement on measures of oral reading and a course vocabulary test.

For students who take the Mastery course, gains on group-administered measures of vocabulary and comprehension average about one year of growth for one semester of instruction. Students' ability to recognize and use the course vocabulary words in writing also improves. Students who take the Explorations course average about six months' growth for eighteen weeks of instruction on group-administered comprehension measures. Students' ability to use study skills taught in the course, such as note taking and summarizing, also show improvement. For those students who have taken all four courses in the curriculum, gains on individually administered tests of basic reading and vocabulary improve from below the fourth-grade level to the eighth-grade level and above within a two-year period (Father Flanagan's Boys Home, 1996).

Resources

Curtis & Longo, 1999. *When Adolescents Can't Read: Methods and Materials That Work.* (Brookline Books: 1-800-666-BOOK)
Curtis, M. B., & Longo, A. M. (n.d.). *Reversing Reading Failure at Boys Town.* (Available on request from Boys Town)

Professional Development

Boys Town staff members will come to your site and train teachers to use the program's methods and materials. Boys Town Center staff will also return to your site once implementation has begun to observe in classrooms and address any questions or concerns.

Program Information

Boys Town Reading Center
Father Flanagan's Boys Home
Boys Town, Nebraska 68010
(402) 498-1075

REASONING AND WRITING

(CS)

Reasoning and Writing (Arbogast, Davis, Engelmann, Grossen, & Silbert, 2001) features well-thought-out scripted lessons that enable teachers to present skills in a way that is easy for students to assimilate; tightly sequenced instruction offering ample opportunities for concepts to be continually applied and consolidated; relevant practice in mechanics, usage, and grammar to refine students' editing skills and improve their writing; and careful teaching of analysis and logic skills to improve the way students communicate in all subject areas.

Professional Development

Contact Dr. Bonnie Grossen at the University of Oregon for professional development options. She can be reached at bgrossen@oregon .uoregon.edu or (541) 686-9185.

Program Information

SRA-McGraw Hill
(888) SRA-4543
www.sra4kids.com

REWARDS (READING EXCELLENCE: WORD ATTACK AND RATE DEVELOPMENT STRATEGIES)

(PH, F)

Rewards (Archer et al., 2005) is an intervention program that teaches students how to decode long words and increases oral and silent reading fluency, particularly in content-area passages. It is an excellent supplemental program for students in general education that have missed key instructional pieces of reading at some point during their elementary school years. It is also useful for students in special education who have mild phonological deficits or for students who have completed a program such as Wilson or Spalding and need to build reading fluency.

Resources

Archer, Gleason, & Vachon, 2003. Decoding and Fluency: Foundation Skills for Struggling Older Readers. *Learning Disability Quarterly.*

Archer, Gleason, Vachon, & Hollenbeck, 2001. *Instructional Strategies for Teaching Struggling Fourth and Fifth Grade Students to Read Long Words.*

Vachon & Gleason, 2001. *The Effects of Mastery Teaching and Varying Practice Contexts on Middle School Students' Acquisition of Multisyllabic Word Reading Strategies.*

Professional Development

Three levels of training are provided. Implementation training, offered in half- or full-day sessions, provides insight into the research behind the program and helps teachers and reading specialists gain the tools necessary for implementation. Training of Trainers to build internal capacity is a two-day workshop for general and special education curriculum directors, reading specialists, staff developers, and teachers who are familiar with the Rewards program and are ready to train staff at their school or district.

Program Information

Sopris West
4093 Specialty Place
Longmont, CO 80504
(303) 651-2829
www.sopriswest.com

THE SPALDING METHOD

(PA, PH, SP, CS)

The Spalding Method is based on the work of Romalda Bishop Spalding, who trained directly under Samuel Orton. Romalda Spalding received degrees at the University of Illinois and Columbia University but discovered that her preparation was not adequate for teaching all students to read and write successfully. Her search for a better method led her in 1938 to the distinguished neurologist, Dr. Samuel T. Orton. Spalding soon realized that the children taught using Dr. Orton's technique experienced more success than her regular education students. Drawing on what she learned from Dr. Orton and her own experience working with children at Massachusetts General Hospital, Children's Hospital at Harvard Medical School, and public and private schools as a classroom teacher, she wrote the textbook, *The Writing Road to Reading* (Spalding & Spalding, 1957/1990).

The Spalding Method is a total-language-arts approach that incorporates the following five features (North, 1995, p. 217): (a) The teacher provides an exemplary model of pronunciation of speech sounds; (b) students accurately reproduce speech sounds; (c) the teacher shows written symbols with simultaneous presentation of speech sounds; (d) students simultaneously say speech sounds and write symbols; and

(e) students blend sounds to produce words, apply pronunciation skills to oral reading, and use strategies to enhance comprehension. "A rather significant and up to date body of data has been assembled showing the indisputable success that many schools are enjoying with the Spalding Method" (Aukerman, 1984, p. 541). Farnham-Diggory (1987), director of the Reading Study Center at the University of Delaware, selected the Spalding Method for use in the reading clinic there because of its well-developed theories of reading processes, reading development, skill learning, and instruction.

NOTE: This description the Spalding Reading Program has been adapted by permission from Spalding promotional literature.

Resources

North, 1995. The Effects of Spalding Instruction on Special Education Students.

Spalding & Spalding, 1957/1990. *The Writing Road to Reading: The Spalding Method of Phonics For Teaching Speech, Writing & Reading* (4th rev. ed.).

Professional Development

Spalding offers a professional development plan for certifying tutors, teachers, and teacher-instructors in The Spalding Method. The plan includes observations, evaluations, coaching, and inservice tailored to specific needs.

Program Information

The Spalding Education Foundation
2814 West Bell Road, Suite 1405, Phoenix, AZ 85023
Dr. Mary North, Director of Research
(602) 866-7801

SPELLING THROUGH MORPHOGRAPHS

(SP, V)

Spelling Through Morphographs (Dixon & Engelmann, 2002) is a remedial program designed to give older students the tools they need to learn to spell. The program teaches a variety of morphographs—prefixes, suffixes, and word bases—and a small set of rules for combining them so that students learn a spelling strategy they can apply to thousands of words. In the first half of the program, students learn over 252 morphographs and the rules needed to spell over 3,000 words. Students learn to generate correct spellings from morphographs, not memorization. Expanded writing and proofreading activities reinforce the connection between spelling and composition.

Resources

Simonsen, Gunter, & Marchand-Margella, 2005. *Spelling Research: Research on Teaching Children to Spell.*

Professional Development

Contact Dr. Bonnie Grossen at the University of Oregon for professional development options. She can be reached at bgrossen@oregon .uoregon.edu or (541) 686-9185.

Program Information

SRA-McGraw Hill
(888) SRA-4543
www.sra4kids.com

Resource C

Creating a Strong Reading Culture

A Process Exercise

DESCRIPTION

This process is designed to help staff members examine and agree on a set of values related to the establishment of a strong reading culture.

APPLICATION

Use this process to create, nurture and monitor positive and professional staff behaviors and attitudes.

TIME REQUIRED

Sixty to ninety minutes

Figure C.1   Sample Set of Basic Beliefs and Core Values

The teaching of strategic reading is the responsibility of every teacher.

We can teach every student in our school how to read.

Every student can learn.

Learners should be treated with respect, even if they are behaving inappropriately.

Teachers make a difference in how, what, when, and why students learn.

Good teaching involves creating as many opportunities as possible for students to achieve mastery.

We must model and then teach strategic reading to our students.

We support and encourage each other through mentoring, coaching, sharing, and cooperating.

Effective two-way communication is the responsibility of every student, teacher, parent, and administrator.

Important decisions must be made collegially.

Time to teach and learn must be protected.

If students work hard, they will achieve.

We have high expectations for every student.

We have high expectations for ourselves as teachers and administrators.

Every teacher shares the responsibility for the behavior and learning of every student in our school.

We respect, value, and welcome the ideas, input, and concerns of parents.

MATERIALS

Make as many photocopies of the Core Values for a Reading Culture as you have groups of five to eight individuals. Cut apart each photocopied set of pages into strips and place them into an envelope. At the end of this copying and cutting process, you should have as many envelopes as you have groups of eight, each one containing separate strips of all of the statements from the sample code of ethics.

ADMINISTRATION DIRECTIONS

1. Count off by eight. Choose a facilitator (e.g., the person with most years of teaching experience) and a recorder (e. g., the person with the smallest pet).

2. Give the following directions to participants:

a. Take the enclosed strips of paper from the envelope. Each strip has a different core value written on it. One by one, read and discuss them.

b. Ask the question, "Do we want this value or belief to be one of our expected beliefs and attitudes?"

c. If your group accepts the statement as it is written, tape it on the chart paper provided.

d. If your group wants to revise or edit the statement, do that *before* you tape it on the paper.

e. If your group doesn't want to include the statement as part of the values and beliefs, lay it aside in a separate pile.

f. Review the list that you have created. Are there any revisions that you want to make or values or beliefs that you want to add?

g. Record your ideas.

h. As you consider the statements you have reviewed, which ones were most important to your group? Your recorder should be prepared to share at least one at the conclusion of this exercise.

i. Turn your work into me, and I will compile your recommendations and submit them to you for final approval.

References

ACT. (2000, May). *Content validity evidence in support of ACT's educational achievement tests.* Retrieved April 21, 2006, from www.act.org/research/curricsurvey.html.

Adams, G. N., & Brown, S. N. (2003). *The six-minute solution: A reading fluency program.* Longmont, CO: Sopris West.

Adams, G., & Engelmann, S. (1996). *Research on direct instruction: 25 years beyond DISTAR.* Seattle, WA: Educational Achievement Systems.

Adams, M. J. (1990). *Beginning to read.* Cambridge: MIT Press.

Adams, M. J. (1998). The three-cueing system. In F. Lehr & J. Osborn (Eds.), *Literacy for all: Issues in teaching and learning,* (pp. 73–99). New York: Guilford.

Afflerbach, P. (1990a). The influence of prior knowledge and text genre on readers' prediction strategies. *Reading Research Quarterly, 22,* 131–148.

Afflerbach, P. (1990b). The influence of prior knowledge on expert readers' main idea strategies. *Reading Research Quarterly, 25,* 31–46.

Afflerbach, P. (2002). Teaching reading self-assessment strategies. In C. C. Block & M. Pressley (Eds.), *Comprehension instruction: Research-based best practices* (pp. 96–111). New York: Guilford.

Afflerbach, P., & Johnston, P. H. (1984). Research methodology: On the use of verbal reports in reading research. *Journal of Reading Behavior, 16,* 307–322.

Afflerbach, P., & Walker, B. (1992). Main idea instruction: An analysis of three basal reader series. *Reading Research and Instruction, 32*(1), 11–28.

Alexander, P. A. (1997). The nature of disciplinary and domain learning: The dynamics of subject-matter knowledge, strategy knowledge, and motivation. In C. E. Weinstein & B. L. McComb (Eds.), *Strategic learning: Skill will, and self-regulation* (Vol. 10, pp. 213–250). Mahwah, NJ: Erlbaum.

Alexander, P. A., & Jetton, T. L. (2003). Learning from traditional and alternative texts: New conceptualizations for the information age. In A. C Graesser, M. A. Gernsbacher, & S. R Goldman (Eds.), *Handbook of discourse processes* (pp. 199–241). Mahway, NJ: Erlbaum.

Allington, R. L. (1977). If they don't read much, how they ever gonna get good? *Journal of Reading, 21,* 57–61.

Allington, R. L. (1980). Poor readers don't get to read much in reading groups. *Language Arts, 57*(8), 872–876.

Allington, R. L. (1983). Fluency: The neglected goal. *The Reading Teacher, 36,* 556–561.

Allington, R.L. (1984). Content coverage and contextual reading in reading groups. *Journal of Reading Behavior, 16,* 85–96.

Alvermann, D. E., & Boothby, P. R. (1983). A preliminary investigation of the differences in children's retention of "inconsiderate" text. *Reading Psychology, 4*(3–4), 237–246.

Alvermann, D. E., & Boothby, P. R. (1986). Children's transfer of graphic organizer instruction. *Reading Psychology, 7*(2), 87–100.

Ananova. (2005, November 19). *2B OR NT 2B?* Leeds, United Kingdom: Author. Retrieved April 21, 2006, from www.ananova.com/news/story/sm_1614625.html.

Anderson, R. C., Wilson, P. T., Fielding, L. G. (1988). Growth in reading and how children spend their time outside of school. *Reading Research Quarterly, 23*(3), 285–303.

Anderson V., & Roit, M. (1993). Planning and implementing collaborative strategy instruction for delayed readers in grades 6–10. *Elementary School Journal, 94,* 121–137.

Andrews, R., & Soder, R. (1987, March). Principal leadership and student achievement. *Educational Leadership, 44,* 9–11.

Apelman, M. (1986). Working with teachers: The advisory approach. In K. Zumwalt, *Improving teaching,* (pp. 115–129). Alexandria, VA: Association for Supervision and Curriculum Development.

Applebee, A. N. (1993). *Literature in the secondary school: Studies of curriculum and instruction in the United States.* Urbana, IL: National Council of Teachers of English.

Arbogast, A., Davis, K. L., Engelmann, S., Grossen, B., Silbert, J. (2001). *Reasoning and writing.* New York: SRA McGraw-Hill.

Archer, A., Gleason, M. M., & Vachon, V. (2003). Decoding and fluency: Foundation skills for struggling older readers. *Learning Disability Quarterly, 26,* 89–101.

Archer, A. L., Gleason, M. M., & Vachon, V., (2005). *Rewards: Multisyllabic word reading strategies.* Longmont, CO: Sopris West.

Archer, A. L., Gleason, M. M., Vachon, V. L., & Hollenbeck, K. (2001). *Instructional strategies for teaching struggling fourth and fifth grade students to read long words.* Retrieved April 21, 2006, from www.rewardsreading.com/PDFs/Intermediate_Study.pdf.

Armbruster, B. B., Anderson, T. H., & Meyer, J. L. (1991). Improving content-area reading using instructional graphics. *Reading Research Quarterly, 26*(4), 393–416.

Armbruster, B. B., Anderson, T. H., & Ostertag, J. (1987). Does text structure/summarization instruction facilitate learning from expository text? *Reading Research Quarterly, 22,* 331–346.

Ashton, P. T., & Webb, R. B. (1986). *Making a difference: Teachers' sense of efficacy and student achievement.* New York: Longman.

Assessment Reform Group. (2002). *Assessment for learning: 10 principles. Research-Based Principles of Assessment for Learning.* London: King's College.

Association for Supervision and Curriculum Development. (2005). Online survey. Retrieved November 17, 2005, from www.ascd.org.

Atwell, N. (1998). *In the middle* (2nd ed.). Portsmouth, NH: Heinemann.

Aukerman, R. C. (1984). *Approaches to beginning reading.* New York: John Wiley.

Bean, T. W., & Steenwyk, F. L. (1984). The effect of three forms of summarization instruction on sixth graders' summary writing and comprehension. *Journal of Reading Behavior, 15*(4), 297–306.

Beck, I. L., & Dole, J. A. (1992). Reading and thinking with history and science text. In C. Collins & J. N. Mangieri (Eds.). *Teaching thinking: An agenda for the twenty-first century* (pp. 3–21). Hillsdale, NJ: Erlbaum.

Beck, I., McKeown, M. G., Hamilton, R. L., & Kucan, L. (1997). *Questioning the author: An approach for enhancing student engagement with text.* Newark, DE: International Reading Association.

Beck, I. L., McKeown, M. G., & Kucan, L. (2002). *Bringing words to life: Robust vocabulary instruction.* New York: Guilford.

Beck, I. L., Perfetti, C. A., & McKeown, M. G. (1982). *Effects of long-term vocabulary instruction on lexical access and reading comprehension.* Pittsburg, PA: Learning Research and Development Center, University of Pittsburgh.

Beers, D. E. (1984). *School-based management.* Paper presented at National Convention of Elementary School Principals, New Orleans, LA.

Bell, N. (1986). *Visualizing and verbalizing for language comprehension and thinking.* San Luis Obispo, CA: Gander.

Bell, N. (1997). *Seeing stars.* San Louis Obispo, CA: Gander.

Bempechat, J. (2000, May 16). The burden of faulty attitudes: What adults want from schools may not be what children need. *Education Week, 64,* 46.

Benjamin, A. (2003). *Writing in the content areas.* Larchmont, NY: Eye on Education, Inc.

Berkowitz, S. J. (1986). Effects of instruction in text organization on sixth grade students' memory for expository reading. *Reading Research Quarterly, 21,* 161–178.

Berliner, D. C. (1981). Academic learning time and reading achievement. In J. Guthrie (Ed.), *Comprehension and teaching: Research reviews* (pp. 203–225). Newark, DE: International Reading Association.

Berliner, D. C. (2005, August 2). Our impoverished view of educational reform. *Teachers College Record.* Retrieved on August 19, 2005, from http:// www.tc record.org ID Number: 12106.

Biancarosa, G., & Snow, C. E. (2004). *Reading next—A vision for action and research in middle and high school literacy: A report from Carnegie Corporation of New York.* Washington, DC: Alliance for Excellent Education.

Biemiller, A. (2003). Oral comprehension sets the ceiling on reading comprehension. *American Educator.* Spring. Retrieved May 2, 2006, from www.aft.org/pubs-reports/american_educator/spring2003/biemiller.html.

Bishop, J. (1993, November). *Impacts of school organization and signaling on incentives to learn in France, Netherlands, England, Scotland, and the United States.* Philadelphia: National Center on the Educational Quality of the Workforce.

Bishop, J. (1995). The power of external standards. *American Educator, 19*(3), 10–14, 17–18, 42–43.

Bishop, J. (1998a). *Do curriculum-based external exit exam systems enhance student achievement?* Philadelphia, PA: Consortium for Policy Research in Education.

Bishop, J. (1998b). *The effect of curriculum-based external exit systems on student achievement. Journal of Economic Education. 29*(2), 171–182.

Blachowicz, C. L. Z. (1986). Making connections: Alternatives to the vocabulary notebook. *Journal of Reading, 2,* 643–649.

Black, P., Harrison, C., Lee, C., Marshall, B., & Wiliam, D. (2003). *Assessment for learning: Putting it into practice.* Berkshire, England: Open University Press.

Block, J. (1971). *Mastery learning: Theory and practice.* New York: Holt, Rinehart, & Winston.

Block, J. H., & Anderson, L. W. (1975). *Mastery learning in classroom instruction.* New York: Macmillan.

Block, J. H., & Burns, R. B. (1977). Mastery learning in L. Shulman (Ed.), *Review of research in education* (Vol.4). Itasca, IL: Peacock.

Block, J. H., Efthim, H. E., & Burns, R. B. (1989). *Building effective mastery learning schools.* New York: Longman.

Bloom, B. S. (1971). *Mastery learning.* New York: Holt, Rinehart, & Winston.

Bloom, B. S. (1976). *Human characteristics and school learning.* New York: McGraw-Hill.

Bloom, B. S. (1980). *The state of research on selected alterable variables in education.* Chicago: University of Chicago, Department of Education.

Blow, B. (1976, April). Individualized reading. *Arizona English Bulletin, 18,* 151–53.

Borduin, B. J., Borduin, C. M., & Manley, C. M. (1994). The use of imagery training to improve reading comprehension of second graders. *Journal of Genetic Psychology, 155*(1), 115–118.

Borokowski, J. G., Carr, M., Rellinger, E., & Pressley, M. (1990). Self-regulated cognition: Interdependence of metacognition, attributions, and self esteem. In B. F. Jones & L. Idol (Eds.), *Dimensions of thinking and cognitive instruction* (pp. 53–92). Hillsdale, NJ: Lawrence Erlbaum.

Bracey, G. (2002, May 5). Why do we scapegoat the schools? *Washington Post,* B01.

Bracey, G. (2005, February 2). Education's "groundhog day." *Education Week, 24*(21), 38–39.

Bracey, G. (2006, January 7). Fix this flawed test. *Washington Post.* Retrieved January 7, 2006 from www.washingtonpost.com.

Bransford, J. D. (1983). Schema activation—schema acquisition. In R. C. Anderson, J. Osborn, & R. C. Tierney (Eds.), *Learning to read in American schools* (pp. 258–272). Hillsdale, NJ: Lawrence Erlbaum.

Bransford, J. D., Brown, A. L., & Cocking, R. R. (Eds.). (2000). *How people learn: Brain, mind, experience, and school.* Washington, DC: National Academy Press.

Bresnahan, M. V. (2001). *How students in middle school with reading disabilities experience reading instruction: Three case studies.* Unpublished doctoral dissertation. Northern Illinois University, DeKalb, IL.

Brown, A. L., & Campione, J. C. (1994). Guided discovery in a community of learners. In K. McGilly (Ed.). *Classroom lessons: Integrating cognitive theory and classroom practice* (pp. 229–270). Cambridge, MA: MIT Press.

Brown, A. L., & Day, J. D. (1983). Macrorules for summarizing texts: The development of expertise. *Journal of Verbal Learning and Verbal Behavior, 22,* 1–14.

Brown, A. L., Day, J. D., & Jones, R. S. (1983). The development of plans for summarizing texts. *Child Development, 54,* 968–979.

Brown, R., & Coy-Ogan, L. (1993). The evaluation of transactional strategies instruction in one teacher's classroom. *Elementary School Journal, 94,* 221–233.

Brown, R., Pressley, M., Van Meter, P., & Schuder, T. (1996). A quasi-experimental validation of transactional strategies instruction with low-achieving second-grade readers. *Journal of Educational Psychology, 88*(1), 18–37.

Bryk, A. S., & Schneider, B. (2002). *Trust in schools: A core resource for improvement.* New York: Russell Sage Foundation.

Burke, C., Howard, L., & Evangelou, T. (2003, November). *Lindamood-Bell® Center in a school: Preliminary evaluation report.* San Diego, CA: SANDAG.

Canfield, J., Hansen, M. V., Hansen, P., & Dunlap, I. (2000). *Chicken soup for the preteen soul.* Deerfield Beach, FL: Health Communications.

Carnine, D. W., Silbert, J., Kameenui, E. J., & Tarver, S. (2004). *Direct instruction reading* (4th ed.). Upper Saddle River, NJ: Prentice Hall.

Carr, E., & Wixon, K. K. (1986). Guidelines for evaluating vocabulary instruction. *Journal of Reading, 29*(7), 588–595.

Carroll, J. (1963). A model for school learning. *Teachers College Record, 64,* 723–733.

Carter, S. C. (1999). *No excuses: Seven principals of low-income schools who set the standard for high achievement.* Washington, DC: Heritage Foundation.

Cavanagh, S. (2005, May 23). *NAEP board postpones decision on 12th grade test.* Retrieved April 29, 2006, from www.edweek.com.

Cavanagh, S. (2005, June 8). NAEP board delays decision on mandatory 12th grade test. *Education Week.* Retrieved April 21, 2006, from www.education week.org.

Cavanagh, S., & Robelen, E. W. (2004, April 14). Bush backs requiring NAEP in 12th grade. *Education Week.* Retrieved April 21, 2006, from www.education week.org.

Chall, J. S. (1983). *Learning to read: The great debate.* New York: McGraw-Hill. (Original work published in 1967)

Chall, J. S. (1986). *Stages of reading development.* New York: McGraw-Hill. (Original work published in 1983)

Chall, J. S., & Dale, E. (1995). *Readability revisited: The new Dale-Chall Readability Formula.* Cambridge, MA: Brookline.

Chambers, A. (1985). *Booktalk: Occasional writing on literature and children.* London: Bodley Head.

Chan, L. K. S. (1994). Relationship of motivation, strategic learning, and reading achievement in grades 5, 7, and 9. *Journal of Experimental Education, 62*(4), 319–339.

Coleman, J. (1966). Equality of educational opportunity. Washington, DC: U.S. Department of Health Education and Welfare, Office of Education.

Collins, A., Brown, J. S., & Holum, A. (1991, Winter). Cognitive apprenticeship: Making thinking visible. *American Educator, 6–11,* 38–41.

Cooper, G. (1990). Cognitive load theory as an aid for instructional design. *Australian Journal of Educational Technology, 6*(2), 108–113.

Coxhead, A. (2005). *The academic word list.* Wellington, New Zealand: Wellington University. Retrieved April 21, 2006, from www.vuw.ac.nz/lals/research/awl/.

Craig, M. T., & Yore, L. D. (1995). Middle school students' metacognitive knowledge about science reading and science text: An interview study. *Reading Psychology, 16*(2), 169–213.

Cubberly, E. P. (1909). *Changing conceptions of education.* Boston: Houghton, Mifflin.

Curtis, M. E., & Longo, A. M. (1997). *Reversing reading failure at Boys Town.* Boys Town, NE: Father Flanagan's Boy's Home.

Curtis, M. E., & Longo, A. M. (1999). *When adolescents can't read: Methods and materials that work.* Cambridge, MA: Brookline.

Curtis, M. B., & Longo, A. M. (n.d.). *Reversing reading failure at Boys Town.* (Available on request from Boys Town.)

D'Anna, C. A., Zechmeister, E. G., & Hall, J. W. (1991). Toward a meaningful definition of vocabulary size. *Journal of Reading Behavior, 23,* 109–122.

Darling-Hamond, L., Ancess, J., & Falk, B. (1995) *Authentic assessment in action: Studies of schools and students at work.* New York: Teachers College Press.

Darmer, M. (1995). *Developing transfer and metacognition skills in educationally disadvantaged students: Effects of Higher Order Thinking Skills (HOTS) program.* Unpublished dissertation, University of Arizona.

Davey, B. (1983). Think aloud—Modeling the cognitive processes of reading comprehension. *Journal of Reading, 27*(1), 44–47.

Davey, B., & McBride, S. (1986). Effects of question-generation on reading comprehension. *Journal of Educational Psychology, 78,* 256–262.

Delpit, L. (1995). *Other people's children: Cultural conflict in the classroom.* New York: The New Press.

Denton, C. A., Vaughn, S., & Fletcher, J. M. (2003). Bringing research-based practice in reading intervention to scale. *Learning Disabilities Research & Practice, 18*(3), 201–211.

Deshler, D. D., & Schumaker, J. B. (2006). *Teaching adolescents with disabilities: Accessing the general education curriculum.* Thousand Oaks, CA: Corwin Press.

Dickinson, D. K., & Smith, M. W. (1994). Long-term effects of preschool teachers' book readings on low-income children's vocabulary and story comprehension. *Reading Research Quarterly, 29,* 105–122.

Dillon, J. T. (1988). *Questioning and teaching: A manual of practice.* New York: Teachers College Press.

Dillon, S. (2005, November 26). Students ace state tests, but earn D's from U. S. *The New York Times.* Retrieved November 26, 2005 www.nytimes.com.

Dixon, R., & Engelmann, S. (2002). *Spelling through morphographs.* New York: SRA McGraw-Hill.

Dole, J. (2000). Explicit and implicit instruction in comprehension. In B. M. Taylor, M. F. Graves, & P. van den Broek (Eds.), *Reading for meaning: Fostering comprehension in the middle grades* (pp. 52–69). New York: Teachers College Press.

Dole, J. A., Valencia, S. W., Greer, E. A., & Wardrop, J. L. (1991). Effects of two types of prereading instruction on the comprehension of narrative and expository text. *Reading Research Quarterly, 26*(2), 142–159.

Donahue, P., Voelkl, K., Campbell, J., & Mazzeo, J. (1999). *NAEP 1998 reading report card for the nation and states.* Washington, DC: U.S. Department of Education, Office of Educational Research and Improvement. Retrieved May 2, 2006, from http://www.nces.ed.gov/nationsreportcard/pubs/main1998/1999500.asp.

Duckworth, A. L., & Seligman, M. E. P. (2005). Self-discipline outdoes IQ in predicting academic performance of adolescents. *Psychological Science, 16,* 939–944.

Duffy, G. (2002). The case for direct explanation of strategies. In C. C. Block & M. Pressley (Ed.), *Comprehension instruction: Research-based best practices* (pp. 28–41). New York: Guilford.

Duffy, G. G. (1993). Rethinking strategy instruction: Four teachers' development and their low achievers' understandings. *Elementary School Journal, 93*(3), 231–247.

Duffy, G. G., & Roehler, L. R. (1987, January). Teaching reading skills as strategies. *The Reading Teacher, 40,* 414–418.

Duffy, G. G., Roehler, L. R., Sivan, E., Rackliffe, G., Book, C., Meloth, M., Varus, L., Weselman, R., Putnam, J., & Basiri, D. (1987) The effects of explaining the reasoning associated with using reading strategies. *Reading Research Quarterly, 16,* 403–411.

Durkin, D. (1993). *Teaching them to read* (6th ed). Boston: Allyn & Bacon.

Edmonds, R. (1979). Effective schools for the urban poor. *Educational Leadership, 37*(1), 15–24.

Edmonds, R. (1981). Making public schools effective. *Social Policy, 12,* 53–60.

Educational Research Service. (1998). *Reading at the middle and high school levels.* Arlington, VA: Author.

Educational Testing Service. (1996). *The comprehensive needs assessment: A basis for making school wide decisions.* Tucker, GA: Author.

Education Trust. (2005). *Stalled in secondary: A look at student achievement since the No Child Left Behind Act.* Retrieved April 21, 2006, from http://www2.edtrust.org.

Ekwall, E. E., & Shanker, J. L. (2000). *Ekwall/Shanker reading inventory* (4th ed.). Boston: Allyn & Bacon.

Elley, W. B. (1992). *How in the world do students read?* Hamburg, Germany: International Association for the Evaluation of Educational Achievement.

Elley, W.B. (1999). *Raising literacy levels in third world countries: A method that works.* Culver City, CA: Language Education Associates.

Elley, W. B., & Mangubhai, F. (1983). The impact of reading on second language learning. *Reading Research Quarterly, 19,* 53–67.

Engelmann, S., Hanner, S., & Johnson, S. (1999). *Corrective reading.* New York: McGraw-Hill.

English, F. (1992). *Deciding what to teach and test: Developing, aligning, and auditing the curriculum.* Thousand Oaks, CA: Corwin Press.

Farnham-Diggory, S. (1987, July). *From theory to practice in reading.* Paper presented at the annual meeting of the Reading Reform Foundation, San Francisco.

Father Flanagan's Boys Home. (1996). *Boys Town reading curriculum research results.* Unpublished paper. Boys Town, NE: Author.

Feldman, K., & Kinsella, K. (2005). *Narrowing the language gap: The case for explicit vocabulary instruction.* Scholastic Professional Paper. Retrieved May 2, 2006, from www.fcoe.net/ela/pdf/Narrowing%20Vocab%20Gap%20KK%20KF%201.pdf.

Fielding, L., Kerr, N., & Rosier, P. (2004). *Delivering on the promise of the 95% reading and math goals.* Kennewick, WA: The New Foundation Press.

Fisher, C.W., & Berliner, D.C. (1985). *Perspectives on instructional time.* New York: Longman.

Fries, C. C. (1963). *Linguistics and reading.* New York: Holt, Rinehart, & Winston.

Fullan, M. G. (1994). *Change forces: Probing the depths of educational reform.* New York: Falmer.

Fullan, M. G. (2001). *Leading in a culture of change.* San Francisco: Jossey-Bass.

Fullan, M., & Miles, M. (1992). Getting reform right: What works and what doesn't. *Phi Delta Kappan, 73*(10), 745–752.

Fuller, T. (1929). In E. Rhys & L. Vaughn (Eds.), *A century of English essays: An anthology ranging from Caxton to R. L. Stevenson & the writers of our own time,* pp. 24–25. New York: E. P. Dutton. (Original work published in 1642)

Gabbert, B. D., Johnson, D. W., & Johnson, R. (1986). Cooperative learning, group-to-individual transfer, process gain, and the acquisition of cognitive reasoning strategies. *Journal of Psychology, 120,* 267–278.

Gall, M. (December, 1970). The use of questions in teaching. *Review of Educational Research, 40*(5), 207–220.

Gallagher, K. (2003). *Reading reasons: Motivational mini-lessons for middle and high school.* York, ME: Stenhouse.

Gambrell, L. B., & Bales, R. J. (1986). Mental imagery and the comprehension-monitoring performance of fourth and fifth-grade poor readers. *Reading Research Quarterly, 21,* 454–464.

Gardiner, S. (2005). *Building student literacy through sustained silent reading.* Alexandria, VA: Association of Curriculum and Supervision.

Gaskins, I. W., & Elliot, T. T. (1991). *Implementing cognitive strategy instruction across the school: The Benchmark manual for teachers.* Cambridge, MA: Brookline.

Gaskins, I. W., Satlow, E., Hyson, D., Ostertag, J., & Six, L. (1994). Classroom talk about text: Learning in science class. *Journal of Reading, 37*(7), 558–565.

Gentile, J. R., & Lalley, J. P. (2003). *Standards and mastery learning: Aligning teaching and assessment so all children can learn.* Thousand Oaks, CA: Corwin Press.

Gentile, J. R., Voelkl, K. E., Mt. Pleasant, J., & Monaco, N. M. (1995). Recall after relearning by fast and slow learners. *Journal of Experimental Education, 63,* 185–197.

Gilbar, S. (Ed.). (1990). *The Reader's quotation book: A literary companion.* Wainscott, NY: Pushcart.

Glickman, C. D. (1990). *Supervision of instruction: A developmental approach.* (2nd ed.). Boston: Allyn & Bacon.

Glickman, C. D. (1993). *Renewing America's schools.* San Francisco: Jossey-Bass.

Goldring, E., & Rallis, S. F. (1993). *Principals of dynamic schools: Taking charge of change.* Thousand Oaks, CA: Corwin Press.

Goodrich Andrade, H. (2001, April 17). The effects of instructional rubrics on learning to write. *Current Issues in Education, 4*(4). Retrieved May 2, 2006, from http://cie.ed.asu.edu/volume4/number4/.

Graham, S., & Miller, L. (1979). Spelling research and practice: A unified approach. *Focus on Exceptional Children, 12*(2), 75–91.

Graves, M. F. (2005). Theories and constructs that have made a significant difference in adolescent literacy—but have the potential to produce still more positive benefits. In T. L. Jetton & J. A. Dole (Eds.), *Adolescent literacy research and practice* (pp. 433–449). New York: Guilford.

Graves, M. F., Juel, C., & Graves, B. B. (2004). *Teaching reading in the 21st century* (3rd ed.). Boston: Allyn & Bacon.

Greaney, V., & Clarke, M. (1973). A longitudinal study of the effects of two reading methods on leisure-time reading habits. In D. Moyle (Ed.), *Reading: What of the future?* (pp. 107–114). London: United Kingdom Reading Association.

Greene, J. F. (2004). *Language!® The comprehensive literacy curriculum.* Longmont, CO: Sopris West.

Greene, J. P. (2006, Winter). A "comprehensive" problem. *Education Next.* Retrieved April 21, 2006, from www.educationnext.org.

Greene, J. P., & Forster, G. (2003). *Public high school graduation and college readiness rates in the United States.* New York: Manhattan Institute.

Grossen, B. (1999). *The REACH System.* New York: SRA McGraw-Hill.

Guthrie, J. T., Van Meter, P., McCann, A. D., Wigfield, A., Bennett, L., Poundstone, C. C., Rice, M. E., Faibisch, F. M., Hunt, B., & Mitchell, A. M. (1996). Growth of literacy engagement: Changes in motivations and strategies during concept-oriented reading. *Reading Research Quarterly, 31*(3), 306–325.

Guthrie, J. T., & Wigfield, A. (2000). Engagement and motivation in reading. In M. Kamil, P. Mosentha,l, P. D. Pearson, & R. Barr (Eds.), *Handbook of reading research* (Vol. 3, pp. 402–422). Mahwah, NJ: Erlbaum.

Haberman, M. (2003, March). *Who benefits from failing urban school districts: An essay on equity and justice for diverse children in urban poverty.* Retrieved April 21, 2006, from www.educationnews.org.

Haifiz, F., & Tudor, I. (1989). Extensive reading and the development of language skills. *English Language Teaching Journal, 43,* 4–11.

Hall, S. (2006). *I've DIBEL'd, now what.* Longmont, CO: Sopris West Educational Services.

Hand, B., Prain, V., & Wallace, C. (2002). Influences of writing tasks on students' answers to recall and higher-level test questions. *Research in Science Education, 32*(1), 49–34.

Hanushek, E. A. (2003). The importance of school quality. In P. E. Peterson (Ed.). *Our schools and our future: Are we still at risk?* (pp. 142–173). Stanford, CA: Hoover Institution Press.

Hardwick, E. (1990). Quoted in S. Gilbar (Ed.), *The reader's quotation book: A literary companion.* Wainscott, NY: Pushcart Press.

Harmin, M. (1994). *Inspiring active learners: A handbook for teachers.* Alexandria, VA: Association for Supervision and Curriculum Development.

Harrison, C. R., Killion, J. P., & Mitchell, J. E. (1989). Site-based management: The realities of implementation. *Educational Leadership, 46*(8), 55–58.

Hart, B., & Risely, T. R. (1995). *Meaningful differences in the everyday experience of young children.* Baltimore: Brookes.

Harvey, J., & Housman, N. (2005). *Crisis or possibility? Conversations about the American high school.* Washington, DC: National High School Alliance.

Hasbrouck, J. E., Ihnot, C., & Rogers, G. (1999). Read Naturally: A strategy to increase oral reading fluency. *Reading Research Instruction, 39*(1), 27–37.

Heck, R., Larson, T., & Marcoulides, G. (1990). Principal instructional leadership and school achievement: Validation of a causal model. *Educational Administration Quarterly, 26,* 94–125.

Heck, R., Marcoulides, G., & Lang, P. (1991). Principal instructional leadership and school achievement: The application of discriminant techniques. *School Effectiveness and School Improvement, 2,* 115–135.

Heinlein, R. A. (1961). *Stranger in a strange land.* New York: Putnam.

Heward, W. L., & Dardig, J. C. (2001). What matters most in special education. *Education Connection.* Amherst: University of Massachusetts School of Education.

Hirsch, E.D., Jr. (Ed.). (1989). *A first dictionary of cultural literacy.* Boston: Houghton Mifflin.

Hirsch, E. D. Jr. (2000, Spring/Summer). You can always look it up or can you? *Common Knowledge, 13*(2/3). Retrieved April 29, 2006, from www.core knowledge.org/CK/about/articles/lookItUp.htm.

Hirsh, D., & Nation, P. (1992). What vocabulary size is needed to read unsimplified texts for pleasure? *Reading in a Foreign Language, 8,* 263–284.

Holt, J. (1964). *How children fail.* New York: Pittman.

Honig, B. (1996). *Teaching our children to read.* Thousand Oaks, CA: Corwin Press.

Hwang, S. (2005, November 19). The new white flight. *The Wall Street Journal.* Retrieved November 30, 2005, from www.wsjclassroomedition.com.

Hyerle, D. (2004). *Student successes with thinking maps.* Thousand Oaks, CA: Corwin Press.

Hynds, S. (1997). *On the brink: Negotiating literature and life with adolescents.* New York: Teachers College Press.

Innes, R. (2005, June 15). NAEP's 12th grade test: Another validity problem. Letter to the Editor. Retrieved November 19, 2005 from www.education week.org.

International Reading Association. (2006). *Standards for middle and high school literacy coaches.* Newark, DE: Author.

Irvin, J. L. (1998). *Reading and the middle school student: Strategies to enhance literacy.* Boston: Allyn & Bacon.

Jago, C. (2000). *With rigor for all: Teaching the classics to contemporary students.* Portland, ME: Calendar Islands.

Jetton, T. L., & Alexander, P. A. (2005). Domains, teaching, and literacy. In T. L. Jetton & J. A. Dole, (Eds.) *Adolescent literacy research and practice* (pp. 15–39). New York: Guilford.

Jetton, T. L., & Dole, J. A. (2004). *Adolescent literacy research and practice.* New York: Guilford.

Johnston, R. C (2005, October 26). States urged to focus on adolescent literacy. *Education Week, 32.*

Jones, B.F., Pierce, J., & Hunter, B. (1988/1989). Teaching students to construct graphic representations. *Educational Leadership, 46*(4), 20–25.

Jones-Gayle, M. Y. (2006) *Professional development and school achievement through the national staff development council standards.* Unpublished dissertation, Florida Agricultural and Mechanical University.

Juvonen, J., Le, V., Kaganoff, T., Augustine, C., & Constant, L. (2004). *Focus on the wonder years: Challenges facing the American middle school.* Santa Monica, CA: RAND Corporation. Retrieved April 21, 2006, from http://www.rand.org/pubs/monographs/2004/RAND_MG139.pdf.

Kameenui, E., & Simmons, D. (1990). *Designing instructional strategies: The prevention of academic learning problems.* Columbus, OH: Merrill.

Karlin, R. (1984). *Teaching reading in high school: Improving reading in the content areas.* New York: Harper & Row.

Kibby, M. W. (1993). What reading teachers should know about reading proficiency in the U.S. *Journal of Reading, 27*(1), 38–51.

King, A. (1990). Improving lecture comprehension: Effects of a metacognitive strategy. *Applied Educational Psychology, 29,* 331–346.

King, A. (1992) Comparison of self-questioning, summarizing, and note taking-review as strategies for learning from lectures. *American Educational Research Journal, 29,* 303–325.

King, J. R., Biggs, S., & Lipsky, S. (1984). Students' self-questioning and summarizing as reading study strategies. *Journal of Reading Behavior, 16*(3), 205–218.

Klein, B., McNeil, J. D., & Stout, L. A. (2005, November 16). The achievement trap. *Education Week, 32.*

Kobrin, D. (1996). *Beyond the textbook: Teaching history using documents and primary sources.* Portsmouth, NH: Heinemann.

Kohn, A. (2000). *The case against standardized testing: Raising the scores, ruining the schools.* Portsmouth, NH: Heinemann.

Krashen, S. (1993). *The power of reading.* Englewood, CO: Libraries Unlimited.

Krogness, M. M. (1995). *Just teach me, Mrs. K.: Talking, reading, and writing with resistant adolescent learners.* Portsmouth, NH: Heinemann.

LaBerge, D., & Samuels, S. J. (1974). Toward a theory of automatic information processing in reading. *Cognitive Psychology, 6,* 293–323.

Learning First Alliance. (2000). *Every child reading: A professional development guide.* New York: Author.

Lewis, C. S. (1994). *The lion, the witch, and the wardrobe.* New York: HarperCollins.

Lindamood, P., Bell, N., & Lindamood, P. (1997). Sensory-cognitive factors in the controversy over reading instruction. *Journal of Developmental and Learning Disorders, 1,* 143–182.

Lindamood, P., & Lindamood, P. (1998). *Lindamood phoneme sequencing program.* San Luis Obispo, CA: Gander.

Lyon, G. R. (1995). Towards a definition of dyslexia. *Annals of Dyslexia, 45,* 3–27.

Lysynchuk, L. M., Pressley, M., & Vye, N. J. (1990). Reciprocal instruction improves standardized reading comprehension performance in poor grade-school comprehenders. *Elementary School Journal, 90*(5), 469–484.

Marliave, R., & Filby, N. N. (1985). Success rate: A measure of task appropriateness. In C. W. Fisher & D. C. Berliner (Eds.), *Perspectives on instructional time* (pp. 217–235). New York: Longman.

Marshall, J. D. (1987). The effects of writing on students' understanding of literary texts. *Research in the Teaching of English 21*(1), 30–63.

Marzano, R. J. (2004). *Building background knowledge for academic achievement: Research on what works in schools.* Alexandria, VA: Association for Supervision and Curriculum Development.

Marzano, R. J., & Pickering, D. J. (2005). *Building academic vocabulary: Teacher's manual.* Alexandria, VA: Association for Supervision and Curriculum Development.

Mason, B., & Krashen, S. (1997). Extensive reading in English as a foreign language. *System, 25,* 91–102.

Mayer, R. E., Hegarty, M., Mayer, S., & Campbell, J. (2005). When static media promote active learning: Annotated illustrations versus narrated animations in multimedia instruction. *Journal of Experimental Psychology: Applied, 11*(4), 256–265.

McEwan, E. K. (1997). *Leading your team to excellence: How to make quality decisions.* Thousand Oaks, CA: Corwin Press.

McEwan, E. K. (1998). *The principal's guide to raising reading achievement.* Thousand Oaks, CA: Corwin Press.

McEwan, E. K. (2002). *Teach them all to read: Catching the kids who fall through the cracks.* Thousand Oaks, CA: Corwin Press.

McEwan, E. K. (2003). *Ten traits of highly effective principals: From good to great performance.* Thousand Oaks, CA: Corwin Press.

McEwan, E. K. (2004). *7 strategies of highly effective readers: Using cognitive research to boost K–8 achievement.* Thousand Oaks, CA: Corwin Press.

McEwan, E. K. (2006). *How to survive and thrive in the first three weeks of school.* Thousand Oaks, CA: Corwin Press.

McEwan, E. K., & McEwan, P. J. (2003). *Making sense of research: What's good, what's not, and how to tell the difference.* Thousand Oaks, CA: Corwin Press.

McGuinness, C., & McGuinness, G. (1998). *Reading reflex.* New York: Simon & Schuster.

McGuinness, D. (1997). *Why our children can't read and what you can do about it.* New York: Free Press.

McIntosh, R., Vaughn, S., Schumm, J. L., Haager, D., & Lee. (1993). Observations of students with learning disabilities in general education classrooms. *Exceptional Children, 60*(3), 249–261.

McKeown, M. G., & Curtis, M. E. (Eds.). (1987). *The nature of vocabulary acquisition.* Hillsdale, NJ: Erlbaum.

Meichenbaum, D., & Biemiller, A. (1998). *Nurturing independent learners: Helping students take charge of their learning.* Cambridge, MA: Brookline.

Mertler, C. A. (2003). *Classroom assessment: A practical guide for educators.* Los Angeles: Pyrczak.

MetaMetrics, Inc. (1998). *About the lexile framework.* Durham, NC: Author.

Miller, G. A. (1956). The magical number seven, plus or minus two: Some limits on our capacity for processing information. *Psychological Review, 104,* 3–65.

Moats, L. (2004). Module 4: The mighty word: Building vocabulary and oral language. In *Language essentials for teachers of reading and spelling (LETRS).* Longmont, CO: Sopris West.

Moody, S. W., Vaughn, S., Hughes, M. T., & Fischer, M. (2000). Reading instruction in the resource room: Set up for failure. *Exceptional Children, 66*(3), 305–316.

Nagy, W. E., & Anderson, R. C. (1984). How many words are there in printed school English? *Reading Research Quarterly, 19,* 304–330.

National Academy of Education, Commission on Reading. (1985). *Becoming a nation of readers: The report of the Commission on Reading* (Prepared by R. C. Anderson, E. H. Hiebert, J. A. Scot, & I. A. G. Wilkinson). Washington, DC: National Academy of Education, National Institute of Education, Center for the Study of Reading.

National Committee on Excellence in Education. (1983). *A nation at risk.* Washington, DC: Author.

National Defense Education Act. (1958). Public Law 85–804. Retrieved July 6, 2006, from http://www.ed.gov/about/overview/fed/role.html?src=ln.

National Endowment for the Arts. (2004). *Reading at risk.* Washington, D.C.: Author. Retrieved April 21, 2006, from http://www.arts.gov/about/NEARTS/ReadingatRisk2.html.

National Governors Association. (2005). *Reading to achieve: A governor's guide to adolescent literacy.* Washington, DC: Author. Alexandria, VA: National Association of State Boards of Education.

National Institute of Child Health and Human Development (NICHD). (2000). *Report of the National Reading Panel: Teaching children to read: An evidence-based assessment of the scientific research literature on reading and its implications for reading instruction: Reports of the subgroups* (NIH Publication No. 00-4754). Washington, DC: U.S. Government Printing Office.

Neill, A. S. (1960/1995). *Summerhill school.* New York: St. Martin's. (Original work published in 1960)

Nevo, D. (1991, October). *An evaluation-minded school: Developing internal evaluation systems.* Paper presented at the annual meeting of the American Evaluation Association, Chicago.

No Child Left Behind Act. (2002, January 8). Public Law 107–110 115 Stat.1425 H.R. 1. Retrieved April 21, 2006, from www.ed.gov/nclb/landing.jhtml.

Nolte, R. Y., & Singer, H. (1985). Active comprehension: Teaching a process of reading comprehension and its effects on reading achievement. *The Reading Teacher, 39,* 24–31.

North, M. (1995). The effects of Spalding instruction on special education students. In C. W. McIntyre & J. S. Pickering (Eds.), *Clinical studies of multisensory structured language education for students with dyslexia and related disorders* (pp. 217–224). Salem, OR: Multisensory Structured Language Education Council.

Northwest Evaluation Association. (2006). *Measures of academic progress (MAP) test.* Retrieved May 1, 2006, from www.nwea.org.

Novak, J. D. (1998). *Learning, creating, and using knowledge: Concept maps as facilitative tools in schools and corporations.* Mahwah, NJ: Lawrence Erlbaum Associates.

Novak, J. D., & Gowin, B. (1984). *Learning how to learn.* Cambridge, UK: Cambridge University Press

Oakes, J., & Guiton, G. (1995). Matchmaking: The dynamics of high school tracking decisions. *American Education Research Journal, 32,* 3–33.

Olson, L. (2005, November 30). Benchmark assessments offer regular checkup on student achievement. *Education Week,* 13–14.

Owen, K. (2004). Effects of Lindamood-Bell on third and fourth grade reading achievement in Pueblo School District No. 60. Doctoral dissertation. University of Denver.

Owen, K. (2005). *Lindamood-Bell Annual Report to the Board of Education, Pueblo School District No. 60.* Pueblo, CO: Pueblo School District No. 60. Unpublished document.

Paas, F., Renkl, A., & Sweller, J. (Eds.). (2003). Cognitive load theory: A special Issue. *Educational Psychologist, 38*(1).

Palincsar, A. S., & Brown, A. L. (1984). Reciprocal teaching of comprehension fostering and monitoring activities. *Cognition and Instruction, 1*(2), 117–175.

Palincsar, A. S., & Brown, A. L. (1986). Interactive teaching to promote independent learning from text. *The Reading Teacher, 39*(8), 771–777.

Parker, G. M. (1990). *Team players and teamwork.* San Francisco: Jossey-Bass.

Pearson, P. D. (1996). Reclaiming the center. In M. F. Graves, P. van den Broek, & B. Taylor (Eds.), *The first R: Every child's right to read* (pp. 259–274). New York: Teachers College Press, and Newark, DE: International Reading Association.

Pearson, P. D., Roehler, L. R., Dole, J. A., & Duffy, G. G. (1992). Developing expertise in reading comprehension. In J. Samuels & A. Farstup (Eds.), *What research has to say about reading instruction* (pp. 145–199). Newark, DE: International Reading Association.

Perfetti, C. (1989). There are generalized abilities and one of them is reading. In L Resnick (Ed.), *Knowing, learning and instruction: Essays in honor of Robert Glaser* (pp. 307–335). Hillsdale, NJ: Lawrence Erlbaum Associates.

Perfetti, C. A. (1985). *Reading ability.* New York: Oxford University Press.

Perfetti, C. A. (1995). Cognitive research can inform reading education. *Journal of Research in Reading, 18*(2), 106–115.

Petty, W., Herold, C., & Stoll, E. (1967). *The state of knowledge about the teaching of vocabulary.* Champaign, IL: National Council of Teachers of English.

Pilgreen, J., & Krashen, S. (1993). Sustained silent reading with English as a second language high school students: Impact on reading comprehension, reading frequency, and reading enjoyment. *School Library Media Quarterly, 22*(1), 21–23.

Pogrow, S. (1995). *A revalidation of the effectiveness of the HOTS program prepared for the National Diffusion Network.* Unpublished paper.

Pogrow, S. (2004, October 24). The missing element in reducing the learning gap: Eliminating the "blank stare." *Teachers College Record.* Retrieved October 24, 2004 from www.tcrecord.org/Content.asp?ContentID=11381.

Pogrow, S. (2005). HOTS revisited: A thinking development approach to reducing the learning gap after grade 3. *Phi Delta Kappan, 87*(1), 64–75.

Pogrow, S. (in press). Redesigning high poverty elementary schools for success: The traditionalist and progressive approach of the Hi-Perform School Model.

Policy Studies Associates. (1998, October). *An idea book on planning* (Vol.1). Washington, DC: U.S. Department of Education.

Pollock, E., Chandler, P., Sweller, J. (2002). Assimilating complex information. *Learning and Instruction, 12,* 61–86.

Pressley, M. (1998). *Reading instruction that works: The case for balanced teaching.* New York: Guilford.

Pressley, M. (2000). What should reading comprehension instruction be the instruction of? In M. Kamil, P. Mosenthal, P. D. Pearson, & R. Barr (Eds.), *Handbook of reading research: Volume III* (pp. 545–561). Mahwah, NJ: Erlbaum.

Pressley, M. (2004). The need for research on secondary literacy education. In T. L. Jetton & J. A. Dole (Eds.), *Adolescent literacy research and practice,* (pp. 415–432). New York: Guilford

Pressley, M., & Afflerbach, P. (1995). *Verbal protocols of reading: The nature of constructively responsive reading.* Hillsdale, NJ: Erlbaum.

Pressley, M., Burkell, J., Cariglia-Bull, T., Lysynchuk, L., McGoldrick, J. A., Schneider, B., Snyder, B., Symons, S., & Woloshyn, V. E. (1990). *Cognitive instructional strategies that really work.* Cambridge, MA: Brookline.

Pressley, M., El-Dinary, P. B., Marks, M. B., & Stein, S. (1992). Good strategy instruction is motivating and interesting. In K. A. Renninger, S. Hidi, & A. Krapp (Eds.). *Role in interest in learning and development* (pp. 333–358). Hillsdale, NJ: Erlbaum.

Pressley, M., Gaskins, I. W., Solic, K., & Collins, S. (2005). *A portrait of Benchmark School: How a school produces high achievement in students who previously failed.* East Lansing, MI: Literacy Achievement Research Center, Michigan State University.

Pressley, M., Johnson, C. J., Symons, S., McGoldrick, J. A., & Kurita, J. A. (1989). Strategies that improve children's memory and comprehension of text. *Elementary School Journal, 90*(1), 3–22.

Pressley, M., Raphael, M., Gallagher, J. D., & DiBlla, J. (2004). Providence-St. Mel School: How a school that works for African-American students works. *Journal of Educational Psychology, 96,* 236–235.

Pressley, M., Wharton-McDonald, R., & Mistretta, J. (1998). Effective beginning literacy instruction: Dialectical, scaffolded, and contextualized. In J. L. Metsala & L. C. Ehri. (Eds.), *Word recognition in beginning literacy* (pp. 357–373). Mahwah, NJ: Erlbaum.

Pressley, M., & Woloshyn, V. (1995). *Cognitive strategy instruction that really improves children's academic performance* (2nd ed.). Cambridge, MA: Brookline.

Purkey, S., & Smith, M. (1983) Research on effective schools: A review. *Elementary School Journal, 83,* 427–452.

Raphael, L. M., Pressley, M., & Mohan, L. (2004). *What does motivating and engaging instruction look like in middle school?* Technical Report: East Lansing, MI: College of Education, Literacy Achievement Research Center.

Raphael, T. (1984). Teaching learners about sources of information for answering questions. *Journal of Reading, 27*(4), 303–311.

Ravitch, D. (2003). A historic document. In P. E. Peterson (Ed.). *Our schools and our future: Are we still at risk?* Stanford, CA: Hoover Institution Press.

Reeves, D. B. (2004). *Accountability in action: A blueprint for learning organizations.* Englewood, CO: Advanced Learning Press.

Renzulli, J. (2000, June 19). In B. Kantrowitz & D. McGinn, When teachers are cheaters. *Time,* 48–49.

Resnick, L. (1999, June 16). Making America smarter: A century's assumptions about innate ability give way to a belief in the power of effort. *Education Week,* 38–40.

RMC Research Corporation. (1995). *Schoolwide programs: A planning manual.* Portland, OR: Author.

Robbins, C., & Ehri, L. C. (1994). Reading storybooks to kindergartners helps them learn new vocabulary words. *Journal of Educational Psychology, 86,* 54–64.

Rose, C., & Nicholl, M. (1998). *Accelerated learning for the 21st century: The six-step plan to unlock your master mind.* New York: Dell.

Rosenshine, B. (1979). Content, time, and direct instruction. In J. Peterson & H. Walberg (Eds.), *Research on teaching: Concepts, findings and implications.* Berkeley, CA: McCutchan.

Rosenshine, B. (1986). Synthesis of research on explicit teaching. *Educational Leadership, 4,* 60–69.

Rosenshine, B. (1997a). Advances in research on instruction. In J. W. Lloyd, E. J. Kameenui, & D. Chard (Eds.), *Issues in educating students with disabilities,* (pp. 197–221). Mahwah, NJ: Lawrence Erlbaum.

Rosenshine, B. (1997b, March 24–28). The case for explicit, teacher-led, cognitive strategy instruction. Paper presented at the annual meeting of the American Educational Research Association, Chicago, IL.

Rosenshine, B., & Meister, C. (1994). Reciprocal teaching: A review of nineteen experimental studies. *Review of Educational Research, 64*(4), 479–530.

Rosenshine, B., Meister, C., & Chapman, S. (1996). Teaching students to generate questions: A review of the intervention studies. *Review of Educational Research, 66*(2), 181–221.

Roswell, F. G., & Chall, J. S. (1992). *Diagnostic assessments of reading.* New York: Riverside.

Rouse, C. (2005, September). The labor market consequences of an inadequate education. A paper presented at the Equity Symposium on "The Social Costs of Inadequate Education." New York: Teacher's College, Columbia University.

Rutter, M., Maughan, B., Mortimore, P., & Ouston, J. (1979). *Fifteen thousand hours.* Cambridge, MA: Harvard University Press.

Sadowski, M., & Willson, V. L. (2006). Effects of a theoretically-based large scale reading intervention in a multicultural urban school district. *American Educational Research Journal, 43*(1), 137–154.

Samuels, S. J. (1979). The method of repeated readings. *The Reading Teacher, 32,* 403–408.

Santa, C. M. (1986). Content reading in secondary school. In J. Orasanu (Ed.), *Reading comprehension: From research to practice* (pp. 303–317). Hillsdale, NJ: Lawrence Erlbaum.

Saphier, J., & Gower, R. (1987). *The skillful teacher: Building your teaching skills.* Carlisle, MA: Research for Better Teaching.

Saphier, J., & Haley, M. A. (1993). *Summarizers: Activity structures to support integration and retention of new learning.* Acton, MA: Research for Better Teaching, Inc.

Sarason, S. (1990). *The predictable future of educational reform: Can we change course before it's too late?* San Francisco: Jossey-Bass.

Schmoker, M. (1999). *Results: The key to continuous school improvement* (2nd ed.). Alexandria, VA: Association for Supervision and Curriculum Development.

Schoenbach, R., Greenleaf, C., Cziko, C., & Hurwitz. (1999). *Reading for understanding.* San Francisco: Jossey-Bass.

SchoolMatters. (2005). *The National Assessment of Educational Progress and State Assessments: What do differing student proficiency rates tell us?* New York: Standard & Poor's. Retrieved November 27, 2005 from www.schoolmatters.com.

Scriven, M. (1967) The methodology of evaluation. In R. W. Tyler, R. M. Gagne, & M. Scriven (Eds.), *Perspectives of curriculum evaluation* (AERA Monograph Series on Curriculum Evaluation No 1, pp. 39–82). Chicago: Rand McNally.

Shanahan, T. (2004). Overcoming the dominance of communication: Writing to think and to learn. In T. L. Jetton & J. A. Dole (Eds.), *Adolescent literacy research and practice* (pp. 59–74). New York: Guilford.

Share, D. L., & Stanovich, K. E. (1995). Cognitive processes in early reading development: Accommodating individual differences into a mode of acquisition. *Issues in Education: Contributions from Educational Psychology, 1,* 1–57.

Shinn, M., Good, R. H., Knutson, N., Tilly, W. D., & Collins, V. (1992). Curriculum-based measurement of oral reading fluency: A confirmatory analysis of its relation to reading. *School Psychology Review, 21*(3), 459–479.

Shriberg, L. K., Levin, J. R., McCormick, C. B., & Pressley, M. (1982). Learning about "famous" people via the keyword method. *Journal of Educational Psychology, 74,* 238–247.

Sillins, H. (1994) The relationship between school leadership and school improvement outcomes. *School Effectiveness and School Improvement, 5,* 272–298.

Simonsen, F., Gunter, L., & Marchand-Margella, N. (2005). *Spelling research: Research on teaching children to spell.* Cheney, WA: Eastern Washington University.

Sinatra, G. M., Stahl-Gemake, J., & Berg, D. N. (1984). Improving reading comprehension of disabled readers through semantic mapping. *Reading Teacher, 38*(1), 22–29.

Snow, C. E., Burns, M. S., & Griffin, P. (Eds.). Committee on the Prevention of Reading Difficulties in Young Children. Commission on Behavioral and Social Sciences and Education. National Research Council. (1998). *Preventing reading difficulties in young children.* Washington, DC: National Academy Press.

Sopris West. *Implementation results with Language!® at the middle and high school grades.* Longmont, CO: Author. Retrieved January 19, 2006 from www.teach language.com/PDFs/Implementation_Data_Middle&High_%20School .pdf.

Sopris West. *Research base for Language!®.* Longmont, CO: Author. Retrieved January 19, 2006 from www.teachlanguage.com/PDFs/Research_Base% 20_for_LANGUAGE!.pdf.

Sopris West. *Implementation results with Language!® of students who are limited English proficient.* Retrieved January 19, 2006 from www.teachlanguage. com/PDFs/Implementation_Data_Limited_English_Proficiency.pdf.

Spalding, R. B., & Spalding, W. T. (1990). *The writing road to reading: The Spalding method of phonics for teaching speech, writing & reading* (4th rev. ed.). New York: William Morrow. (Original work published in 1957)

Spinelli, J. (1990). *Maniac Magee.* New York: Little, Brown.

Spinelli, J. (1994). *Who put that hair in my toothbrush?* New York: Little, Brown.

Stahl, S. A., & Shanahan, C. (2004). Learning to think like a historian: Disciplinary knowledge through critical analysis of multiple documents. In T. L. Jetton and J. A. Dole (Eds.), *Adolescent literacy research and practice* (pp. 94–115). New York: Guilford.

Stanovich, K. E. (1986). Matthew effects in reading: Some consequences of individual differences in the acquisition of literacy. *Reading Research Quarterly, 21,* 360–406.

Stanovich, K. E., & Cunningham, A. E. (1993). Where does knowledge come from? Specific associations between print exposure and information acquisition. *Journal of Educational Psychology, 85,* 211–229.

Stebbins, L. B., St. Pierre, R. G., Proper, E. C., Anderson, R. B., & Cerva, T. R. (1977). *Education as experimentation: A planned variation model. Vols. 4A, 4C: An evaluation of follow through.* Cambridge, MA: Abt Associates.

Stenner, A. J. (1996, February). *Measuring reading comprehension with the Lexile framework.* Paper presented at the Fourth North American Conference on Adolescent/Adult Literacy, Washington, DC. Retrieved April 21, 2006, from www.lexile.com.

Sternberg, R. J. (1987). Most vocabulary is learned from context. In M. G. McKeown & M. E. Curtis (Eds.), *Nature of vocabulary acquisition.* Hillsdale, NJ: Lawrence Erlbaum.

Sullivan, A. M. (1988). The personal anthology: A stimulus for exploratory reading. *English Journal, 77*(1), 27–30.

Sunderman, G. L., Kim, J. S., & Orfield, G. (2005). *NCLB meets school realities.* Thousand Oaks, CA: Corwin Press.

Swanson, C. (2004). *Projections of 2003–2004 high school graduates.* Washington, DC: The Urban Institute.

Sweller, J. (1994). Cognitive load theory, learning difficulty, and instructional design. *Learning and Instruction, 4,* 295–312.

Taylor, B. M., Pearson, P. D., Clark, K. F., & Walpole, S. (1999). Effective schools/accomplished teachers. *Reading Teacher, 53*(2), 156–159.

Teachers College Columbia University. (2005, November 9). The price of inequity. News release. Retrieved April 21, 2006, from http://www.tc.columbia.edu/news/article.htm?id=5350.

Teddlie, C., & Reynolds, D. (Eds.). (2000). *The international handbook of school effectiveness research.* New York: Falmer Press.

Teddlie, C., & Stringfield, S. (1993). *Schools make a difference. Lessons learned from a 10-year study of school effects.* New York: Teachers College Press.

Their, M., & Daviss, B. (2002). *The new science literacy.* Portsmouth, NH: Heinemann.

Thompson, S. T. (1999, October 6). Confessions of a "standardisto." *Education Week.* Retrieved April 21, 2006, from http://www.educationweek.org.

Tomlinson, T. (1992). *Hard work and high expectations: Motivating students to learn.* Washington, DC: U.S. Department of Education, Office of Educational Research and Improvement.

Torgesen, J. K., Alexander, A. W., Wagner, R. K., Rashotte, C. A., Voeller, K., Conway, T., & Rose, E. (2001). Intensive remedial instruction for children with severe reading disabilities: Immediate and long-term outcomes from two instructional approaches. *Journal of Learning Disabilities, 34,* 33–58.

Tovani, C. (2004). *Do I really have to teach reading? Content comprehension, Grades 6–12.* Portland, ME: Stenhouse.

Trabasso, T., & Bouchard, E. (2000). *Text comprehension instruction. Report of the National Reading Panel, Report of the Subgroups* (Chap. 4, Pt. 2, pp. 39–69). NICHD Clearinghouse.

Trabasso, T., & Bouchard, E. (2002). Teaching readers how to comprehend text strategically. In C. C. Block & M. Pressley (Eds.), *Comprehension instruction: Research-based best practices* (pp. 176–200). New York: Guilford.

Tsang, W. K. (1996). Comparing the effects of reading and writing on writing performance. *Applied Linguistics, 17*(2), 210–233.

Underwood, T., & Pearson, P. D. (2004). Teaching struggling adolescent readers to comprehend what they read. In T. L. Jetton & J. A. Dole (Eds.), *Adolescent literacy research and practice,* (pp. 135–161). New York: Guilford.

U.S. Department of Education, Institute of Education Sciences, National Center for Education Statistics, National Assessment of Educational Progress (NAEP), 1992, 1994, 1998, and 2002 Reading Assessments.

Vachon, V. L., & Gleason, M. M. (2001). The effects of mastery teaching and varying practice contexts on middle school students' acquisition of multisyllabic word reading strategies. Retrieved April 21, 2006, from www.rewardsreading.com/PDFs/Middle_School_Study1.pdf.

van den Broek, P., & Kremer, K. E. (2000). The mind in action: What it means to comprehend during reading. In B. M. Taylor, M. F. Graves, & P. van den Broek (Eds.), *Reading for meaning: Fostering comprehension in the middle grades* (pp.1–25). New York: Teachers College Press.

Vaughn, S., Moody, S., & Schumm, J. S. (1998). Broken promises: Reading instruction in the resource room. *Exceptional Children, 64*(2), 211–225.

Viadero, D. (2005a, November 9). GAO revises estimates of students excluded from NAEP. *Education Week.* Retrieved April 21, 2006, from www.educationweek.org.

Viadero, D. (2005b, November 2). States vary on students excluded from NAEP tests. *Education Week.* Retrieved April 21, 2006, from www.educationweek.org.

Wade, S. E., & Moje, E. B. (2000). The role of text in classroom learning. In M. L. Kamil, P. B. Mosenthal, P. D. Pearson, & R. Barr (Eds.), *Handbook of reading research* (Vol. 3, pp. 609–627). Mahwah, NJ: Erlbaum.

Wagner, R. K., Torgesen, J. K., & Rashotte, C. A. (1994). Development of reading-related phonological processing abilities: New evidence of bidirectional causality from a latent variable longitudinal study. *Developmental Psychology, 30*(1), 73–87.

WestEd. (1997). *Schoolwide reform: A new outlook* (Vols. 1 & 2). San Francisco, CA: Author.

Whatis.com. (2006). Retrieved April 21, 2006, from whatis.techtarget.com/definition/0,,sid9_gci212216.00.html

Whipple, G. (Ed.). (1925). *The twenty-fourth yearbook of the National Society for the Study of Education: Report of the national committee on reading.* Bloomington, IL: Public School Publishing.

Wilhelm, J. E. (1997). *You gotta be the book: Teaching engaged and reflective reading with adolescents.* New York: Teachers College Press.

Wiliam, D. (2003). *Assessment for learning: Putting it into practice.* Berkshire, England: Open University Press.

Wise, B. W., Ring, J., & Olson, R. K. (1999). Training phonological awareness with and without explicit attention to articulation. *Journal of Experimental Child Psychology, 72,* 271–304.

Wood, E., Woloshyn, V. E., & Willoughby, T. (Eds.). (1995). *Cognitive strategy instruction for middle and high schools.* Cambridge, MA: Brookline.

Wooden, J. (with Jamison, S.). (1997). *Wooden: A lifetime of observations and reflections on and off the court.* Chicago: Contemporary Books.

Worthington, P. (2005, February 19). *Lindamood-Bell Learning Processes: Comprehensive district reform through professional development in reading— Leaving no child behind.* Speech at American Association of School Administrators Conference. San Antonio, TX.

Zimmerman, S., & Keene, E. O. (1997). *Mosaic of thought: Teaching comprehension in a Reader's Workshop.* Portsmouth, NH: Heinemann.

Index

CORWIN PRESS